A
Newark

Childhood
A memoir

David Hugo Barrett

© 2020 by David Hugo Barrett. All rights reserved.

No part of this book may be reproduced in any written, electronic, recording, or photocopying without written permission of the publisher or author. The exception would be in the case of brief quotations embodied in the critical articles or reviews and pages where permission is specifically granted by the publisher or author.

Although every precaution has been taken to verify the accuracy of the information contained herein, the author and publisher assume no responsibility for any errors or omissions. No liability is assumed for damages that may result from the use of information contained within.

Books may be purchased at Amazon.com, select bookstores, or www.davidhugobarrett.com

Cover Design: Kerry Johnson of Caricaturebykerry
Interior Design: Angela Harris of Kokopelli Marketing
Publisher: DHugo Publishing
Editor: Susan Thornton-Hobby
Library of Congress Catalog Number: TX5-919-773
ISBN: 978-1-7331122-1-5
ISBN: 978-1-7331122-0-8
1. Memoir 2. American History
First Edition
Printed in United States of America

Contents

Part I	**The Neighborhood**
Chapter 1	In the Beginning
Chapter 2	Religion
Chapter 3	Discovery
Part II	**Leaving the Security of the Neighborhood**
Chapter 4	Webster Junior High School
Part III	**Outside Interventions**
Chapter 5	Learning the Hard Way
Chapter 6	Bloomfield Technical High School
Part IV	**Central High School and Beyond**
Chapter 7	Ernie
Chapter 8	The Bel Chords
Chapter 9	From Camp to College

Dedication

This book is dedicated to my sons: *Tehuti, Issa, and Brandon; to my five grandchildren, Brianna, Jasmin, Allen Hugo, Aria, and Bahia Barrett; and to my wife, Sandy, whom I abandoned for a countless number of hours to retreat to my office to write.*

Preface

My wife and I were guests of friends, Donald and Michael Williford, at their villa in Cancun, Mexico, in November of 2003. I had decided to take part of this time away to edit the completed chapters of this book. On the second or third day of our stay, and while our wives were out, Donald asked me what the target audience for the book was. Up to that point I had not given it any thought; only that I had a story I wanted to tell and had decided two years earlier to tell it.

As I began to tell him, I recalled the interest my three sons had taken in the project and their requests to let them read my completed chapters. My middle son, Issa, was particularly persistent in this regard; while Tehuti, the oldest, and Brandon, the youngest, were content to wait for me to dole out a page or two whenever I was ready. Reflecting on their interest in the project, I continued with my answer: I said I wanted to do it for my sons and the children they might someday, have. I went on to say that my father had died in August, 1984, nine months after Brandon was born and that my mother had died on June 28, 1978, one day before Tehuti's eighth birthday. None of my older sons got to know them very well and Brandon not at all. I added that as my story developed, it became also a story about my parents, especially my mother, and, to a lesser extent, my siblings. I concluded that at least some of the experiences I had as a child growing up in Newark were universal, and, as such, I thought a high school student growing up in a city would be able to relate to my story and so might some parents. The story would have special meaning if the parents too, were products of an urban upbringing.

The idea for the book came to me after I read Robert Hayden's poem, "Those Winter Sundays." The lines reminded me of the sacrifices my mother had made for my siblings and me, and how we had taken for granted what she did for us. I wanted to write something that would recall what she did for me, and by extension, for my siblings as well. I supposed that whatever I wound up writing would be my way of belatedly thanking her and maybe suggesting to other parents that their children, too, might eventually acknowledge them for the sacrifices they made for them. My advice to parents is be patient and when the acknowledgement of your love and sacrifice comes, spills, unexpectedly from your child's lips, be ready to receive it.

For my sons, I hope this story at least partially answers one of the questions every parent is eventually asked by a son or daughter, "What were things like when you were growing up?" I hope that it inspires them to write their own stories at some point and to bridge the intra-family generations.

On his seventieth birthday, I sent my Uncle Hugo a draft copy of the first chapter, because my first day in kindergarten in Newark contrasted sharply with his in Portsmouth, Virginia. But both of those first days of school had one element in common — the guiding hand of his sister, who became my mother. After he read the chapter, he sent an email from his home in Chesapeake, Virginia; it is quoted below in its entirety.

Hi Dave! I just finished reading your "first day in school"!! I loved it. I did not know how great an impact my experiences had on me until I was told by my father's sisters, who had gone to New York to work, [because] they did not accept the treatment we tolerated from white folks down here! Their courage and the anger that Uncle George kept before us helped prepare us for the battles that we undertook to bring about the change that they could not make. We still have a long way to go.

Tell Brandon that I am betting on him to hurry and come out and join the battles yet to be won to make real the unfulfilled promises that are still (for us) dreams deferred.

By all means finish,

Unk (He frequently signed his name with this moniker.)

I suppose I should say a word about my approach to telling this story. As I began to formulate the idea for the story, I knew there were a number of events I had witnessed or heard about, as well as experiences I had lived through, that though often separated by time, space and circumstance, were nonetheless related, and I wanted to connect them in the telling of my story. For example, my late uncle was 27 years my senior (my Uncle Hugo A. Owens died at age 92 in July 2008 before I had completed the manuscript). He and I were separated by time (he was 27 years ahead of me); space (he was in Portsmouth and I was in Newark), and circumstance (he was born into, raised, and lived under legal racial segregation and I wasn't). Yet, he and I had kindergarten experiences in which my mother played a key role. Though these events occurred 27 years apart, I talk about them in the same place in the book. I take the reader back to the relatively distant past to establish the link, and then resume my story in the more recent past, where I left off. A computer programmer would recognize this in principle as behaving very much like a subroutine in a computer program. This is an observation I am qualified to make. I was first a teacher and then worked as a mathematician/computer programmer for General Electric, Lockheed and the Computer Science Corporation (CSC) for a combined total of ten years. I was ten years after the" Hidden Figures" made popular by the book and film both titled "Hidden Figures". At CSC, I was one of a trio of senior programmers (Today called coders) who were assigned the task of developing a simulator for the space shuttle. It was to be called the Approach Landing Test or ALT. No one told us it was supposed to be hard, so we just did it and had fun doing so. We spent three weeks commuting from our motel 19 miles one way to the NASA operations center located at Edwards Air Force base in the blazing hot (average temperature 88 degrees F) Mojave Desert. where the live testing would be conducted. I later learned that Mojave was also the home of the appropriately-named Death Valley.

My former student and mentor for this project, Komozi Woodard, a professor of African American history and culture, as well as public policy, at Sarah Lawrence College, upon reading the manuscript informed me that, "It jumps around quite a bit. But it's okay; just make sure you warn the readers so you set their expectations."

I did not consciously set out to tell my story in a nonlinear fashion. In fact, I began trying to tell it in sequence, but found it did not feel right; I felt I was forcing myself to be a kind of storyteller that I was not. Please take the story as it is, because there is no other way I could have told it.

I have omitted the last names of some of the book's characters out of respect for their privacy. In only one case do I not use the full real name of a person. He is John Pollard a classmate in kindergarten. Other than that, everyone and everything are for real. No joke.

It's difficult, if not impossible to know precisely who or what influences play the most significant role in shaping a developing child. This question is a subject of ongoing debate among social scientists (nature or nurture?). The child is touched by so many people, including parents, siblings, grandparents, other close relatives, teachers, and peers, as well as the environment of the very town or city in which he or she is raised. Truth be told, the city could also be a character. In fact, it is the one that provides the context for the human characters in my story.

It could be that those who are in most frequent contact with the child and whom he respects are the greatest influences. But ultimately, it's a combination of influences that puts the child on a productive or destructive course.

In this memoir of my childhood in Newark, New Jersey, I have tried to identify and describe the influences — good and bad — as best I could recall -- that played a role in my development. Had it not been for the constant echo of the voices of my mother and my Uncle Hugo surfacing in my head at opportune times, trying to intervene when I found myself going off course, I might have wound up in jail or dead at a very young age, as was the fate of a few boys in my neighborhood and two of my best friends in high school. To be sure, I did not always listen to those voices, but when I didn't, I suffered the consequences.

I have used the language of black and Italian adolescents and teenagers in my neighborhood and at the schools I attended during the period covered by the story. Moreover, I use phonetic spellings to recreate the sounds. Some words are just plain "Jersey" such as "youze" for "you second person plural. The reader will notice that I use both the words "colored" and "Negro." when referring to African Americans. This is a reflection of my evolving identity due to political and social dynamics defined and accelerated by the civil rights and black power movements.

Finally, I played the music of my favorite R&B singers of the time as I wrote about events through middle school. Towards the end of middle school, I discovered jazz and my interest in it and its creators took root and began to redefine me. Once I started high school and formed a new circle of friends who shared my affinity for jazz, I fully embraced it. Thus, I played through high school the music of Miles Davis, John Coltrane, Gerry Mulligan, Art Blakey, Benny Golson, Nancy Wilson - "Guess Who I Saw Today" and others. When I started writing about my high school events, I played their music to help me experience again the feelings I had back then to help me lend authenticity to my language.

It is my hope that in these pages parent or guardian readers will find something of value- an anecdote or lesson that might help some young person get on and stay on a positive path to being a responsible and productive citizen. If you are a young person still trying to find your way, know that the force that fuels this story is an undying love.

David Hugo Barrett
Ellicott City, Maryland
February 3, 2019

Part 1
The Neighborhood

Chapter 1
In the beginning

(1)

James Luther Barrett was born March 6, 1911, in Franklyn, Virginia. Less than a month later that same year, Annie Owens was born April 5, in Portsmouth, Virginia. Somehow their paths crossed and they met and married 19 years later. Annie, who was to become my mother, was a high school graduate, but James, an only child and my future father, had completed only the eighth grade. None of my siblings knew how it came to be that our parents had moved from Virginia to New Jersey. But like many Southerners migrating north during the 1930s, James was probably searching for economic opportunity so he could support his growing family. We do know that the family had moved several times around New Jersey in the towns of Bloomfield and Montclair, where one of James's maternal aunts, Rose, lived. They settled in Newark in 1942 with a family of three girls and one boy. They moved to a five-room, cold-water flat on the first floor of a three-story, nine-family tenement at 67 Clay Street in the North Ward — the section of the city known as Little Italy because of its high concentration of Italian immigrants. The tenement was a half-mile west of the Passaic River, which separated the blue-collar city of Harrison from Newark. The Clay Street Bridge connected the two New Jersey cities.

Within two years of the family's moving to Clay Street, my younger brother, Melvin, and I were born 15 months apart, at Beth Israel Hospital in the heavily Jewish Weequahic section of the South Ward of Newark.

The neighborhood in which we lived encompassed an area bound roughly by High Street on the west, Eighth Avenue on the south, Crane Street on the north and McCarter Highway on the east. The residential part of Clay Street extended three blocks -- from High Street, crossing Broad and Spring streets and stretched all the way down to McCarter Highway.

On the other side of Clay Street, beginning in my block and heading east, were the Clay-Bro Diner (so named because it was at the intersection of Clay and Broad streets); Bruno's used car lot, where my older brother, James, Jr., was employed; four or five garages owned by Bruno that were rented to the few neighborhood families that had cars; a succession of linoleum stores and another used car lot where Clay Street intersected with Mount Pleasant Avenue. Extending for another block and on both sides of the street, there were even more linoleum stores clear down to the Amoco station at the southwest corner of Clay Street and McCarter Highway; and finally, the Passaic River.

On one side of cobble-stoned Spring Street were a sweltering steel foundry, a scissor manufacturer and a dress factory (where my mother worked for a short time), while on the other side were a pair of row houses and the parking garage for the Bell Telephone Company service trucks, the Flamingo Lounge (formerly the Fireplace Tavern) and Newman's grocery and deli at Eighth Avenue and Spring Street. Because of the presence of these businesses, there was a large influx of white people into our neighborhood during the day to work at the steel foundry, the telephone company, or to shop at the many linoleum stores that lined Clay Street. Invisible to these intruders, I would watch with rapt curiosity as they looked for parking spaces, took lunch and coffee breaks, and rushed home after work. I used to wonder what the neighborhoods they lived in looked like and what they thought of mine.

Each of Newark's five wards had its own mix of racial, religious, and ethnic groups. The Central Ward was as colored as the north was Italian, while the West Ward was second only to the North in its Italian demographic, though there were a significant number of colored people and a few other white ethnic groups living there as well. The East Ward boasted a Polish and Portuguese population, the latter being the third-largest in the world after Lisbon and Boston; and a growing Puerto Rican community. The South Ward, once virtually entirely Jewish, and birthplace of Philip Roth (born 11 years before me), was slowly becoming a colored ward as the Jews moved farther west into the Weequahic section and finally out of the city altogether into the suburbs of Orange, West Orange, East Orange and Millburn.

Broad Street was the longest street completely contained within Newark. Other streets were longer, but they stretched into other jurisdictions such as Bloomfield, Montclair, and Irvington. The three-mile stretch along Broad Street between Clay and Camp streets was populated with businesses and public spaces that contributed to the character of the street and the city.

It stretched north and south and intersected with Market Street to create a space Newarkers called Four Corners. It was largely residential north of Clay Street; but southbound from Clay it revealed more variety as it made its way right through the heart of downtown Newark. Like a spine, it passed through a bustling shopping and business district that featured multiple banks, retail stores and offices. Among them were the administrative offices and communications nerve center of Bell Telephone, an over-the-top nouveau building at 540 Broad Street; the Lackawanna railroad station; and the Studebaker automobile dealership, behind which were stabled the

Budweiser Clydesdale horses, fixtures in the Thanksgiving Day parades. Then there were the Mutual Benefit Life Insurance Company and Washington Park, where a bronze statue showed George Washington standing proudly next to his horse, addressing the troops after a victory at Rocky Hill, New Jersey. Four hundred yards northwest of General Washington on Washington Street were the Newark Public Library, once the best in the state; and part of the Newark campus of Rutgers University. Continuing south on Broad Street, one would pass the Loews movie theater and S. Klein's, Bamberger's and Hahne's department stores. Military park was directly across from the three stores.

Just south of Hahne's was the corporate headquarters of the Prudential Insurance Company. At 24 stories; it was the most imposing structure in downtown Newark's Four Corners. Continue a few more blocks and you'd find Teddy Powell's Lounge, the most popular jazz club in New Jersey and frequented by those who considered themselves well-schooled in jazz and blues. Nearby was the Potamkin Chevrolet dealership, and the Continental and Terrace ballrooms. If you traveled south two more blocks, you would be greeted by a statue of Abraham Lincoln standing tall in a small park. Bearing his name, the park was directly across from the federal office building at the intersection of Camp and Broad streets.

In the 1950s and '60s, downtown during the week in the daytime gave a distorted view of the proportion of colored people living in Newark, because the city was populated largely with white people on foot, in cars and peering out of the windows of buses. A few lived in Newark, but the vast majority commuted from Newark's Essex County suburbs, mainly those west of Newark such as the Oranges (East, West and South); Livingston; Short Hills; Montclair and Bloomfield. At 7 a.m. or 5 p.m., one need only stand on any one of the in/outbound thoroughfares -- West Market Street, South Orange Avenue or Springfield Avenue -- to watch the steady, slow, flow of traffic out of the city ferrying white faces to even whiter spaces to fully appreciate this curious phenomenon.

While Newark was dotted with several small parks, the two largest ones were Branch Brook in the North Ward and Weequahic in the South Ward. These were the parks that many families frequented on weekends for cheap recreation of swings, row boating, softball, and picnicking. Curiously, Weequahic even had tennis courts and a golf course.

On hot summer days, we could take advantage of five swimming pools, one in each of Newark's five wards. On Clifton Avenue, Rotunda was the pool that served my neighborhood and one that we would frequent at our own risk; it was in Little Italy and we had to walk through densely populated Seventh Avenue to get there. Gangs of Italian teenagers and young adults would occasionally be hanging on the corners and, depending on the mood of the group, they would be inclined to "get some niggers" when they saw colored boys passing through their neighborhood. But we sometimes wanted relief so badly from the summer heat that it was a risk we were willing to take. We attempted to mitigate that risk by traveling in a group whenever we could.

I was nine years old when Newark's mayor, an Irishman named Leo P. Carlin, started his first term. He was the first mayor whose name I knew because he was the centerpiece in a 8 x 10 black and white photograph my father cherished. It pictured him, nattily dressed, sitting next to Carlin with a small group of other white men, each hoisting a glass of liquor at an affair at Newark's Terrace Ballroom. "The mayor's my friend," my father would casually mention. I surmised that this could not possibly be true since the other men my father called his friends were men with whom he drank, played cards or shot craps. These men would occasionally show up at our apartment to engage in these activities. They were named One-Eyed Phil; a dancer called Hucklebuck Shorty; biracial Donald Boston and

Oscar Singletary, who carried a .45 caliber pistol in a shoulder holster. The mayor was never among them.

During one of his visits, Oscar, a bachelor who lived at 65 Clay Street, took me to our back yard and fired his pistol into the air. The loud noise and flash of fire were so frightening; the recall of the experience still makes me uncomfortable. I wondered where the bullet would fall and if it would injure someone. How would they know who fired the gun? The next day, I worriedly scanned the *Newark Star-Ledger* for any report of someone being struck by a stray bullet, not knowing what I would do if I had found such a report.

Like most families on Clay Street in the 1950s, my family did not have an automobile or telephone — it would be 1954 before the first family, the Keys, and most everyone else would get a telephone. In the interim, the public telephone at the Old Oak Tavern around the corner on Broad Street southwest of our tenement served that purpose. It also served as the neighborhood hangout for my father when his funds were low. On payday, he would move upscale, going to the Novelty Bar and Grill downtown on Market Street and, on special occasions, to Teddy Powell's Lounge to hang with the hipsters. Of all of the fathers in my neighborhood, mine was the only one who hung out in bars.

My mother got the news of her father's death over the line in the telephone booth of the Old Oak. He had been sick and one evening my mother went "to call home" to check on him. When she returned, she called Melvin and me into the kitchen and announced in a sad voice, that "Papa's dead."

Ten years earlier, when she learned she was pregnant (with me), she had used the same telephone to share the heavy burden with her younger brother, Hugo. With children ages 12, 11, and 7 (one child, Rose Marie, had died of pneumonia as a toddler) and on welfare, she was overwhelmed by the prospect of having yet another mouth to feed and was seeking Hugo's advice. She was the only girl of five children born to James and Grace Melvin Owens, the children of enslaved Africans who were raised in the Deep Creek area of Norfolk County, Virginia. My mother's brothers called her "baby" even though she was older than two of them. The younger boys got their cue from the older ones and the name stayed with her until her death from an angina attack on June 28, 1978.

"What must I do?" she cried.
After a short pause, he said, "If it's a boy, name him Hugo."

With the exception of three families that lived in the Eighth Avenue row houses, everyone in the neighborhood was a renter. In our block, there were three red brick tenements with slate stoops. Each was three stories high and encompassed the street numbers 65, 67, and 69. All of the apartments had five rooms and one bathroom, which was entered from the kitchen. This particular style of apartment was known as a shotgun or railroad flat, so called because you could walk from one end to the other in a straight line and see the entire apartment just as you could walk through the cars of a train. At the north and south ends of the apartments were the kitchen and the front (living) room which faced Clay Street. The three rooms in between served as bedrooms. My parents slept in the room next to the living room and my older brother, James, and I slept in the same double bed in the room next to theirs. A door separated the rooms. On the other side of our room was another bedroom adjacent to the kitchen where my sisters slept in a double bed and Melvin slept in a folding bed. Once my sisters left home, though, my parents bought a convertible sofa bed for Melvin. His room would then double as a sort of family entertainment center, since it was there, we kept our television and record player, both acquired in 1955.

Though Melvin had wanted a Castro Convertible sofa bed, but we could not afford one. My brother had been captivated by their catchy jingle, whose first line was, "Who was the first to conquer space?" "Castro Convertible," was the answer. Ultimately, my mother bought a convertible sofa that she said "would sleep just as well as a Castro."

My mother bought a record player after she heard "The Great Pretender" by The Platters; she bought the television because Melvin and I had been spending too much time next door at the Carters' watching "Howdy Doody," "The Rootie Kazootie Club" and "Captain Midnight" on Saturday mornings on a TV Mr. Carter, had built. She reminded us that the Carters already had nine children of their own and had no extra room for us. I do not know where Mr. Carter acquired the skills to build a television, since for a living he was a delivery truck driver for the Schickhaus meat packing company on Orange Street., a few blocks east of the Baxter Terrace housing development.

We heated our apartment with three kerosene stoves. One was built into the kitchen and had been converted from a wood-burning stove in the late 1930s. Standing three feet high by three feet deep by four feet wide, it was a sturdy, black iron structure nestled in a corner next to our gas stove and opposite the small pantry, in which we stored not only our food, but also our dishes, pots and pans. The stove had an oven and four top burners. The burners' tops were removable with the aid of a portable handle that fit neatly into slots designed for that purpose. Once the tops were removed, I could see the dancing flames rising from the kerosene-soaked wicks. This stove provided not only heat for the kitchen, but also, in the winter my mother would sometimes use it for cooking. This convenience saved us money, of which it seemed we never had enough.

I have two distinct memories of that old stove: warming my hands over it when I came in from playing in the snow, and polishing it with a special black wax. It wasn't the actual polishing that I relished; rather, it was the slightly pungent smell of the burning wax that filled my nostrils after I lit the stove following a good polishing. So I did not mind when my mother asked me to polish the stove because experiencing that unique smell was my reward.

The second stove-related ritual was one I performed with Melvin -- clipping and then placing our finger- and toenails to burn on the stove's hot surface. Once, when he had athlete's foot, Melvin peeled the infected skin from his feet and burned it too. We were surprised that the skin smelled the same as the toenails.

On cold winter school mornings, my mother would get up an hour or so before anyone else and light the stove so the kitchen would be warm for breakfast. Decades later, I would discover the poem, "Those Winter Sundays" by Robert Hayden that forced me to reflect on my mother doing just this. She would also heat a kettle of water so Melvin and I could wash our faces and hands before we got dressed. We did not have pajamas (I thought that clothing item was worn only by white people on television and in the movies), so it did not take us long — five minutes max—to perform this task.

Neither did it take us very long to get dressed in the morning. I suppose it helped that we had a sparse wardrobe, which made it possible for us to spend very little time each morning trying to decide what to wear. While I changed my underwear every day, I wore the same pair of corduroy or khaki pants to school for an entire week, and I wore the same shirt for two days straight. Then I would change to another shirt for the next two days. The shirt that I wore on the fifth day, I would wear again on Monday, but with a different pair of pants for that week. With these outfits, I wore my only pair of school shoes, always black, from Thom McCan's, a store known for its sturdy, affordable shoes. I continued this ritual through sixth grade. As an "upperclassman," I thought I was God's gift to Burnet Street

School, but once I got to junior high school, I was the lowliest of the low as a seventh-grader. I needed to rise to a new standard of hipness. Being hip was the most important thing — not elementary school hip, but junior high school hip, which was a whole 'nother thing. And the most obvious way to advertise that you had arrived at hipdom was to dress the part. Corduroy pants, plaid flannel shirts and Blockbuster shoes got you attention, but not the kind you wanted.

The second oil stove was dirt-brown and stood about three-and-a-half feet tall in Melvin's room; it provided heat, such as it was, for that room and the next bedroom where James and I slept. The third stove was in the living room, which had no door between it and my parents' room, which was next to James' and my room. Since we were so poor, we would light it only on special occasions, such as Thanksgiving and Christmas, or when relatives visited. Except for those occasions and during summer, the living room was as cold as it was outside. In fact, my mother nicknamed it "the refrigerator" because when she had to store food, such as a turkey or large ham that was too big to fit in our icebox, (in 1952, we got a Hotpoint refrigerator, a low-end model made by GE), she would place the meat, ironically, on top of the living room stove. This put it out of reach of hungry mice. Fortunately, the holidays that we celebrated with big meals occurred in the winter months. I don't think any food ever spoiled in "the refrigerator."

There were only two sets of windows through which any significant amount of light was admitted into our apartment. They were in the refrigerator and the kitchen, whose windows looked out onto Clay Street and the backyard, respectively. I don't know why we called it the "backyard" because there was no front yard from which to distinguish it. Instead, we had sets of stairs that led to the building. The bedroom windows faced the east wall of the building at 69 Clay Street and the buildings were so close you could reach through an open window and nearly touch the opposing wall.

As was the case with the other apartments in the neighborhood, ours was a cold-water flat. To get hot running water, we had to light a small gas water heater that stood adjacent to the hot water tank located in the kitchen. We performed this ritual weekly on Saturdays in preparation for our Saturday-night baths and the week's clothes-washing. Melvin and I had to take the baths even if we did not need them. To show that we were wrong about that, after our baths, my mother would point out the black ring lining the tub as proof. If we needed hot water for a "bird bath," we would heat it on the gas stove in a gray tea kettle and pour it into the wash basin. During the week, we would wash hands, faces, armpits, private parts, and feet (I sometimes skipped this latter step) in the basin, which we placed in the kitchen sink because we had no sink in the bathroom, only a toilet and bathtub.

In 1956, my mother once told me that she had read in the newspaper that the Newark Housing Authority was planning to build a multiple-building, high-rise housing project, the Christopher Columbus Homes, only a few blocks from Clay Street, in Little Italy. With suppressed excitement, she said the apartments would have steam heat and hot water all of the time and that we could all have our own rooms. She said we might take out an application to get in. It sounded like heaven to me — I had already begun to imagine myself in my own room reading comic books.

She did apply, but our application was rejected because we "made too much money." That was the year my father earned $3,500! My mother was floored. She said they did not want us, but it was because we colored. I secretly thought it seemed white people could do anything they wanted to colored people and get away with it. Hadn't they done so with Emmitt Till?

The year before we tried for that public housing, Till, a fourteen-year-old boy visiting relatives from his Chicago home, just as Melvin and I would visit our grandparents in

Portsmouth and Franklin, had been brutally murdered by a pair of men in Mississippi. The news put both fear and hatred of white men deep in my bones. In the relative safety of Newark, adults whispered of the tragedy among themselves in a failed attempt to shield us youngsters from the horrible news.

Being rejected by the Columbus Homes turned out to be a blessing in disguise, because over time, these and other such high-density housing developments proved to be federally- financed, rat-infested incubators of crime.

In addition to being just plain drafty, our apartment was on the first floor, directly over the cellar, a dark, damp place that had a dirt floor and contained six lockable storage bins, one for each family. Each storage bin housed a 50-gallon oil drum which was also lockable. My mother used to say that the reason our linoleum-covered floors were so cold was that we were directly over the cellar. However, the heat from our apartment rose to heat our ceiling which, in turn, heated the floors of the second-floor tenants; so if our apartment was warm, so were their floors.

In good times (this meant when my mother was working to supplement my father's income) our oil drum was filled with kerosene delivered by Mr. Curtis, the oilman; one of four delivery people who were neighborhood fixtures; the other three being the paperboy, the Italian "policy man", or numbers runner, Tony, and the milkman. Mr. Curtis looked as though he had washed both his brown, crusty-hard hands and coveralls in oil. He always smelled like oil — even in the summertime when he was delivering ice for our ice box before we got our Hotpoint refrigerator.

In the winter months, Melvin and I were overjoyed when Mr. Curtis showed up because it meant for a few weeks, anyway, we would not have to trek the two blocks east toward the Passaic River to the Esso gas station on McCarter Highway to fill our five-gallon kerosene can. It also meant we could have uninterrupted heat for 30 days or so. Except at night, as I have said, when all stoves were shut down.

In between the "good times", about which Lucille Clifton speaks in her poem, "Good Times", Melvin and I would have to take turns carrying the heavy oil can until we got the beautiful, red Radio Flyer wagon, which not only made the task easier, but it also meant only one of us was needed to do it.

That wasn't the only use to which we put the red wagon; I used it to haul groceries to the homes of the many people, almost exclusively women, who shopped at the Acme supermarket on Broadway near Bloomfield Avenue. It seemed to be the norm that most shoppers did not own a car, or preferred not to drive it to the Acme. Many of those who did drive still required assistance getting their groceries to wherever they had parked.

Friday evenings and all-day Saturday were the Acme's busiest times, as most people got paid on Fridays and did their major shopping on these two days. Ranging in age from ten to thirteen, our group of budding entrepreneurs parked our wagons in front of the store, in a neat little line parallel to the curb as we waited to approach a potential customer with the words, "May I take your order, ma'am or sir?"

It was not unusual for one of the other boys to try to bogart (elbow in on) your order. I could not rely upon my customers' remembering me, so to avoid the "my-word-against-yours game," I made a point of wearing some distinctive piece of clothing (usually a brightly colored cap) so my customers could readily recognize me when they finally emerged with their groceries. "Remember me," I would say, "I'm the boy with the red cap."

Like the other boys, I had no fixed fee that I charged my customers; they pretty much gave us whatever they wanted, which was between a quarter and a dollar. There seemed to be no correlation between pay and the number of bags hauled, number of flights of stairs climbed, or the distance traveled.

Over time, I got to know who the big spenders were and also who lived so deep in Little Italy that no size tip would get me to go there. Garside Street was as far west as I would go.

The first and only time I took an order above Garside was uneventful until I had made my delivery and headed home. As I pushed myself in my wagon, left knee planted firmly inside while I propelled myself with my right leg, a little boy, who could not have been more than eight years old, threw his teddy bear and hit me in the face. I suspected it was a set up to see what I would do, so I ignored the assault and kept my eyes glued straight ahead and whistled as I pushed on. I thought of the movie *The King and I* and the song "I Whistle a Happy Tune," so no one would suspect I was afraid. But that tactic did not cut any ice with the pint-sized punk. Thinking that it was only the start of a bad situation, I lifted myself out of my wagon and, walking as fast as I could, began to pull it south toward home. Before long, I heard someone shout, "git that nigger!" I looked back to see what seemed to be seven or eight boys whose ages I could not even guess; it had gotten dark and they must have been thirty or forty yards behind me. My heart jumped into my throat and I took off as fast as my legs could carry me. I thought about another movie that featured the colored actor Stepin Fetchit, who had found himself in a haunted house. When he heard a strange noise, he shouted, eyes bulging, "Feets don't fail me now!" before he lit out, safety-bound like Slim Greer in the Sterling Brown poem "Slim Greer in Hell."

Like most colored boys my age, I thought nothing of Hollywood's portraying our people as fools, in fact I had come to expect it. So, of course I thought the scene in the movie was funny. But I wasn't laughing now. I ran so fast; the wheels of my wagon barely touched the ground. I ran past curious adults and teenagers who seemed to be amused at the fun the kids were having at my expense. I prayed that none of them would try to intervene to stop me. I continued running, made a left onto Seventh Avenue and continued a few more blocks before I noticed I had not heard any screaming in a while. I looked back and, seeing I was no longer being pursued, I slowed to a brisk walk. I do not know how much longer I could have kept up my fear-fueled pace, but it did not matter now, I had shaken them and I was near home.

Emboldened, I thought, *them mothahfuckas better not follow me to Clay Street if they know what's good for them*. In a short-lived fit of fantasy, I imagined myself calling together all of my boys to go to our "secret hideout," (the cellar) to plot how we would get even with my would-be attackers. But never having gotten a look at them, I would not have been able point them out even if we had been bold enough (which we were not) to go into Little Italy to hunt them down.

That cellar was more than a place for storing oil; it was also a place of limitless possibilities for acting out the ignoble proclivities of adolescents, from responding to our hormonal impulses to having secret meetings to plot an attack against real or imagined enemies. I had become curious about what was under the skirts of little girls and took them there to explore. When I grew bored with experimenting in the cellar, I worked my way up to the roof. I felt a greater sense of adventure up there and I could see almost to Branch Brook Park to the northwest and to the Prudential Building downtown to the south. It also seemed as though it was more respectful to go three stories above ground than it did to go one story below. "Shall we go to the penthouse or the basement?"

You could be halfway slick about rendezvousing in the cellar because it had two entrances — one at each end of the building — so the girl and the boy could enter from a separate entrance without attracting attention. Going to the roof was not so simple. First, you had to climb -- very quietly -- three flights of stairs and hope no one else was coming down at the same time, because everyone knew where everyone else lived. So someone would know you were not going to your apartment or to visit anyone once you passed the second floor because there were no little kids on the third floor, except Pee Wee Wilson and his sister Sylvia and they were too weird to hang out with. (Their parents would not allow them to hang out after school. The only time we saw them was when they were running errands or going to school or to church.) But as far as playing softball, tag, hide-and-go seek, they were not a part of any of that. Also, if the third-floor families heard footsteps through the paper-thin walls, they justifiably thought that one of them was about to have a visitor. When no knock came on either door, it was a sure sign that something was up and that would bring some curious adult to his door to check things out.

Once you survived all of that, you then had to ascend a short, narrow flight of stairs leading directly to the roof, lift the heavy skylight cover, quietly remove it and then place it back so as not to draw attention to the spot. When you were ready to leave, you would have the same challenge in reverse.

This early sexual experimentation was ironic. I was indulging in this exploration when I would not kiss or even dance with a girl! In fact, when among my boys, I would pretend to hate girls, even though my boys knew I was lying as all of us had done at one time or another.

(2)

Except one, every family in our neighborhood consisted of parents in their first marriages and their children. The one exception was the family of my best friend, Larry, who lived directly over us on the second floor. There was one characteristic about Larry's family that set it apart from all the other 30 families that lived in our neighborhood: his mother's sister, her husband and their three children and his mother's parents all lived with them. Not only that, but also his mother's brother periodically lived there too.

One thing that Larry and I had in common was that we were named for one of our uncles. My uncle was married with children and was a successful dentist who owned his own home. But Larry's uncle was a "fag" This was the derogatory term to refer to homosexuals who dressed in outlandish clothes the likes of which I had not seen anyone else wear: brightly colored shoes made of patent leather, saddle-stitching down the outside seams of his pants, and outrageous shirts seemed to be staples of his wardrobe. "Fag" still a derogatory word today, was the only term I knew to refer to a man who, as the myth held, hated girls and who was believed to attack them at night to cut off their hair. In my little, parochial world, I believed gay men could be objectively identified by the loud clothes they wore, the way they held their wrists, and their style of talking and walking. Also, they could not fight. It was this latter characteristic that we implied when we would insult someone by calling him a fag. This was the ultimate expression of disregard for someone. And if someone called you a fag and you did not defend yourself by saying something mean to him, or if you weren't quick with words, punching him out to prove you were not a fag, well, that was cool.

I was clueless as to the sexual implications of the term fag. At age 10 or 11, I was still trying to figure out boy-girl relationships. I could not conceive of a boy-boy connection. It was an issue I did not have to struggle with because I had not yet met boys who displayed these indicting tendencies.

I was equally ill-informed about lesbians, whom we referred to as "bulldaggers or butches" (street talk for lesbians). Some myths about them were that they hated men, carried knives and would cut a man's throat if he tried to mess with them, i.e., make a play for them as if they were regular girls. There was one single woman named Bobbie who always wore pants and kept her hair cut short. I never saw her in the company of anyone else when she left or came home to her apartment in the Clay Street tenement building just east of Spring Street. She was a fine, shapely woman with bronze-colored skin and when she passed by a group of us boys, we would knock each other over trying to be the first to speak to her. "Hi Bobbie," we would pipe almost in unison, and she would invariably respond, "Hi baby." Then, we would argue amongst ourselves trying to establish at whom she had directed the return greeting. After all, she did say "baby," which was singular! I suspected she was a lesbian, but could not accept that someone so fine could prefer other women. Secretly, I wished I were older so I could find out for sure. Even if she was, I thought I would be able to "convert" her.

I was of the age where sexuality — my own and that of others' — was a frequently discussed topic. Although "homo" and "lesbian" did not find their way into my adolescent lexicon until years later, I did not know that homo was short for homosexual. I have already said the only person we suspected of being a "fag" was Larry's uncle. But none of us cats who hung out with Larry had the nerve to ask him if was true because we did not want to risk losing his friendship. More importantly, we did not want to risk an ass-whipping. But behind his back we would point out how funny his uncle walked. He swiveled his hips and flapped his pigeon-toed feet as if he were wearing swim fins. Larry was pigeon-toed too, but only in one foot. I quietly wondered if he might turn into a "fag" too when he grew up.

I would also poke fun at his uncle's processed hair. My mother used to say, with disdain, his head reminded her of patent leather. This I found a bit perplexing because she loved Nat King Cole and never commented one way or another about his processed head. But then Nat could sing!

Larry used to boast, or so it seemed to me, that his grandparents were not colored because they were from the West Indies. I didn't even know where the West Indies were and neither did he, because when we asked him, he dismissed us by calling us dummies. "Don't you dummies know anything?" he would blurt out. When Harry Belafonte's recording of the banana boat song was released, all of us kids liked it, but we couldn't understand all of the lyrics. When Belafonte sang "Come Mr. tally man, tally me banana," we did not understand what he was talking about. We did know that Belafonte was from the West Indies (my sisters had told me), so I asked Larry to ask his grandparents what "tally" meant, - they being West Indian and all. Carrying out his assignment, he reported back to me that the words were really "Come Mr. Yellow man and carry me banana." I was so glad that we had a friend whose grandparents spoke "West Indian" and I authoritatively set about correcting the kids outside our immediate circle whenever I heard them singing the "incorrect" lyrics.

Larry's given name was Lawrence. But up until the third grade, all the kids called him Brussy. His older brother, Jun, (short for junior, we kids called him Fat Junny) called him by that name because when Larry was born, his parents would refer to him as "brother" to Jun but Jun could not get the "th" sound down and settled for "brossa" which later became just Brussy. I remember the day "Larry" was dropped on him. It was the first week of third grade and the teacher, Miss Warren, a silver-haired, ruddy-complexioned white woman, had begun to read the names on the class roster. When she got to "Lawrence," she said "I think I'll call you Larry, wouldn't you like that?" Larry said, "I guess so." That was it. He had been Brussy for eight years and now in about eight seconds, he had become Larry for the rest of his life! To everyone except Junny, that is, who continued to call him Brussy well into his adulthood.

Larry and I were the best of friends, at least until we entered high school, where we ultimately went our separate ways. We both took note of the fact that he was exactly 40 days older than I. He seemed especially proud of this fact; I never knew why, but maybe it was because of the Biblical significance (40 days and 40 nights). We were also knee babies (As we used the term, next to last in birth order) and liked and participated in the same sports. He was by far the better athlete — and for a while, like me, really liked school, though I was the better student. To pick a fight with one was to invite a fight with both of us. We had no secrets between us and shared everything. The one physical characteristic that set us apart was our teeth.

Though I had a slight overbite, my teeth were Pepsodent white just like in the TV commercials; while Larry had thoroughly yellow, rotten teeth and bleeding gums (He was always spitting blood.) and while everybody noticed, no one talked about it (to his face). At the time, there was a toothpaste product on the market called Pepsodent that boasted in one of its commercials, "You'll wonder where the yellow went when you brush your teeth with Pepsodent." If this claim had been true, I know Larry would have taken advantage of the product.

The only kid who could talk about Larry's dental hygiene was an older cousin of his named Joe, who used to say that Larry had breath like a blowtorch and that he could clear out a movie theater just by blowing across the room. Joe was a heavyset, dark-skinned boy about two years older than Larry and me. He was a born comedian who could find humor in almost anything. He had big round eyes that had a way of drawing your attention to his face. He was the kind of person who could effortlessly make you laugh no matter how much you tried not to — even if the joke was on you.

He once said that my glasses were so thick that they gave me X-ray vision and I would slyly sneak stares at girls so I could see beneath their clothes. It was difficult and sometimes impossible to strike back at Joe because his cracks were always fact-based, though exaggerated to absurdity. And even if you were able to come back with something really strong, it would take you so long to put it together that no one would appreciate it. Then there were the matters of timing and delivery. Joe had already gotten the advantage by striking first and at the most opportune time and always with an element of surprise. All of these factors conflated to make a frivolous atmosphere only Joe could create. One such occasion was Larry's twelfth birthday party.

Larry had invited a few close friends and his local cousins to the party; unfortunately for him, one of these cousins was Joe. Larry's mother had made a big, beautiful yellow cake covered with chocolate icing and dotted with twelve candles. We had been having a grand time playing games and telling stories when Larry's mom called us; it was time to cut the cake and sing "happy birthday." We assembled around the kitchen table, in the center of which she had placed the cake. At her signal, we began to sing the song. At the song's conclusion, Larry's mom asked him to blow out the candles; whereupon, Joe said, "Well we won't have to cut the cake because when he blows on it, the cake's gonna turn into cupcakes." I immediately looked at Larry's mom, thinking she was going to bust Joe in the mouth, but it was apparent that this remark had passed right over her. Sensing that she was clueless, the entire assemblage (minus Larry and Joe, who kept a straight face) burst into boisterous laughter. I felt guilty for laughing at my friend on the joyous occasion of his birthday, but I just could not control myself. Larry, darting his eyes across all of our faces, did manage to blurt out defensively, "I fail to see the humor in what Joe said, Hugo." But he was too late. Even if Pepsodent had been able to live up to its claim, not even it could have helped Larry at that point.

(3)

Many of the kids who lived in Little Italy lived with families that were first- and second-generation Italians whose non-English-speaking grandparents lived with them and clung to the ways of "the old country." Most often, or so it seemed, the surviving grandparent was the grandmother who, in apparent perpetual mourning, was always dressed in black. To my young eyes, these women seemed so old. Their long dresses hung unevenly over their ankles and they covered their white-haired heads with long, black scarves whose ends they held together with one hand. Their olive-colored skin, probably once very beautiful, was now wrinkled, prune-like; their curved backs - question-mark like, and missing teeth gave them the appearance of characters in a horror movie. They looked like no other women I had ever seen.

The more affluent Italians lived in neighborhoods north and east of Park Avenue, not far from Bloomfield, in single-family homes that sat on small, nicely kept lawns that complemented the clean streets. The nicer parts of Branch Brook Park extended into these neighborhoods and added to their beauty.

All of the close-by amenities — swimming pool, Boys Club, playground and Branch Brook Park — that attracted me were located in Little Italy. Of special interest to me were the Catholic feast festivals, at which there were all kinds of food vendors and amusement rides all up and down Seventh Avenue, a main artery in Little Italy. There would also be a small parade that featured a statue of person standing erect being transported on a float pulled slowly by a car. The faithful would place money on this statue. Not being Catholic, I didn't know why they had these feasts, but I believed it had something to do with saints. For me, it just meant I could look forward to having a good time. During these feasts, my friends and I roamed freely among the crowds without fear of harm.

As I got older though, things began to change. I began to notice in the Italian boys an open, unexplainable hostility toward colored boys. The very sight of a colored boy walking through their neighborhood would inflame them. Often, I was faced with the prospect of a severe beating from a gang of vicious, usually older boys, admonishing me to stay out of "the ward" as they called it, or get an asskicking. They often hid their real motives by using a younger, smaller boy as bait the way they had done me on my fateful trip to Garside Street mentioned earlier, or so I surmised. The bait would walk up to you and start calling you names. If you reacted, the older boys, ensconced somewhere close by and watching clandestinely, would move in to defend the little guy from the "menacing nigger."

Coming back from the Rotunda Pool one hot summer day, Melvin and I were accosted by a group of five or six boys bearing menacing grins who silently began to surround us. Melvin and I had a ready-made plan for such an event. We would target the smallest one in the group who was standing between us and home and run toward him and hit him in the nose. After that we would have to depend on speed of foot. One of the kids, who like me, wore glasses, was only a bit taller, but smaller in stature. I honed in on him, and was surprised at how easy it was. I led the charge, slamming my elbow into the unsuspecting boy's nose and knocking him to the ground. The element of surprise had to have played a significant role in their response because they did not pursue us right away. Instead, they went to the aid of their fallen goomba. "Did you see that? The nigger hit Sal. He hit Sal," I heard as I looked over my right shoulder to see how much of a lead we had gotten. Melvin was only a step behind me as we ran two abreast. In a few seconds, we heard a chorus of "Get dem niggers. Stop dem niggers." A small group of old Italian men was standing in front of a store as we sped down Seventh Avenue and one of them, responding to the chorus, attempted to trip me by sticking out his foot as we approached. But I was going so fast the impact caused him to lose his balance and fall onto the hood of a parked car. I stumbled forward, but somehow managed to regain my balance. The boys chased us all the way to Broadway — the northwest perimeter of our neighborhood — before they slowed their pace and turned around to head back home, cussing and threatening us still.

Though this was a common occurrence, it was impossible to predict when we might be attacked. Sometimes, we could walk the five blocks — four of them on Seventh Avenue — to the pool and there would not even be so much as a hint of provocation. Someone might call you a "nigger" but as long as you did not look in the direction of the name-caller, you could sometimes make it all the way to the pool without incident. Once you arrived at the pool, there was never a problem — not even name-calling. I knew that white people in the South — "crackers" is what we called them — hated colored people, but as far as I knew they didn't go to church. So, I presumed they were just naturally evil and had no fear of divine retribution; something my mother validated every now and then. After relating in the newspaper, a story of yet another injustice suffered by a colored person at the hands of white people, she would often sigh and say, "White folks are just plain evil."

When we weren't fighting our way to Rotunda for a swim, we would visit the Boys' Club or go to Branch Brook Park. The club was located at the intersection of High Street and Eighth Avenue, a bit south of Clay Street and just off the southeast tip of Little Italy. Membership was 35 cents a year and we got a membership card in a small plastic case that doubled as a key chain. Recreational activities included basketball, shuffleboard, pool, bingo, and boxing. The club was in neutral territory and staffed entirely by Italian men who tried to deal fairly with all the boys. They were very strict and took no nonsense from anybody. They had a one-strike rule about fighting. It did not matter who was at fault, if you were involved in a fight, you would be barred from the club for one year. It was attributable to them that I felt none of the abject fear that haunted me while I was making my way to Rotunda. In fact, I actually felt secure.

During the school year, I was limited to attending the club only on Fridays after school and on Saturdays. I was a member until I was twelve or thirteen, and during that entire time, I witnessed only one fight: Michael Palante, in a dispute over a game of pool, had spit in Pedro Carter's face (we pronounced it Pee-dro). Pedro was one of nine children in his family, who lived at 69 Clay Street. Only the boys in the immediate area had witnessed the assault and I was the only other colored boy from Clay Street present that night. Pedro ran into the bathroom to clean up and returned, appearing angry, but saying nothing. Palante was a big kid who was at least a year older than the frail Pedro. I eased over to Pedro and asked him if he was going to report the incident to Abalou (I do not know if that was his first or last name, but that's what everyone called him), the club's disciplinarian. Pedro replied he would handle it himself. I sensed Pedro was not going to disclose what he had planned. But I thought if he were going to fight Palante, he would have done so already and just taken the suspension. On the other hand, there was no way Pedro could beat the much bigger Palante.

About ten minutes before the eight o'clock-closing time, Pedro announced he was ready to go home. I was just finishing up a game of shuffleboard, so I was ready as well. Once we were outside, Pedro said, "I'm gonna knock that mothafuckah's head off." I said, "Who you talkin' 'bout, man?" "Palante," was his response and he pulled a three-foot piece of tubing from under his jacket. Somewhat in disbelief, I said, "Oh, shit. Where did you get that?" At the same time I was thinking Pedro would never be able to return to the club not because of suspension — he would have to be caught fighting for that to happen. Rather, it was because I thought he would be ganged up on and beaten to within an inch of his life if Palante's friends decided to teach Pedro a lesson. A few minutes later, Palante emerged from the club with one of his friends. He saw Pedro standing at the bottom of the stairs and through a laugh said, "I thought you went home. You must want another bath," and he advanced toward Pedro who, like somebody in a Western like Lash LaRue or Whip Wilson, swung the tubing back over his right shoulder in an arc aimed at Pallante's left temple. Then he pulled back to follow up with a second swing. This one knocked Pallante's eyeglasses from his face, sending them flying past his friend, who instinctively caught them. Then Pedro just stood there and said, "Nobody spits in my face, you wop bastard, nobody!" It seemed everybody was in shock except Pedro; but no one more than Palante who was stunned with disbelief as he grasped both sides of his face, screaming, "The nigger's crazy, he's crazy!" as he and his friend took off running north on High Street toward Little Italy.

What Pedro did was truly heroic. He received much praise from the Clay Street gang once I spread word of his brave actions. A few weeks passed before any Clay Streeters would risk returning to the club. We had feared that every one of us would be in for a beating in spite of the fact it was only Pedro who had gone up side Palante's head. "Any nigger would do," we thought they would say. To my surprise, there were no repercussions and I never saw Palante again. I speculated he was ashamed to tell anyone what a beating he had suffered at the hands of a smaller, colored boy from Clay Street.

The Boys Club provided me with opportunities to attend summer camp free or subsidized, not once but three times. The first experience was at a camp ironically named Camp Goodwill. At Goodwill there was a culture among the counselors that permitted anyone who wanted to abuse the campers in the name of discipline to do so with impunity. We had to address the counselors by their first names preceded by the handles, Mr. or Miss.

One night during a campfire sing-along, Mr. Al, without provocation, grabbed Melvin by his arm with such force that he began to cry. When I attempted to intervene, he grabbed me, twisting my arm behind my back with one hand and with the other placed his hunting knife at my throat demanding to know what I was going to do about it. I screamed for him to let me go. I had gotten his attention off Melvin and that was my goal. I did not believe he would kill me before so many witnesses, which included both fellow campers and counselors, although none of the counselors even took a step to cool down Mr. Al. After he had made his point, he called me a sissy and pushed me to the ground.

At the end of the two weeks, after I returned home, I told my mother of the incident, she was shocked. She was double shocked when I corrected her assumption that Al was white. "He was culid," as I pronounced the word then.

The camp did not reopen the next summer. Apparently, other campers had reported their own woeful tales to their parents who, like my mother, reported them to the Boys Club officials.

The following summers I spent two weeks each at Camp Brady, where I learned to swim and to dive off the diving board; and Camp Princeton, where while canoeing, I knocked my glasses into the murky lake while attempting to swat a wasp that had been buzzing my head. I also learned some sexually suggestive drinking songs about young maidens and lewd jokes from campers from Long Island. These two camp experiences more than made up for the bad memories of Camp Goodwill. I was surprised that my mother let Melvin and me attend camp again, but since it got us out of her hair for two weeks, it was probably worth the risk. I was glad she took it.

Before our first camp experience, my mother would take Melvin and me to Portsmouth, Virginia, to visit her parents. I do not recall that my father ever accompanied us on these visits. Carrying the shoe boxes of fried chicken, potato salad, and cake that my mother had packed for us, the three of us would board the Greyhound at Newark's Penn Station and travel the eight hours or so to Norfolk. By ferry boat, we crossed the James River to Portsmouth, where we would be met by one of my mother's brothers, usually Uncle Hugo or Uncle Cornelius.

We called Cornelius, whose middle name was Charles, Uncle C.C. Uncle Hugo told me that he was named for a brother of my maternal grandmother who was murdered by white thugs enraged with jealousy over his success as a Deep Creek merchant. No one was ever charged with the crime. Moreover, no one in the family ever spoke of this tragedy until I was in my forties, when Uncle Hugo told me about it. When I asked him why they did it, he succinctly replied, "he was too successful."

(4)

My first day at Burnet Street School did not live up to the billing the older kids had promised. The summer before I started kindergarten, they had begun to fill my head with frightening tales of what I could expect — arithmetic, social studies, and homework, as I recall, were supposed to be so hard they made you cry. I was not looking forward to school at all. It never occurred to me that if school was so hard, how was it that they were surviving it?

That same summer, I recall my mother coming home from the hospital to a welcoming chorus of my siblings and me. My father had gone to get her and they arrived home in a taxicab. I do not remember her being away, just coming home. Some months later, I noticed her right arm had swollen to nearly twice the size of her left. I was told she had had an operation and since the only thing different about her that I could see was in the size of her arm, I assumed the surgery had been on her arm. It was not until I was in college that I learned she had had breast cancer and the arm swelling was a permanent side effect of her mastectomy.

I don't remember at all the walk to school on my first day of kindergarten, although we must have passed the Lackawanna railroad station and the Westinghouse factory along the one-mile route. However, I do recall that it was my mother who took me. When we arrived at the first-floor classroom that would be mine for the next ten months, I was struck by the sight of a stately woman who looked like a movie star. I remember her being so tall and having golden blond hair and milky white skin. She was the most beautiful woman I had ever seen in person. The smile she flashed revealed a perfect set of white teeth (Pepsodent, I was sure) that looked like those of the models I had seen in toothpaste ads in *Life* magazine. A mixture of sweet smells wafted from her body. I was awestruck.

She greeted us with a warm smile that was encircled by bright red lipstick. "Well, hello there, young man. My name is Miss Matoronna. What's yours?" she asked. I was puzzled that she had not greeted my mother first. I tried to speak, but my words, while in my head, could not find their way out of my mouth. My mother looked at me. "His name is David Hugo, but we call him Hugo at home. What do you want Miss Matoronna to call you, David or Hugo?" my mother asked. Now I certainly knew my first name, but no one had ever called me David, so I was perplexed by my mother's question. For all of my five years on earth, everyone had been calling me Hugo. Why is it now that I have an option on what I should be called? Why would I say David? And if I did, would everyone start calling me David or would it be just Miss Matoronna? This was the first question I was being asked in school and already I was flunking. School was going to be hard after all.

Tentatively, and meekly I told her, Hugo. My voice was barely audible. "Hugo it is then." She turned to the class and said, "Children, I want you all to meet our newest pupil,

Hugo Barrett." All I could think of when she said "pupil" was someone's eye. She asked a girl named Olivia to raise her hand. When she complied with the request, Miss Matoronna directed me to sit right at the empty desk behind Olivia. She pointed to an olive-skinned, wavy-haired girl who smiled shyly as she raised her hand. I was to have a crush on her right up through sixth grade.

Like many of the students at Burnet, Olivia lived in Baxter Terrace, a public housing project that was a cluster of neat, well-maintained, three-story walk-up garden apartments. There were really two clusters of buildings. The ones north of James Street were where only colored families lived, while those south of James Street had only white residents and a mere sprinkling of colored ones. The James Street students were in the district for Central Avenue School, with its mostly white enrollment. I didn't think there was anything odd about this. In fact, we quite casually referred to the "white and colored" sides of Baxter Terrace. It was just a fact, and, to the children anyway, devoid of judgment.

I hesitated to take my seat because I suddenly realized my mother was going to leave me there with these strange children and the beautiful teacher. She must have sensed it because she said, "It's going to be alright. I'll be right here to take you home when school is out. Be a good boy." I slowly ambled in the general direction of my seat, looking over my shoulder at my mother as I did, and sat down. Once I was seated, my mother walked quietly out of the classroom, waving and flashing a reassuring smile as she exited.

The kindergarten classroom was on the east side of the building and it ran parallel to Eagle Street. About 10 a.m. most days, the sun would peek over the rooftops of the two-story tenements that lined the street and spread its golden rays across our eager faces. The classroom's atmosphere was warm, friendly, and inviting.

Years later, my Uncle Hugo told me his sister took him to his first day of school at the Deep Creek colored elementary school in Norfolk County, Virginia. Like many of the schools for colored children in the South at that time, it was a one-room schoolhouse. His experience contrasted sharply with mine. Both his mother and grandmother had constantly reminded him of the dangers he would face if he got involved with white people. Moreover, he was told that if he were to have anything to do with a white woman, white men would pour tar on him, cover him with feathers and set him on fire. He should stay out of the way of white men because they would shoot him or put a rope around his neck and hang him from a tree just for sport and no one would do anything about it.

He started school in 1922, and these images had planted themselves so deeply in his six-year-old mind that the telling of this tale at age 39 would send him into a short trance as he brought them into the present. The only girl among four boys, his older sister, who was to become my mother, had been asked to take him to his one-room schoolhouse because her own one-room schoolhouse was right next door to his. He had been looking forward to attending school and was very eager to start. On the way, he repeatedly asked his sister how much longer it would be before they would arrive, making the one-mile walk seem more like two. When they finally arrived, Hugo froze in the doorway. The teacher was white! She had reddish hair, freckles that dotted her face, and blue eyes that seemed to glow like the eyes of a cat reflecting moonlight. He began to hear the voices of his mother and grandmother and see images of himself being murdered by an enraged white mob. He was terrified. How could his mother send him to the very people about whom she had so sternly warned him? He felt betrayed. He had to escape. His sister, Annie, took his hand and led him toward the teacher and introduced him. He was unable to speak, yet he fixed his gaze on this intimidating stranger in case she tried anything that might get him in trouble. He was shown his seat, which he obediently sat in, but as soon as Annie left the room, he jumped up and ran after her as fast as he could. Repeated attempts to get him to go back were unsuccessful, so, in victory, he spent that day with Annie in her classroom.

When they went home after school, it took his mother and his grandmother to convince him that Miss Nellie Boyd was not white. "Everybody who looks white is not white," he recalls the women explaining. How was a six-year-old to tell the difference? Suppose he made a mistake and addressed a white woman he thought was colored. Would he be punished? "Baby's (my mother's nickname) explanation did not make him any more comfortable," he told me.

Not a one-room schoolhouse by a long shot, Burnet Street School had a student body of about 400 and went up to the sixth grade at the time I enrolled, and among all of these kids, I was the only person who had the name Hugo, and I paid dearly for it. The older kids called me "I go, you go, you gone," and other variations on the name. For the first time I had begun to hate my name. In fifth grade, a Puerto Rican kid from the Archbishop Thomas J. Walsh public housing project named Lugo enrolled at Burnet. Drawing attention to his name, I tried to transfer the taunting to him, but it didn't work. I was greeted with the reminder of my own name and told I was in no position to poke fun at Lugo. Of course, they were right. I was just trying to get some relief, even if at someone else's expense.

Miss Matoronna played the big, black grand piano that occupied one corner of the room. She seemed to love all of the kids. I never detected any hint of favoritism or harshness toward any of the kids on her part. Even when John Pollard had an accident that stunk up the whole classroom and she had to take him into the cloak room to clean him up. Even then, she was compassionate as she tried to comfort the distraught and embarrassed John.

Kindergarten also provided me with my first exposure to so many white children. I had been in the presence of white children before -- they were in my Sunday School class during church services attended by the adults upstairs. However, at no time were there more than five kids in the entire class, including Melvin and me, but since I had not learned there was actual value associated with skin color, I didn't think anything of it any more than I did the different colors in a box of crayons, they were just colors. But in time, the cumulative effect of the horrors of Little Italy, the mean spirits of white telephone workers in my neighborhood at the Bell Telephone Company, the summer vacations at my grandparents' in the segregated Virginia towns of Portsmouth and Franklin, and the horrific lynching of Emmett Till would change all of that. Those traumas shaped my view of the world and my place in it as a colored boy.

My studies at Burnet were not hard for me. I liked the idea of learning about new things and having so many new friends. The boys and girls had separate entrances to the school through what were known as the girls' and boys' courts. This arrangement seemed odd to me. What was it about us that we could sit in class together but we had to enter and leave the school through separate entrances? You could actually be disciplined if you were caught even in the girls' court, much less trying to enter the building via this route. The presence of a boy in the girls' court could mean only that he was up to no good, or so we were told. I would trespass every now and then just for the hell of it, but I never got caught. Ironically, the only entrance that was open for access to after-school activities was through the girls' court.

Girls could enter their court from Burnet Street by walking a short distance down a fenced walkway or from Eagle Street through an unlighted, street-level tunnel that was about fifty yards long. We had to use this same tunnel to gain access to the playground. The tunnel was the perfect location for engaging in socially unacceptable behavior. If there were going to be a fight planned for after school, the tunnel was where it would inevitably take place. Spontaneous fights, of course, could and did take place anywhere and at any time, without regard to consequences.

The most indulged-in activity in the tunnel was not fighting but feeling girls, an activity in which I had begun to participate by fourth grade. I never thought I could get in trouble for it because no girl had ever reported it. The most severe reaction we would get from the victim (though at the time, I did not see them as victims) was a punch accompanied by some name-calling and threats of more physical harm, which were never carried out. I thought it was all in fun. As I approached from behind, I would run quickly by the unsuspecting girl, squeeze her buttocks and keep on running, looking back and laughing as I sped away. "Hugo, you nasty thing. Wait 'til I catch you!" some would yell. If a girl had a big brother, it was insurance that she would never be bothered in this way. I heard that one girl expressed that she hated having a big brother for just that reason. Apparently, in her mind, it deprived her of a way to get attention.

I had a soft side to my hard exterior. A girl named Shirley was in my fourth-grade art class, taught by Miss Sabroski. (Miss Sabroski later became Mrs. Stanford; she had gotten married over the summer and never told us of her plans — just showed up one day with a new name.) Shirley had suffered third-degree burns on her face and both arms after she was caught in an apartment fire the year before. She was out of school for nearly a year while she healed. I felt really sorry for her and out of this sympathy, I helped her with her art projects when no one else would even go near her. I secretly wished she would become a Christian Scientist so she could pray and make the burnt skin go away.

I would later pray for myself after my sister, Hilda, discovered that I was nearsighted. To correct my vision, I was prescribed thick eyeglasses that I hated with a passion. I was to wear these monstrosities for the next fifty years, but in the interim, I thought, through Christian Science, I could pray up 20-20 vision. But in my sixtieth year, the Almighty would use science in the form of cataract surgery to give his delayed response to my prayers. Delayed or not, I was extremely grateful. My sister, Hilda, discovered my need for glasses one day while observing how close to my face I held the comic book as I sat reading at the kitchen table. She asked me to hold the book further away and then asked me to read. I couldn't. Actually, my sister wasn't the first to discover my myopia; but she was the one to act upon it by telling my mother, who was present at the time, "Mama, this boy needs glasses."

In third grade, I remember failing to do an in-class assignment that had been written on the blackboard and when I was confronted by the teacher about it, tears ran down my cheeks, as I confessed, "I can't see from here." Her solution was to move me to the front of the class. Why she did not refer me to the school nurse, I never found out.

My first pair of eyeglasses were a failure. We got them through the Board of Health where some incompetent wrote a prescription so far wrong, I would not even wear the glasses. In disgust, my mother then took me to a private optometrist, Mr. Bedford, downtown on Broad Street near S. Klein's department store. The prescription was so good, I was astonished at how much better I could see. But like anything else, whenever you solve one problem, it creates yet new one or a few new ones. Now my problems would be failing to take off the glasses when I went to bed only to wake up the next morning to discover that one of the lenses had been dislodged; the second was being teased by my friends that my lenses resembled the bottom of a Coke bottle. It was not long before my friends renamed me the age-old "four eyes."

(5)

There were two major peer influences in my adolescent years. In 1955, a new family moved into the neighborhood. They were a Brady Bunch whose stepparents were not married. They were the first adults living together, in my experience, to have this distinction. To be sure, I had overheard my parents and other adults whispering disapprovingly of "common law" marriages, but I did not know what the term meant. I had deduced it could not have been anything positive, or else why did they find it necessary to whisper in my presence? In addition, I thought, *What did law have to do with marriage anyway? Preachers married people.*

When I told my mother about the new family, she just grunted "humph" and said she did not think it was a good idea to play with children from such a family. She also observed that "If people like that are moving into this neighborhood and they are moving up, can you imagine what they must be moving up from?" I did not see the relevance, because the way I saw it, I would be playing with the kids, not the parents. So her disapproving tone fell on deaf ears.

Billy and Carolyn were the children of the man of the house and shared his name, Johnson; while Barry and Bunt (never did know his real name) were children of the lady of the house. And they shared her last name, Siegel. Both sets of children called their parents by their first names! This was unheard of in our neighborhood and some of us kids had mixed emotions about this. I, for one, felt very uncomfortable just thinking about calling the parents of my friends by their first names and would not do it with Billy's parents, despite them urging me to do so.

Billy's apartment was located over a linoleum store at the northeast intersection of Clay Street and McCarter Highway, about a quarter mile west of the Clay Street bridge. The crowded, untidy apartment smelled of urine, as did Billy, so we suspected he was a bedwetter. We never mentioned it because Billy was bad; he took no shit from anyone and he'd just as soon split your head as look at you. He could cuss and fight.

At 13, Billy was closer in age to those in our core group than he was to his siblings and we all looked up to him. He was a gangly character with a dark brown complexion and earlobes that jutted out like ice cream scoops turned sideways. He attended Montgomery Street School, a school for children who had been labeled "slow learners." His different abilities might have accounted for why he found comfort hanging with kids much younger than he; and who had inferior street smarts. He seemed to know so much more than any of us about topics our parents had not found the time to tell us about. These included "secrets" about girls, hormonal changes in our own bodies, and the power of bananas. He said that eating bananas would make you have more cum. Even if it were true, I never thought why I would *need* more.

It did not take very long for him to establish himself as our leader. Billy introduced us to some strange games. The objective of one, which had no name, was to catch one of your buddies unawares. Say, as we were hanging out on the block, you would stand behind your mark as he was preoccupied with something else, take out your johnson and piss on him. This would put everyone else in stitches. That was the game. Peer pressure made everyone a participant and, of course, ensured that everyone would abide by the simple rules.

If you opted not to participate, you were subject to get pissed on anyway, but you did not have piss-back rights. If you got pissed on you could not get physical with the cat who got you because the rest of the cats would kick your ass. But one kid, Larry, my best friend at the time, did not have the temperament to be on the receiving end of this stuff, even though he had earned the reputation for being one of the most ruthless members of the club.

On one of the occasions when he became the victim, we were standing around listening to Larry telling us lies about one of his sexual exploits when Lefty slowly crept up on Larry and started emptying his bladder. It was a cold, gray November day and Larry was wearing the thickest corduroy pants I had ever seen. He did not react for what seemed like minutes. The rest of us were unable to contain our laughter, and it seemed for a time that Larry thought we were laughing at his story. It wasn't until the urine began to run down his pant leg and into his sock that Larry realized what had been happening. He let out a string of cuss words and went after Lefty to kill him, I was sure.

The faster runner, Lefty took off headed southbound on Spring Street, pacing himself and glancing periodically over his left shoulder to shout at Larry, "I got you fair and square, man. What 'chu mad about?" The rest of us chased after Larry until we caught and wrestled him to the ground. Once he was immobilized, we made him admit that he had gotten fairly pissed on. We reminded him of the time he had once stood on a car and pissed on Raymond's head. Raymond had been a good sport and that was far worse than what Lefty had done to him. Larry finally calmed down and agreed not to bother Lefty, who was observing from a safe distance. This development notwithstanding, Lefty, apparently thinking discretion was the better part of valor, went home.

While this game was unique, we also played some of the same games played by kids in other cities. Newark was not a place teeming with green space, but it had as much outdoors as any place else, and outdoors is where my friends and I spent most of our unstructured time. Except for the occasional softball game organized by Frank Jones, one of the neighborhood parents, we had no organized sports, so most everything we did was kid-initiated and executed.

We played kick the can and contact football sans pads. But since no one could afford a football, we used an old sailor hat stuffed with rags held together with shoe laces. Our football field was a grassy island that was in the middle of Clay Street near McCarter Highway, a street heavily used by commercial vehicles.

We also frequented a field on the Newark side of the Passaic River that had a steep hill down which we would ride our sleds after a winter snowfall and in the summer, our homemade summer sleds crafted from large cardboard boxes that we had gotten from Bell Telephone's trash and flattened to suit our needs. We would make our way down this hill, seated on our rumps and screaming at the tops of our lungs as our cardboard sleds picked up speed, sometimes hurling us onto our faces. Groups of us would stay at this play place until we were too exhausted to walk the half-mile home or in winter when our hands had gotten too cold to steer our sleds.

We also played hide-and-go seek (we would say "hang go seek"), marbles, and hopscotch. When we felt adventurous, and thought it safe to do so (always a risky proposition), we walked the mile or so to Branch Brook Park to catch pollywogs; watch old Italian men fish from the shore of the small man-made lake; and ride on the swings, merry-go-round, and see-saw.

Lefty was my other adolescent influence. Lefty, ironically, was right-handed. He got his nickname from one of the older boys, George Davis, whose nickname was Hooksie, when, one day, he appeared wearing two matching, but left sneakers. His wardrobe error branded him with that nickname; it stayed with him all the way through high school and into adulthood. Lefty was a street-wise but marginal student who compensated for his lack of academic prowess by sharing his worldly knowledge with his peers. He was such a convincing rascal that if our parents told us one thing and he told us something else, we believed him.

"I know, Ma, but Lefty said ...," we would tell our parents. My mother nicknamed him "the professor" because he would also argue so self-assuredly with her. He would conduct himself as if he was an adult and he was slow to yield. When the adults got tired of him, they would just dismiss him with a "Boy, get out of my face!"

There was one area in which he excelled and for which we all admired him: his recitation of the urban, African-American folk epoch "The Sinking of the Titanic." He could recite the entire poem from memory and on demand. I have since learned that there are several versions of the story, as is often the case with a work that lives through oral tradition. Lefty's version was among the vulgar ones that I had heard and, during my childhood, the only one I knew.

The main character in the ballad was named Shine. It happened that Shine, who worked in the ship's boiler room, as the only colored person aboard, since racial segregation barred colored passengers. Shine was the first to discover that the ship had sprung a leak. Dutifully, he reported the problem to the captain, who, in turn, rebuffed him. The captain was convinced of the ship's indestructibility and just knew that Shine had to be mistaken. Finally, disgusted at the white folks' arrogance and to save his own life, Shine dives overboard and begins his long swim for shore. Along the way, the drowning captain, his wife, and daughter make offers to Shine of money and sexual favors if he would only save them. Even a shark is impressed with Shine's swimming ability:

> Shine, shine, you swimmin' fine
> Miss one stroke and your ass is mine.
> Shine said, you may be king of the ocean
> You may be king of the sea
> But you got to be a strokin' mothafuckah
> If you gonna catch me.
> And Shine swam on.

Though a hero in our neighborhood, Lefty's poetic prowess got him into trouble in Miss Plummer's sixth-grade class. We had been studying the Irish folk art form called the limerick. As a class project, we all had to make up one of our own and recite it before the class. On the day of the presentations, none of which had been screened, Miss Plummer, a sickly person, had been pleased with everyone's performance even though some of them got a little personal, as the one about me by Carolyn Johnson:

> There once was a boy named Hugo
> Who loved to blow the bugle
> He blew so well
> His lips began to swell
> That poor, poor, Hugo.

Carolyn, a blotchy-faced girl, was one of about eighty-five students being bused in from the Bishop Walsh public housing project in north Newark while they awaited the completion of what was to be their school, Broadway Junior High School. She was a friend of Rose Urciolli, who had died of a heart attack in an elevator in her building the year before. We had left school on a Friday looking forward to the weekend, and when we returned on Monday morning, our teacher, Miss Battersby, solemnly announced that Rose had had a heart attack while riding in the elevator of her apartment building and had died. I never knew a child could have a heart attack. *That was something that happened to old people*, I thought, and I hated God for letting Rose die. I had learned in Christian Science that God was omnipotent, omniscient, and omnipresent; I thought if he was ever-present, he was right there in that elevator with her and if he knew everything, he knew she was sick; if he was all-powerful, then why couldn't or wouldn't he save her? My sister, Rose Marie (another Rose), died when she was only a toddler before I was born. From time to time I had thought of what she might have been like had she lived; but I had actually known the Rose from my school, from third through fifth grades she sat right behind me. Though I was mad at God, still, I did as Miss Battersby told us.

Rose's parents had delivered prayer cards to our class and asked that we read them every night after we said our prayers. *Rose was already dead and they wanted us to read a prayer to the God who let her die?* I found all of it very confusing.

Until her recitation of the limerick about me and the bugle, Carolyn had not uttered an unkind word about me. I did not even play the bugle or any other instrument. Miss Plummer had not given us any guidelines. So, I guess that's why she did not discipline Carolyn, even though the class snickered and I was embarrassed. When it was Lefty's turn, he took it boldly.

> There once was a boy named Red,
> Who loved to pee the bed.
> He peed one day
> And floated away.
> That poor, soaking boy named Red.

Miss Plummer turned redder and redder as Lefty navigated his way through his short recitation. You could see her struggling to get her words out and wheezing as she slowly raised her fragile body from the chair. In the meantime, the class was rolling in the aisles, overcome by laughter. It was by any measure the funniest thing we had heard all day. When Miss Plummer finally was able to speak, she blurted, "Well, I never. You disgusting, filthy-mouthed little…. Get down to the principal's office right this minute!"

Lefty, as well as the rest of the class, was bewildered at her reaction. What was his offense? I wondered. His was, without question, the best limerick rendered. We all of us knew kids who peed the bed, some of us on occasion still did ourselves. I imagined Red being lifted right out of his bed and floating in a stream of his own golden urine clear down Spring Street, arms flailing wildly and screaming for help. Wasn't this an apt punishment for an incurable bedwetter? Anybody who had an experience like that would never pee the bed again!

Lefty was suspended until one of his parents came in to get a lecture from our author/mathematician/principal, Dr. Skolnik, who had written a geometry book used by the Newark School System. But Lefty was our hero, no matter what the school officials or Miss Plummer thought!

(6)

Under Billy Johnson's leadership, we formed our first gang, the Fire Birds. Our sole mission was to protect our turf from invasion by other gangs. When too much time passed without an invasion, we got bored and we would set out to invade some other gang's turf, hoping to be challenged so we could fight them. I had heard of people getting killed in gang fights in New York City — shot with zip guns, stabbed — and I did not want any parts of this. Being in a gang was cool, but being killed or maimed for life was not. So, I lobbied successfully to be the warlord. The warlord was the only one empowered to declare war on another gang. I figured that in this role, I could keep the rest of the gang and myself alive. I did all I could to discourage everybody from going onto other gangs' turf. Little did I know how hard this would be.

Every now and then we would hear about a gang fight in the predominantly colored Central Ward. I could not figure out why these colored gangs — the Nomads, Cherokees, Dukes, and Outlaws — would be fighting *each other*. Here I was on the cusp of Little Italy, risking my life every day I ventured out of my neighborhood to go to Rotunda Pool or to the Boys Club. We didn't have to do anything but just be conveniently around whenever some of the Italians wanted to "kick a nigger's ass." We wished the Central Ward gangs would stop fighting each other and team up and help us teach the Italians a lesson. Billy convinced us we did not need the Central Ward's gangs help. Well, we stumbled upon a reason for Billy to prove it.

One warm summer night, about five of us were out walking near a highway construction site (now Route 280), just on the southwest perimeter of Little Italy, when we ran into a group of Italian kids who had strayed too close to our turf. As we approached, an eerie silence gripped us all, as if we knew that something was about to go down. As we passed each other, Billy stopped and asked, "What are y'all doin' over here?" One of the boys raised his head as if he intended to respond, but then thinking better of it, said nothing. Billy said "Hey, man, I asked you a question." At that point the boys broke into a run. One of them shouted, "Youse niggers are gonna be sorry. I'll remember your faces and we gonna come back and wipe youse out." Angered by this outburst and wanting to make an impression on my fellow Fire Birds, I hurled a rock I had earlier picked up, and with surprising accuracy, I hit the kid in the back of his head. He stumbled down the hill and fell while his buddies kept gettin' up. We caught up to him and beat him till his mama wouldn't recognize him (or so we reported when we told others of our adventure). Billy was especially brutal. While everybody else was content to get in one or two licks, Billy seemed to get angrier each time he hit our victim. Then when the boy went down, he began to kick him over and over again. Afraid he might kill him, we pulled Billy away, saying, "C'mon, man you gon' kill the dude." To which Billy said, "the mothafuckah need to die. Don't no white mothafuckah call me no nigger and live." Then somebody said he thought he saw a police car and that got Billy's attention. We split up running in different directions.

About an hour later, we met in the cellar of one of the Clay Street tenements to gather ourselves and talk about what we would do if the Italians were to come looking for us. Among ourselves, we had certain rules of engagement when it came to fighting. You had to fight fair.

This sort of gentleman's agreement meant you could not use weapons, you could not scratch or put your fingers in someone's eyes or kick your opponent, especially when he was down. Though you could punch him while he was down. These were the rules for one-on-one fighting.

But when it came to gang fighting, so Billy told us, none of these rules applied. "In a gang fight, you got to take a cat down as fast as you can and in any way you can because while you standin' tryin' to be fair, some other cat could take your head off. That fair shit just don't play," he concluded. "Plus [Billy was fond of using "plus" as a transitional word]," he continued, "them Italians don't fight fair no way. They use bats, chains, and brass knuckles. Y'all remember the time they were on a rampage at Webster [Street Junior High)? When they cornered that culid cat in the playground and he tried to escape by climbin' the fence 'cause they had all the exits blocked. There were even some grown men ready to join in on the nigger beatin' and the boy was only thirteen. They shook the fence till he came fallin' down on his head. I wish them Italians would come lookin' for us and I wish y'all had let me kill the mothafuckah tonight."

I had heard about the boy who had been shaken from the fence at Webster, but since nobody had seen it or could say when it had happened or even knew the victim's name, I never fully believed it. But the way Billy talked, it sounded like it could have been true. And suddenly, I did not feel so bad about beating up that kid. After all, it was not our fault his punk buddies left him. Had they stayed, it might have been a real gang fight and we still would have won, I reasoned. That was the only "gang fight" we actually had. Though on another occasion, we did come close to having another. But the other gang, some white boys from Harrison, did not show. I was relieved: This idea of gang fighting just did not sit right with me. Now that we had had an actual encounter, I was even more convinced this was a sure way to get killed. I had been successful at keeping us out of planned gang fights but I couldn't control the impromptu stuff. Maybe we could find some outlet for our testosterone. Billy responded to the need with a solution.

Four blocks south of the Clay Street bridge was the Stickel Bridge, or the new bridge as we kids called it, because it was newer than the Clay Street bridge. In fact, I watched steadily its progress as it was being built. Unlike its gray, turnstile cousin, the Clay Street Bridge, the new bridge was a towering drawbridge. On the Newark side, it started at the east end of Grant Street and did a steady rise over McCarter Highway, across the Passaic River and on into Harrison. Led by Billy, and standing on the bridge, we used to amuse ourselves by urinating on cars southbound on McCarter Highway. We would get a special thrill when a convertible would approach, like the time a Chevy full of white teenagers neared the overpass. One of the female occupants looked up and anticipating what was about to happen, covered her head and started screaming to the driver to warn him, but it was too late. He did not react quickly enough and the streams of golden water drenched them.

That wasn't the only mischief I managed to get into with the bridge as a prop. Under the bridge, at the point where it began its ascent, there were alcove-like openings homeless men — bums we called them — used as beds in warm weather. The only one we knew by name was called Shorty, or Shorty the Bum. Others would float in and out, but Shorty was the only regular. He was about 5' 2" tall, had a full head of gray crew-cut hair and a ruddy, wrinkled complexion. What his age might have been never occurred to us, but we knew he was old and that was close enough. He always greeted us with a toothless smile and friendly "Hello, boys." When he was drunk, which was most of the time; he would often soil his pants. I wondered how he could walk around with wet pants, where he kept his other clothes, and where he washed himself and his dirty clothes before he wore them again. I had heard on the radio a song titled

"Bad, Bad Whiskey (Made Me Lose my Happy Home)." I wondered if Shorty once had a happy home, or a home at all, and if we might lose our home because of my father's love of the bottle. I couldn't say our home was happy, but I still didn't want to lose it.

I learned that in the winter, Shorty joined other homeless men to take up residency at the Goodwill Rescue Mission home on Plane Street. On the Plane Street side was the entrance to the store and on the Eagle Street side was the entrance to the mission. There was big neon sign hanging next to a crucifix over the mission door that read, "Jesus Saves." I used to think the message was to encourage us to put our money in the savings accounts we opened through the school at the Howard Savings Bank. You know, like, Jesus saves and by association, so should we.

The mission entrance was right across the street from Burnet Street School. On Fridays, they would invite us to attend after-school Bible lessons in the form of stories. They would illustrate the story-telling with Biblical scenes they would stick on a felt board as the story developed. Afterwards, they would give us candy as a reward for attending.

The homeless men got food and shelter in exchange for doing some menial work and attending religious services. I suppose those who needed it also got some treatment for their alcoholism, though I cannot say for sure.

Occasionally, we would play a game that had no name, but involved us going to the alcoves under the new bridge and throwing stones at whatever homeless men we found there. I don't think I ever intended to hurt anyone, or maybe I just did not think about the consequences of our cruel actions. I always aimed for the body though, taking care not to hit the head. In some sick, adolescent way, I had considered myself humane for sparing a blow to the heads of these defenseless men. I felt very powerful when our victims begged us to stop as they ran for cover.

One late afternoon, when three of us decided to engage in this diversion, we met our match. A really big guy, whom we had not seen before, was sleeping soundly, snoring so loudly we could hear him from a distance of 15 yards or so. We crept up to him just to get a good look at our target. Then we took our positions behind the supporting beams of the bridge and released a hail of stones in his direction. Two or three stones hit him, abruptly waking him. He must have had a strong survival instinct; because as soon as he was able to determine from which direction the missiles were coming, he immediately began to return the fire with surprising accuracy. I was not prepared for this defense, and at first was frightened. But I soon recovered and urged my boys to redouble our attack. To my amazement, the man did not retreat. Instead, he picked up some more stones and charged us while throwing his missiles. This was too much, so we hatted up towards McCarter Highway, away from home because we would have had to head in his direction to go directly home and we did not want to risk that.

We ran north towards Clay Street, turned left and left again when we got to Spring. I don't know about anyone else, but I never looked back. Once we were sure he was not pursuing us, we came to rest. We briefly discussed rounding up some more boys and going back to get even. But I realized if we gathered reinforcements, it meant we would have to admit that three of us had been scared off by only one man. I knew we could never live that down; so, we kept it cool, to ourselves. I quietly decided right then I would never again participate in this game.

Some months later, after a long summer evening of playing in the recreational center at Burnet school, we started to head for home. It was around 8 o'clock and it had just gotten dark. There were about five of us and Billy was heading the pack. Instead of going directly home, Billy suggested that we go by Maxie's, the candy store directly across the street from the Goodwill mission. We went into Maxie's and stole about as much as we bought and headed out. On the way, somebody, I think it was Larry, shouted, "There's the bum who was throwing stones at us." He pointed to a group of three or four men standing in front of the mission that happened to be closed for the day. Billy asked what he was talking about and Larry told the whole story without naming his accomplices. Billy said, in disgust, "Y'all punk-ass mothafuckahs, punk-ass mothafuckahs, I say. Damn! Alright, we gon' even the score right now. Come on sissies."

Reluctantly, we followed as he headed toward the men. Apparently, sensing something bad was about to happen, the men began a rapid retreat — all except the one who had engaged us in the stone fight. He was game. I thought I could minimize the amount of harm that would come to the man if I jumped out front with an act of minimal violence. I thought that would keep Billy from going wild on the man. I threw a wild right cross, leaving my feet like the cowboy Bob Steele, stretching to reach the man's jaw since he was so much taller than I. He fell across the hood of a car behind him and rolled into the street. I thought this would satisfy Billy and the rest of my friends, that they would think the man had been punished enough. Well, my strategy failed because the sight of this guy lying in the street affected Billy like a shark smelling blood. He began to kick the man everywhere he found an opening, the way he had done the Italian kid that summer. We kept telling Billy that he had had enough and to please leave him alone but Billy just would not stop. Finally, when the man was no longer moving, Billy stopped and we all ran up Eagle Street. As we turned the corner at Orange Street heading east, we saw a police car turning into Eagle, whereupon we abruptly stopped running and tried to act as if we had been walking all along. Once the car was out of sight, we took off again and split up as we headed for our hideouts.

Somehow Billy and I wound up together as we made our way east on Grant Street, just south of the Lackawanna railroad station. Once we thought we were in the clear we started walking. Suddenly, two police cars approached from different directions. Guns drawn, the policemen jumped out, and ordered us to freeze and raise our hands over our heads. I could not believe what was happening. These cops were going to shoot us. I just knew it. I was too young to die. They ordered us into one of the cars and began to ask questions. Where we were coming from? What were our names? Why had we been running? Did we know anything about a man being stabbed and robbed? *Stabbed and robbed?* I thought. We didn't stab anyone. And then I heard myself saying aloud, "We just hit him. Somebody else must have come by later and stabbed him." Billy said, "Man what are you saying?"

Soon, we were pulling into the driveway of St. Michael's Hospital on High Street just north of Central Avenue. After they parked, the police ordered us out of the car and to walk in front of them into the hospital. We guided us towards the emergency room where we saw our victim heavily bandaged, his clothes blood soaked, his head hanging low. The sight of what we had done repulsed me and I began to feel great remorse for my participation in the brutal attack. When he looked up, the police asked him if we were "the guys who had assaulted you." *Assaulted? What about the stabbing?* I thought. Then I realized we, or rather I, had been tricked. I was so eager to deny what we had not done that I confessed to what we had done. The man looked at me and then at Billy. He repeated this back-and-forth motion a few more times. I began thinking about what I would say to my mother. How would I explain my involvement in such an odious incident? I was more worried about that than I was about the prospect of going to Jamesburg, the New Jersey juvenile detention center. Finally, the man looked at the policeman and said slowly and deliberately, "It was the tall guy," pointing to Billy. "And it was another big guy." Pointing at me, he said, "This other kid wasn't there.". One of them, a Detective O'Connor, called out to me as I hastily made my way out. The first thought that entered my mind was they had reconsidered and were going to charge me after all. I turned and waited for him. He had something white in his hand. As he approached, he extended his hand and gave me his business card. "Call me, if you need to talk about anything, anything at all." I took the card and read his name. It was the first business card anyone had ever given me, perhaps even the first I had ever seen.

I hurriedly left the hospital, never even bothering to look back to see how Billy was doing. *Why had the man not identified me?* I thought. After all, I was the one who started the whole thing. Even if my intention was to keep something worse than my hitting him from happening, he could not have known that. And it could not have been out of fear of retaliation because he had identified Billy. Yet, in spite of my confession, the police let me go.

As I walked home, I did not worry about Billy being pissed with me because I got away clean. I figured I would cross that bridge when I came to it. Even though I knew I could not beat Billy, I was not afraid to fight him. I still held O'Connor's card in my hand. I glanced at it again and placed in my wallet. I would need it in about two years.

I never mentioned a word of this narrow escape to my mother. I did tell our accomplices what had happened, however. They told me how lucky I was. At the same time, we wondered how much time Billy would get. We figured it would be a lot because he had been in trouble with the law before. Sometime later, we learned from his brother, Barry, he had been sent to Jamesburg.

In a way I was glad Billy was gone. He had had a magical power over my other friends and me that we were unable to resist because we wanted so much to receive his approbation to confirm our worthiness.

I wasn't to see Billy again for some seventeen years. I had become active in Newark Black nationalist organization and local politics. I was on my way to a meeting when I saw Billy, saliva dripping from his mouth and nodding, in the middle of a busy Springfield Avenue near Belmont Avenue. I was stopped in traffic as he stumbled past my car. Tentatively, I called out to him: "Billy?" He seemed to recognize me as he tried to speak, but only jumbled sounds found their way across his lips. Or perhaps, like an infant, he was only responding to the sound of my voice. His eyes were so glazed over that it would have been a miracle if he had been able to recognize himself in a mirror. At that moment, traffic started to move again and I pulled away.

I had not thought about Billy since that fateful night he and I had spent together. Yet, as I guided my car east on Springfield Avenue, glancing in my rearview mirror at this pitiful sight, I could not help but wonder where I might have wound up had that homeless man identified me too

Chapter 2

Religion

(1)

I started attending Sunday School at the Christian Science church in Newark shortly after my mother came home from the hospital. Around that time, the church was renting space in the Wurlitzer piano building on Broad Street in downtown Newark, near Washington Park. Later, the church bought its own building on Mount Prospect Avenue, just north of Bloomfield Avenue in the North Ward.

My Uncle Hugo told me that his mother, the wife of a deacon at Zion Baptist Church, was the one who introduced our family to Christian Science. She had fallen very ill in 1933 and she was so ill that he had to postpone for a year going to college after high school graduation to care for her. He was the logical choice because he was the only one of his siblings still living at home; the others were already married and had families of their own. Uncle Hugo recalls that as the year passed, he underwent remarkable emotional and intellectual growth. Emotional because of the demands placed on him in his role as caregiver, and intellectual because in that year, he read every book in the house. Among them were works by Du Bois and Dunbar and a Great Books series. When he entered Virginia State College, he was only one year older than the other freshmen, but believed himself to be much older in every other way.

My grandfather, whom we called Papa, was a very personable but quiet man. He was a mail carrier who had made many friends along his route. Uncle Hugo told me that one day during his deliveries, he stopped to chat with a lady named Miss Plummer and shared with her that my grandmother was very ill. Miss Plummer offered to come by and sit a spell with her, an offer my grandfather accepted. At the time, he did not know that Miss Plummer was a Christian Scientist, nor do I think it would have mattered to him.

She came by in a few days and brought the Bible and two other books with her. It turned out that Miss Plummer was not any ordinary Christian Scientist, she was a practitioner — a person who had achieved a high level of spiritual growth and had been formally certified. In the Christian Science church, this certification was as close to the concept of minister as one could get, though not in the same sense as in other Christian denominations. Miss Plummer read and prayed with my grandmother for several weeks, at the end of which she was healed. My grandmother was so moved by this experience that she, who had been a Baptist until then, joined the Christian Science church and began to read the daily lessons to my mother and my sisters during their summer visits. Once she converted to Christian Science, my grandmother never received medical treatment or visited a doctor until she had a stroke at age 89. Had she had her wits about her, I doubt she would have agreed to medical treatment even then. But she was no longer calling the shots.

My mother credited Christian Science with her recovery from breast cancer in 1948. Even though, according to Christian Science doctrine, she should have been able to bring about the healing without the intervention of medical science, she believed it was Christian Science that kept her from relapsing.

As for us children, Melvin and I attended Christian Science Sunday School until we turned eighteen. My peers found this odd and a reason to ridicule my brother and me since by the time they were twelve, they were attending church services. However, at the Christian Science church, anyone under the age of eighteen had to attend the Sunday School. Once you turned eighteen you "graduated" from Sunday School and could attend church services. At this time, you were also eligible to join the church.

Sunday School classes were taught in the basement of the new building on Mount Prospect Avenue, where we were grouped according to age. So, Melvin and I had, for the most part, the same classmates, only one of whom was a female, the entire time we attended Sunday School. For years, we had been the only colored kids in the entire Sunday School of twenty to thirty children. Then around 1955, a large colored family, the Johnsons, began to attend services shortly after we moved to the new building. They were somewhat of a curiosity to the congregation, I suspect, because they made such an impression when this family of seven chocolate children and their mother and father stepped off the bus. Nine bus fares! What struck me about them was the father; a short, heavyset man with large hands and a perpetual grin on his face. Or maybe it was a smile, because he always looked happy. Despite his size, his suits (always brown) seemed a little roomy and his jacket sleeves extended to his knuckles. His wife wore plain and simple, soft-colored dresses. The five boys, who appeared to range from four to ten years old, were all dressed alike, as were the girls, who looked about eleven or twelve.

My mother expressed pleasure that they were a "whole family worshiping together" and amazed that they could afford to raise "umm, umm, umm, all of those children so close in age and bringing them to church every week. All that bus fare." I sensed she was wishful that our family could worship together like the Johnsons. Instead ,we were spread out all over the place. My father sporadically attended New Hope Baptist Church in the Central Ward and my sisters worshiped at Mount Zion Baptist Church in the North Ward, the church Sarah Vaughan attended and in whose choir they all sang. When he attended church, my older brother went to church in East Orange with his girlfriend, Judy, whom he married in 1960.

All of my friends attended an Episcopalian church, the House of Prayer, on Broad Street about three blocks south of Clay Street and one block north of the Lackawanna train station. The church had gotten a progressive minister named Father Jensen who had made a conscious effort to extend his ministry to the residents of the neighborhood in which the church was located. My understanding was some of his white parishioners were unhappy about this outreach and threatened to leave if he did not stop recruiting the colored.

I frequented the recreation center that he ran after school and Saturdays. During one of my visits there, he asked me what church I attended. When I told him, he seemed surprised. Eventually he got to the point where he felt comfortable enough to ask me questions about Christian Science. I thought they were designed to get to the reason I was one. I knew I was at a disadvantage going up against an adult, but I tried my best.

The only answer I had was what any ten-year-old would have. "I go with my mother. I go because she says that is our religion." I also thought that through Christian Science, I could cure myself of my myopia; but I didn't tell him that. He seemed to want to engage me in a theological discussion when I didn't even know what theology was. He wanted to know what they taught me there. I wanted to tell to go to the library and read for himself, but out of respect, I did not. I did recite for him a teaching of every Christian Scientist, a passage we all had to commit to memory, even children, called the scientific statement of being.

> *There is no life, truth, intelligence or substance in matter. All is infinite mind and its infinite manifestation, for God is all in all. Spirit is immortal*

truth. Matter is mortal error. Spirit is the real and eternal. Matter is the unreal and temporal. Spirit is God, and man is his image and likeness. Therefore, man is not material, he is spiritual.

Father Jensen asked me what it meant. I told him that it meant we are not really the bodies we are in. That the real "we" is spiritual and, therefore, that makes us immortal because spirit never dies. "How do you know that?" he asked. "I just believe it," was my uneasy reply. I felt as though he was picking on me, mad because I did not attend his church. He did not know it but the conversation we had just had killed any chance that I would even consider it, though I did attend one service at the invitation of my friend, Larry. It was a service in stark contrast to those at the Christian Science church. The smell of incense, the sound of Latin being spoken and lots of ritual are what stood out in my mind about the service.

Christian Science was different from any religion I had ever known. Not that I had studied any other, because I hadn't. But I had attended Baptist services at my maternal grandfather's church in Norfolk County, Virginia, and at my paternal grandfather's Christ's Holy Sanctified Church in Franklin, Virginia. At his church services, people let go of everything in response to the rousing sermons delivered by the minister. The congregation danced in the aisles and shouted out from their seats. Some were so overcome with emotion, they literally passed out. Sometimes the services lasted long into the night. I used to think this was all by design so you would not have any energy to even think about sinning.

In the Christian Science church, the atmosphere was, by comparison, dead. What I mean is the services were opposites in content, music, and expectations of the congregation. Christian Science was an intellectual experience and a religion that could be engaged in by only the (very) literate or at least those who were predisposed to and aspired to being highly literate, as I did. The church service and Sunday School lesson were in session for exactly one hour, 11 a.m. to noon. We always started and ended on time.

Both the Sunday School and church lessons were the same. We had daily, prescribed readings in the Bible and another book written by our founder, Mary Baker Eddy, called *Science and Health with Key to the Scriptures*. The text we were to read each day was listed in a publication called the Christian Science quarterly. Each week, it featured a theme and the Bible readings were selected to illustrate that theme. Then we were directed to *Science and Health* to read Ms. Eddy's interpretation of the Biblical text. The topics were not lightweight stuff. The one topic that has stayed with me was one whose title introduced me to the word necromancy: "Ancient and Modern Necromancy, and Hypnotism Denounced." You can imagine how challenging such a topic was for a Sunday Schooler still reading comic books. I had to look up the word necromancy before I could even begin the reading. We had to read the lessons on our own — one for each day of the week, except Sunday — and discuss in Sunday School what they meant to us.

In church, a person designated as the reader led the lesson. He or she was a practitioner as well. This person's job was to read to us what we were to have read for ourselves during the week. The difference was he or she read the entire lesson in that hour, whereas we were to have read only the portion for the particular day of the week. The readings were punctuated with a few songs. There was no choir, so accompanied by a pianist, only the congregation sang. In addition to the congregation's droll singing, the service always featured a soloist. My mother was very excited once when the soloist was a colored man. I remember the occasion well because he had a rich, deep baritone voice and because it seemed so important to my mother. The church recruited and paid the soloists whether or not they were of the faith. Downstairs, in the basement

Sunday school, we had no such treat. We had to be content with singing *a cappella* from the same hymnal as the adults. We sounded terrible.

Being a follower of Christian Science was very difficult for me for a number of reasons. None of my friends shared the religion and I found it impossible to explain to them what it was. Any attempt on my part was often met with snickers and jabs. It got to the point that I avoided any discussion of it at all. After all, they were my peers and it was important for me to minimize conflict with them. Second, I truly disliked that it was void of any display of emotion. The Sunday readings were dry and not conducive to call and response. There was no choir. It was purely an intellectual experience.

To compensate for this emotional void, I participated in the youth choir's Wednesday evening rehearsals at Mount Zion Baptist Church. Under the thinly veiled threat of quitting the group, one of the members of my R&B group had invited Melvin and me to sing with the choir. At first we declined because we knew we could never perform on Sundays due to our standing Sunday school obligation. But he told us not to worry about it. When I told my mother about it, to my surprise, she encouraged me to go to the rehearsals. "It can't hurt you," I remember her saying. After four or five weeks of Melvin and me rehearsing with the group, the choir director eventually and regretfully gave us an ultimatum to come to church and sing or be booted out of the choir. Eventually, we were asked to leave; but I still continued to attend the rehearsals so I could listen and sing my parts to myself. My two favorite songs were "There Is a Balm in Gilead" and "There's a Tree on Each Side of the River."

My mother must have felt the emotional void too, because after church, she would turn to WNJR 1430 am to listen to the gospel music they always played on Sundays. Having been raised a Baptist, she was familiar with the songs they played and would often sing along in her smooth alto, humming the parts whose words she had apparently forgotten.

I was offended during one of my Sunday school lessons when the topic of Negro spirituals was brought up. Mr. Pedersen, an engineering graduate of Stevens Tech in Hoboken and our teacher at the time, asked the class if we could think of an example of blind faith. When we couldn't, he presented the Negro spiritual as an example. I must have been about eleven and while I had no idea of the history of the Negro spiritual, emotionally and intuitively, I knew they were not expressive of blind faith. In fact, I didn't even know what blind faith was. I had read in one of my Bible lessons that faith was the "substance of things hoped for and the evidence of things unseen" *Was 'not seeing' the same thing as being blind?* I wondered. But I soon concluded, he must have meant blind faith was belief not reasoned nor intellectually realized. As with Father Jensen, I did not challenge him, after all, he was the teacher. But even if these had not mattered, I did not know enough about the subject to provide an informed response.

During the bus ride home, I told my mother what Pedersen had said. She grunted and then said she didn't believe Mr. Pedersen knew what he was talking about: "He might know Christian Science, but I doubt he has any training in Negro spirituals or exposure to them either. You can just forget all about that nonsense. I've got a good mind to speak to him but", her voice trailed off. I could see she was a bit peeved (one of her favorite words to express annoyance) but was trying to control it. I now believed the pain I had felt was justified and my respect for Pedersen dropped a notch after that incident. Though I could not articulate it at the time and even though the spiritual was something that was only tangentially a part of my life, I considered what he said an uncalled-for attack on an aspect of my culture and, therefore, an attack on me.

(2)

When I started high school, my mother let me visit church with my friends. While I was at Bloomfield Tech, my best friend was Maurice Ingram. Maurice was a handsome, honey-colored boy about 5'5" tall, who had an older sister and two older brothers. An excellent sketch artist who also designed clothes, he wanted to be a draftsman. He didn't have to sneak around to smoke because his mother, a smoker herself, allowed him and his siblings to smoke, although during one visit to his apartment, she asked me if I could persuade "your friend to stop smoking." He lived in the Christopher Columbus Homes, the place that rejected my mother's application. I made other friends from Columbus whom I was to be in touch with decades after we graduated from high school; among them, our high school's queen of class reunions Delores McCrae.

Thanks to his brothers, Maurice knew a lot more about jazz than I, and was up on the latest men's fashions. At the time the fad was the so-called Continental look and Maurice had a full wardrobe of these clothes, from shoes to shirts as well as the appropriate coats. I strove to be like him in his taste for clothes, music, hip speech, and girls. He was the hippest of all my peers. And I was proud he was my friend.

Maurice's sister, Barbara, had a good friend named Blanche Lawrence whose younger brother, Rudolph Valentino, had the largest collection of jazz albums of anyone I knew. Rudy had a retreat in the attic of his parents' house that was the coolest place for us to hang out because its walls and ceiling were painted black and red, respectively. On some weekends, our small jazz crowd would assemble at Rudy's and just sit around drinking Kool-Aid, eating potato chips and listening to Miles and Monk, praising every note they played. No drugs or alcohol, just ourselves talking as hip as we could, trying to impress each other.

Maurice would invite me to go with him to churches that were purported to have fine girls. One such church was Abyssinian Baptist on West Kinney Street in the Central Ward. We would show up early and sit in the back so we could see who came in. When they announced the offering, we would get up and go to the bathroom to avoid having to put anything in the plate. Afterwards, we would return to our seats. When church let out, we would stand outside to see what girls we might want to talk to. We got conversation, but never any phone numbers, so after a few weeks of this, I copped out. Deep down inside, I believed what we were doing was sacrilegious, anyway, so it wasn't a hard decision for me.

My mother once encouraged me to invite Maurice to come to Sunday School with us; but I told her there was no way he was going to attend a Sunday School. "He's too old for Sunday School. Christian Science is the only religion I know of that makes you go to Sunday School until you're ready to get out of high school, mom. None of my friends would go for that."

Though I eventually left Christian Science, just as myopic as I had always been (I had prayed from the day we discovered I needed glasses that my vision would be made 20/20 but …), it left an indelible impression on me. Through the readings and Sunday school classes, I was able to increase my vocabulary and sharpen my reasoning skills. I also began to move away from reading just comic books to chapter books. I remember my tenth-grade history teacher, Mr. Schectman, remarking, "There's a reader for you," when I knew the definition of some word (I think it was "omnipotent" in our textbook). That was the first time that I realized there was a correlation between reading and vocabulary. And I knew I had Christian Science to thank for it.

To my social disadvantage, I had begun to use my expanding vocabulary in my everyday speech. My mother had impressed the magic of words upon me through her impromptu recitations of Dunbar's poetry. She used to remind me that we all had access to the same words as Paul Laurence Dunbar (she always called his full name), but he had a gift that "enabled him to own them. He was their master." So, I was ready for the word challenges Christian Science had in store for me. Out of a self-imposed sense of duty, I had also started correcting my friends' grammar. If that wasn't bad enough, I sought to resolve disputes over matters of fact by running home to get, of all things, a reference book. My display of these behaviors made me very unpopular. I remember one dispute we had that was over a word in a Pat Boone song, "'Twixt Twelve and Twenty." We had just come from a movie in which Boone had sung the song and I asked no one in particular, what "'twixt" meant anyway. Somebody said it must mean "ten." Others followed, rendering their own guesses. It became apparent to me that no one really knew, so I went home and brought back a dictionary and looked up the word. I thought my decision would be welcome since we all were clueless, but I was as wrong as two left shoes.

"Damn, Hugo, why you always got to be sticking your nose in some damn book?" It wasn't just one person; they would all chime in with support for such bizarre statements. They wouldn't even let me read the definition to them. The only smarts that mattered to them were the smarts of the street.

Even as a young boy, I could not understand why it seemed they preferred to remain ignorant than learn something. Until I got to high school, I disciplined myself to stop this irksome practice. Once in high school, I would fall into a group of students who welcomed things intellectual, who routinely used sources to support their positions, and who appreciated critical thinking. Smart was okay in my new crowd and we would always push to see who was the smartest, not who was the most ignorant or who merely passed a test. We were about excellence!

Chapter 3

Discovery

(1)

Right up until we entered high school, Larry and I remained best friends. We had our squabbles to be sure; but we would always find our way back to each other. Nothing came between us for long. Even when I had a fight with his older brother and managed to get in a lucky punch that sent him home crying, blood streaming from his nose ("go for the nose", my father had counseled me. The one who lands a solid punch on the other cat's nose will win the fight."). By nightfall, Larry had come gunning for me to get revenge. He came to my apartment to ask if I could come out to play. That he thought I would go for this thinly disguised trick insulted my intelligence. Did he think I didn't know what was going on? I told him my mother said I couldn't come out any more that night. So, he confronted me right in my doorway; yet, I managed to talk my way out of a fight with him. "Whoever heard of a little brother taking up for a big brother?" I remember asking him. I convinced him that if word got around that he had to take up for his big brother, it would just make things worse for him (his brother) — mess up his rep even more. Truth was, while I had no fear of Larry's brother, Fat Junny, we called him — the thought of tangling with Larry terrified me. He was solidly built and robustly muscular. I just imagined that with those big arms he could crush my head even if I had been able to block the punch.

In fact, he had nearly done just that one day when he and I were boxing under the watchful eye of Father Jensen at the House of Prayer's recreation center. I had the disadvantage of being very nearsighted, so I had difficulty seeing his launched punches until it was too late. To make matters worse, Larry was a lefty and my right eye was the weaker one. I had been doing very well for the first two of a three-round match, during which I bobbed and weaved to stay out of his reach, adopting a tag-and-run strategy. I hit him a few times, but none of my blows appeared to do much damage. Then at the opening of the third round, he rushed me and before I could evade him, he delivered a smashing blow to my right temple, forcing me backward into the arms of the small group of boys who had been cheering us on. Father Jensen rushed to my aid and stopped the match. Larry rushed to my side to see if I was okay and apologized for hurting me.

Boxing was a highly regarded skill in our neighborhood. If you got into a fight, you were expected to box your opponent. Rushing, grabbing and wrestling him to the ground were things we expected of white boys, or more specifically Italians, since they were the only white people with whom we came in close contact. In fact, to be accused of fighting like a white boy was a serious insult. We all wanted to be like Sugar Ray Robinson or Joe Louis, not Carmine Basilio or "Two Ton" Tony Galento. It wasn't that you won or even lost the fight, the question was were you cool, slick, smooth? We did not value being able to take a punch as highly as avoiding being punched at all.

We had rules about fighting that were strictly enforced. No dirty fighting; this rule precluded kicking, hitting a man while he was down, biting, scratching, or using anything other than one's fists to hit the other cat. Also, other boys' jumping in was not allowed. This meant you could not gang up on another cat unless you wanted to fight the whole gang. Such a transgression would cause, at least for the moment, friends to turn into enemies of the transgressor as they would beat him to teach him a lesson about values.

We did not observe these rules when we fought boys from other neighborhoods because we did not know if they shared the same values and we did not believe we could trust them even if they said they did. So, the rule for fighting outside of the neighborhood was anything goes.

Larry and I shared everything — candy bars, comic books and what few secrets we had. So, it was not surprising that he came to me with what would turn out to be the biggest secret we ever shared. Bonnie had given him some! I was incredulous. How could this be? How did it happen? And why this popeyed dude? (Behind his back, we called him "Popeyes" because his eyes protruded from his sockets like oversized marbles). We were only twelve years old. She was fourteen and stacked like a brick shithouse. I mean big tits, big hips, and big butt. What the hell would she want with Larry when she could have given it up to any of the older boys who would have been more than glad to help her out? Moreover, even though we bragged about what we would do if we ever got any, it was all jive. It was suspect as to how many of us were even sure where the point of entry was. I certainly didn't. So, strategically, I accused Larry of lying and I told him the only way I would believe him would be if I could get some too. Neither of us could stand not being believed by the other. It put a crack in the armor of our friendship, so I knew he would try to work out something for me. "Otherwise, I know you lying," I told him.

After we parted company, I began to think what it would be like to get some real pussy. I knew what an orgasm felt like — I had learned well from Minnie and her four sisters — but to have an orgasm induced by sticking my penis in a girl, well, I had no idea how that would actually work. How many times would I have to go in and out before I would cum? How would it feel to her?

All I knew about intercourse I had learned from older boys in the neighborhood and the dirty little comic books they showed us. I remember one that featured Popeye,

Bluto, and Olive Oyl. As usual, they were competing for her affection. But this time it was not with their fists, it was with their penises. At a certain point, Bluto pulled his out to impress Olive Oyl, who laughed uncontrollably at its pencil-like size. When it was Popeye's turn, he pulled out what looked like a flesh-covered baseball bat, which, of course, made Olive Oyl crazy with desire and anticipation. The story ended with Olive falling on the bed, legs spread as wide as the Grand Canyon as Popeye, erect penis in hand, approached the eagerly waiting Olive. The comics never depicted a vagina or any act of penetration. Everything was always implied. But for our young minds that was enough.

There were other cartoons that also featured otherwise kid-friendly characters such as Dagwood and Blondie, Nancy and Sluggo, and Superman and Wonder Woman (to make Super Boys and Wonder Girls). The irony of these characters being depicted in sexually explicit situations was not lost on me. It was these extreme departures from their socially acceptable behavior as portrayed on the comic pages and the silver screen that put a certain edge on their escapades and, for the moment, robbed them of their innocence.

I learned in other classes at the sex academy of the streets that eating lots of bananas would cause you to increase the volume of jism or cum when we got a nut. I never even questioned why this was important; but I was sure it had something to do with our manhood. We also learned that jerking off would cause you to go blind. Now, this one I believed a little bit because of my myopia, except I had been myopic for as long as I could remember and way before I discovered masturbation, so I was somewhat conflicted about the full validity of this claim. Add to this the fact that in the early days of masturbation, I got orgasms but nothing ever came out. I continued to shoot blanks until I was about twelve. That was when I had my first wet dream.

I woke up one Saturday morning with my underpants wet with some sticky substance. I initially thought my older brother, with whom I slept, had raped me while I was asleep. But I could not figure out why it had not awakened me. I also could not explain why the mysterious substance was in the front of my briefs. Disturbed, I went to my parents' room to get some clean briefs. I had no place in our room to store my things because James took all of the space in the one dresser in our room. I woke my parents in the process and my father asked me what the matter was. I replied, "There's some sticky stuff in my pants." I heard him and my mother exchange whispers, but neither said anything to me, then or ever.

I do not know how much time had passed before Larry got back to me about Bonnie, but it seemed like an eternity. I kept anticipating and imagining what it would be like. How would we do it? Where would we go to do it? Was he lying after all? Would she agree to give me some too? Why should she? I had been so taken off guard at Larry's news; I never even thought to ask him where they had done it. Options were limited because every adult acted as a surrogate parent to the kids in the neighborhood. If they saw anything suspicious, they would call you out and tell you upfront they were going to report you to your mother. This practice was something that was understood anyway, so I do not know why they felt they needed to say it, unless it was to cause us to fret about our fate until our mothers got home. In my neighborhood, mothers always took the word of each other when it came to reporting the misbehavior of us kids. Otherwise (I figured this out much later), their own credibility might be questioned when it was their turn to report. The mothers who were at home during the day knew the work schedules of the other mothers and they also knew what kids lived in which buildings. So any girl seen entering a building where none of her playmates lived was bound to be reported if she had been seen. "Mrs. Barrett, I think you should know I saw Hugo sneaking a girl into your apartment when you weren't home."

Where had they done it then? Larry lived in the second-floor apartment just over ours. His grandparents lived with him and they were home all of the time, so I know he hadn't taken her to his apartment. And there were no girls Bonnie's age in our building, so she couldn't have pretended to be going to visit one of them on her way to the roof. Besides, the families on the third floor would be able to hear them walking or humping. Moreover, with it being summertime, the tar could get really hot — too hot to lie on. And finally, while you might get away with going to the roof, you could possibly get caught coming down and have some fast explaining to do. I discovered this problem when I was about nine.

I took Ellen to the roof one summer day and damn near burned up from the heat. We had crept up the stairs of the building making our way to the narrow stairwell that led to the roof. At the end of the stairwell, we lifted the lid to gain access to the roof. The heat was so bad we decided to sit on the stairs and explore each other there. The disadvantage was that the stairwell had no light and we could not see each other's private parts. We had to be satisfied with touching without seeing. When we were finished we thought it safer if we would leave separately. We agreed that she should go first and I should count to 100 before coming down myself.

When I came down there was a group of kids sitting on the stoop who had seen Ellen when she came down. They knew I lived on the first floor, and since Larry was among them, they knew I had not been to his apartment. Moreover, Ellen did not even live in the building. Somebody jumped to conclusions and accused Ellen and me of "doing pussy." His pronouncement elicited a chorus of "Ooohhh, I'm gonna tell," but we were adamant in our denials.

For all of my early exploration, the first vagina I saw, or thought I saw, was not that of one of my playmates, but that of an adult. She was one of three neighborhood drunks, as we called them then - today they would be called alcoholics, and was a member of one of five white families that lived around our way. She lived alone and we knew her only as Mrs. Duncan. She lived in the second block of Clay Street in a second-floor apartment. Though she had little to do with the adults, she was friendly and always spoke to us kids on her way to and from the bus stop. I never saw her in the company of anyone else nor did I observe anyone come to visit her.

She would go on drunken binges — sober for a long time, then drunk for days. On one particular day she was really wasted and had come to sit with us kids while we were just hanging around one evening sitting on the stoop of one of the tenements on Spring Street. She had been sitting wide-legged and otherwise unladylike, when some of us boys noticed she was not wearing any drawers. To get a better view, we began to walk casually back and forth in front of her while glancing slyly to steal a peep. Not content to contain the viewing to just those then present, one of the boys began to summon other boys to share the entertainment. This escalation of the process really pissed off the girls in the group who, up to that point, had been tolerating our behavior.

Emboldened, we crossed the line when we began to call even more boys. One of the girls, apparently feeling a sense of sisterhood, or maybe just common decency, shouted out "Mrs. Duncan, those nasty boys are looking up your dress." To everyone's surprise, Mrs. Duncan responded by shouting, "You mean this?" and abruptly pulled her dress up to her shoulders! Well, that was just more than anyone could stand. The boys began to laugh and shout in pure disbelief, "Oh man, oh man, oh man." Some even fell to the ground, laughing so hard they had to hold their sides. What a twist of fate it was. The girls had been trying to protect her and Mrs. Duncan responded by giving us a full, unobstructed view.

While the full view was certainly shocking — all we saw was a mound of pubic hair — it was not as much fun as it had been when we were sneaking peeps. Slyly peeping allowed us to imagine what we could not see. Of course, by the time word got around the neighborhood, the story had grown to unimaginable proportions. One version went so far as to claim that not only had Mrs. Duncan pulled up her dress, but she had also invited the boys to come to her crib to get a little bit. When asked if anyone had taken her up on the offer, the source replied, "No, man she was too old for anybody to mess with."

Sneaking looks up skirts is one behavior that most men, no matter how old they get, cannot seem to let go of. I think this is the point graphically and pointedly made a few decades later in the movie *Basic Instinct*, starring Sharon Stone and Michael Douglas. Stone's character was a murder suspect who had been brought in for questioning by homicide detectives. She was dressed in a short, tight, white dress with a revealing neckline and it was difficult to tell whether she was wearing panties. She sat casually and suggestively in a chair strategically placed about fifteen to twenty feet in front of them. She was being interrogated by an all-male team, led by the character played by Michael Douglas. Very much aware that the men were trying to position themselves to see up her dress (one got the sense that she was counting on it), she teased them by crossing her legs first this way and then that, being careful to reveal just enough to keep them off balance. It got to the point where it became obvious that the team was extending the interrogation way beyond what was necessary. At this point one also became aware that the Stone character was the one really in control of the situation, engaged in a power game that she was winning. While the movie scene itself was a whole world apart from the Mrs. Duncan scene, in many ways, the basic instinct of the sophisticated, worldly, white homicide detectives was the same as that of the naïve, poor, virgin, black boys.

Finally, Larry got back to me and told me the plan. We would meet Bonnie in the back hallway of her apartment building on Saturday at 8:30 p.m. after she had finished washing the dishes. It would be dark by then and we could make our way through her yard under the cover of the warm, summer night without being noticed by neighbors. And even if we were, Lefty lived in the adjacent tenement and we could always claim we were headed to his place. "Then what?" I asked. Larry said we would do it right there in the hallway. This seemed like a high-risk arrangement to me. What if her father, a short, fat, fire hydrant of a man, whose nickname was Moose, were to catch us? I began to have reservations, but Larry assured me that Bonnie had it all figured out. She had chosen the day and time because her folks usually watched television in the living room after dinner and her sister and brother were going out to a party. It sounded okay to me now. Bonnie seemed to have thought this thing through. Besides she was taking a risk too. And if we did get caught, it would be pretty obvious that we would not have been there had we not been invited. So it was all cool with me. The bad news was that it was only Wednesday. How was I going to be able to contain my anticipation? Every time I urinated between Thursday and Saturday, I would look at my penis and talk to it. "It won't be long now. I got a surprise for you coming up and we both are going to have the time of our lives." I did not masturbate while I was awaiting the appointed hour because I wanted to be as strong as possible. I did, however, eat a record number of bananas, just in case.

I woke up Saturday morning with an erection big and stiff enough to pole vault with. I was ready for Bonnie, but still had thirteen hours to go. It was a warm sunny day, not a cloud in the sky, a perfect day for just about any outdoor activity. For breakfast, I ate bananas with my Grape Nuts. I read comic books until I got hungry and then for lunch, I ate two triple-decker peanut butter and jelly sandwiches and a big glass of milk. I avoided my mother as much as I could because, in an eerie sort of way, I was feeling deep shame about what I was planning. I thought she might be able to sense my uneasiness and ask me about it. I was not a very good liar, especially when it came to her. When she suspected I was not being truthful, she had a way of fixing her eyes on mine and asking me to repeat myself. She never accused me of lying, but the look she could give me at times would force out the truth. Even though I knew I could not confess to something I had not yet done, I did not want to take any chances with her.

After lunch, some of my friends came by and invited me to join in a softball game. I was the best shortstop on the block and was always selected in the first round of team-member selection. I wanted to be on Larry's team; but he was nowhere to be found. After the game, which my team won, I jumped on my bike and headed for Burnet Street School's playground in search of a pickup game of basketball. I was not a very good basketball player, but I did have a reasonably good jump shot that I could sink most of the time if I could get open.

Like every boy in my neighborhood, I had wanted a Schwinn Black Panther, the Schwinn being dubbed by my friends and me the "Cadillac of bikes." But my sisters had bought a generic bike for my brother and me to share. Once I got it though, I forgot about the Schwinn, which many years later I learned was, at that time, a symbol of making it in the middle class.

Not allowed to ride in the street, I obediently made my way on the sidewalk, skillfully jumping each curb after I crossed the street. I approached the curb and at just the right moment, I jerked my handlebars upward, forcing the front wheel off the street and onto the sidewalk, smiling to myself at the accomplishment. There was no curb too high for me to jump — something of which I was quite proud. I got a bigger thrill out of putting my leg out while making a sharp left turn around a corner. I had seen motorcycle riders, dressed entirely in black, perform this extremely hip maneuver — left turn, left leg extended; right turn, right leg extended — bike and rider extensions of each other, rider leaning into the turn. No one could tell me that I too was not one of those motorcycle dudes. In reality, the extended leg could not have possibly broken the fall had the motorcycle or my bike taken a spill. But somehow, I think they (and I too) knew that. We did not do it for safety, but for the coolness of it all. So, it didn't matter. What irony! Here I was acting like the child I was, filling time doing childish things, as it were, as I anticipated participating in the adult activity I was so eagerly awaiting. Soon, at least for a time, I would put away my childish things.

Larry came to get me around 8 p.m., according to my Timex. We went to Bonnie's backyard, hid behind the woodshed and waited for the signal. She was to turn the kitchen lights off and on again. We had a clear view of the kitchen from our vantage point because the window looked right on to the yard. There was no yard light. The only light available was from her kitchen window way up on the second floor. At last the signal came. "There it is." Larry said. "Let's go." I did not have to be told. We both wearing our PF Flyer sneakers so we could be quiet and run fast if necessary. I could hear my heart pounding in my chest as we crept up the unlit back stairway of the enclosed porch. I wiped my sweaty palms on my pants. When we reached the top of the stairs, we sat down and waited. Not a word passed between us as we sat. Suddenly, the door to the apartment swung gently open and we heard a soft whisper, "Are you there?" someone asked. It was Bonnie. Larry said quietly, "Yeah." "I'll be right there," she said. I opened my fly and took out my pounding penis. I did not want to waste any time when the golden moment came.

I had been repeating to myself, "I'm going to get some real pussy. I'm going to get some real pussy." As if somehow, I still had to convince myself it was really going to happen. Why did I need the adjective "real"? This impending experience was making me think some weird stuff. I was even reminded of a taunt the girls used to use when they wanted to annoy the boys. "Boys are made of snips and snails and puppy dog tails. Girls are made of sugar and spice and everything nice."

What seemed like an interminable period of time finally came to a close when Bonnie appeared wearing a flowered, patterned skirt and a white, or very light, tight Banlon blouse. I did not know about breast sizes at the time — just small, medium and large. She was definitely large. She selected me to go first. I was hoping like hell that she would help me because I was clueless. Placing her back against the wall, she slid herself down, hoisting her skirt as she descended, and came to rest with her back making a 45-degree angle with the floor. I waited for her to tell or show me what to do. Sounding somewhat imperious, she said, "Come on, get down here." But I did not care about her tone. I just wanted to get inside of her as quickly as I could. Obediently, I got on my knees and placed my body on top of hers. She was not wearing any panties. I don't know why I was surprised to discover this, but I was. She grasped my penis and began to fondle it. No one had ever touched my penis before (except Ellen but I was only nine and, as I recall, my penis was not even erect. Plus, fondling had been the end, not the means), so I was taken aback momentarily by this action, not knowing what I should do. She gently stroked my penis and then slid it inside of her. She swooned and I felt like I was on top of the world, because I was making her respond just like the women in the movies. I moved what seemed to me to be instinctively somehow knowing what to do. Bonnie responded with her body and her words instructing me to do what she wanted — "Go left, go right, go hard and deep.". She told me to feel her tits, but I did not want to do it. I was too focused on our joined centers. She told me again to do it; this time I did. Then she asked me to suck one of them. I did that too. This felt really weird. Why did she want me to do that? Was she practicing for when she had a baby? Well, I was no damn baby, but I kept at it anyway, all the time wondering if I would draw any milk. And if I did, would I swallow it or spit it out. Would she be offended if I did?

At some point, Larry asked me how it felt. Now, while I appreciated his interest, I was in no mood to discuss how I was feeling while I was feeling it, especially with him. There would be plenty of time to compare notes afterwards. So, I ignored him. Besides, I had no words that could describe the feeling. "Good" came to mind, but it somehow fell way short of an accurate description. My peanut butter and jelly sandwich was "good." I had a "good" time reading, playing softball and basketball earlier that day. But the feeling from intercourse transcended "good," yet I lacked the vocabulary to render any other word.

I don't know how long I had been hanging in there when I felt the orgasm approaching. I wanted to hold it so the experience would last longer but; it was too late. Suddenly, my johnson began to spit like a cobra and I felt a sustained, chorus-like sensation like the ripples in a brook, making its way from my toes to my ears and in the process, making every muscle in my body tingle. An extended fission! But I kept on stroking and, shortly thereafter, I noticed a swishing sound coming from Bonnie's vagina. She heard it too. "Did you pee in me?" "Hell no, I wouldn't do that." "Then what's that noise?" she asked. "Damned if I know." When I was finished, it was Larry's turn. Actually, I was not finished. I was still hard and wanted to get another nut. But it wasn't to be — at least not this time. Bonnie just told me to get up because she didn't have all night and she wanted to give Larry some too.

I tried to get my erect penis back into my pants, but I was distracted by how wet it felt. I had the urge to smell my hand — an urge to which I yielded. I thought about neighborhood dogs, including my own Teddy that I had seen sniffing behind other dogs. This gesture could be nothing but anti-climactic. Why did I want to do it? I knew my own cum did not have an odor, so I concluded the pungent smell had to be from her pussy juice or the mixture of the two. Would this stuff stain my briefs? *Would my mother see it when she washed my clothes?* It wasn't long before Sergeant Johnson was no longer at attention, thus allowing me to put him away without snagging him on my zipper.

When Larry got himself into position, she told him to wait a minute and then she did something that I had not even seen in the dirty little comic books. She bent over the banister with her butt facing him and told Larry to stick it in from the back. I thought she meant for him to stick it in her ass and I thought, *Damn this is a nasty girl. I'm sure glad she didn't ask me to do that. Ain't no way I would do no shit like that.* Dutifully, Larry entered her from the rear. "Oh, my goodness," she exclaimed. "It's all the way in. It's all the way in." Then she did something that would remain a sore point for me for years. She reached out and grabbed my hand and placed it behind her so I could feel how deeply Larry had penetrated her. "Give me your hand, Hugo." I thought I knew what she was going to do, but if I did not comply, I was afraid she would get pissed and cut me off.

This was my first time out and already I had already learned two positions! "See?" she asked, as if she had a need to prove it to me. "Yeah," I said, snatching my hand away as soon as I realized what was happening. Larry was to rib me about this for years to come. "Remember the time you touched my dick, man?" It got to the point that I would not even answer him. If he were losing an argument with me (often the case), he would take me south by saying, "at least, I don't go around touching people's dicks."

As I watched the two silhouettes moving in the darkness, I tried to savor my initiation, to relive it, but it was no use. It was gone like the flavor cheap bubble gum too long chewed. I smelled my hand again. It was no use. I had not expected the feeling from the orgasm to fade so soon afterwards. Actually, I did not know what to expect. I had looked only to the moment and had not even considered any aftermath. Another thought came to me as I stood there getting more and more nervous with each passing minute. I had gotten what I came for and was ready to get my hat. Yet, in the middle of all of this, I thought, *There has to be a God.* I don't know why I was thinking about the existence of God right then, but that is the thought that popped into my head.

Seven years later, in my sophomore year in college, the class was engaged in a discussion of the existence of God in philosophy class. Professor H. David Bleich was engaging and challenging us to think critically. "Throw away your old notions, or at least set them aside for now. Reach down inside and try to find something new," he charged us. "Yes, Mr. Barrett, do you have a contribution to make?" "Yes, sir, sex." "I beg your pardon, what do you mean?" asked Bleich. "There is no way the powerful feelings one gets from sexual intercourse could be an accident of nature. And not just the feelings during the act, but all of the emotions leading up to it. If you have been sexually aroused and engaged in intercourse and gotten an orgasm, then you know what I am talking about. What a brilliant scheme! Give humans and other animals something so powerful, so filled with physical pleasure, and make this something the means of reproduction and they will multiply in spite of themselves. What more proof do you need? If we have agnostics among us, they must be virgins." Loud laughter. I added this last remark because I wanted to preempt counter arguments. I figured no one would admit he or she was still a virgin because according to my premise, that would be the only basis for doubt. I was only half-serious, but I did want to see what kind of reaction I would get.

As a teenager, I was to experience sex as a component of love and this combination would nearly drive me crazy. Until then though, all I would experience was lust. Years later, Al Green would record a song that claimed, "Love will make you do right, and make you do wrong. Make you come home early, stay out all night long." Antony and Cleopatra would have related to these lyrics.

"Bonnie? Bonnie?" we heard her mother calling. Our trio simultaneously jumped. "I'm taking out the garbage, Mom. I'll be right back." We did not notice that she had brought a bag of trash out with her when she met us. Apparently, she had anticipated that something like this could happen and the garbage was her cover. Cunning of her. At the same time, Larry pulled himself out of her, and I started downstairs. Larry called softly but forcefully to me to be careful and quiet. But I was shaking in my boots at the prospect of getting caught. In my haste, I missed a step and fell, making a noise that seemed to me could have been heard two blocks away. "Who's out there?" It was her mother. I started to run. "Stay here, man. Don't run, you dummy." Larry said. But fear had overcome me and I dashed out into the yard trying to make my escape. I hid behind the woodshed waiting for things to quiet down before I made my break for home. Mrs. Marshall had gone to the kitchen window, and leaning out of it, she shone a flashlight scanning the yard and calling out to whomever it was to come out into the open. "I got you now. I'm gonna wait right here if it takes all night."

Throughout all of this commotion, Larry remained in the porch hall, lying low. I began to think how stupid I was for not listening to him. But it was too late for that now. How long would her mother stay in that window waiting for me to make a move? Would she send her husband down to flush me out? I didn't want to wait to find out, so I took a deep breath and putting full faith in my PF Flyers, jetted from behind the shed as fast as I could, shielding my face by pulling my shirt over my head. "Ah huh-unh, I see you, I see you, Hugo. Wait 'til I tell your mother." I had been made. In anticipation of my mother's confronting me with the question, I began to concoct a story to explain what I was doing in Bonnie's back yard. We had no telephone (actually, our service had been interrupted), so I knew Bonnie's mother would have to make a special trip to our apartment to make her report since she and my mother were not really visiting neighbors. But for some reason, she never came. Or if she did, my mother never said anything to me.

The experience with Bonnie had an unexpected aftereffect on me. A week later, I masturbated in a vain attempt to recreate the experience. It was a major letdown because it turned out to be weak imitation of the real thing and nowhere nearly as satisfying. Now that I had had the real thing it was all I wanted from then on.

That Saturday night was the only time Larry and I took Bonnie down together. Thereafter, I would not need him to get over. I had established my own relationship with her and could now go for myself (she had gotten over being upset with me for messing up.) That summer, I spent a good deal of my time scheming to find a safe place for us to couple up. We met several times at my apartment after I had carefully figured out the optimum window of opportunity and least risk. No foreplay was necessary. Not even a kiss. We were both always ready when the moment of truth was upon us. She lay on my bed, pulled up her skirt, pulled down her drawers and spread both her arms and legs and said, "Come on." As if I needed encouragement. It got to be almost routine. She wore a cheap perfume the smell of which always lingered after we had been together. Years later I walked by the fragrance counter in McCrory's in downtown Newark. I was looking for a birthday present for my mother and sampled some of the fragrances. When I smelled something called Evening in Paris, I recognized it at once as the fragrance Bonnie wore. When I got to high school, I noticed that other girls wore it too. When I smelled it, I would always think of Bonnie and the education she gave me.

The relationship with Bonnie was purely sexual. We really had no other one-on-one contact, having nothing else in common. She was, after all, at fourteen, two years older than I. Hell, I was still playing hide-and-go seek and hopscotch. And on occasion I would still take out my Erector Set and build something.

Larry had kept up his rendezvous too and we shared these experiences with each other, sometimes lying about encounters that never occurred in an effort to suggest Bonnie preferred the one telling the story. At least I know I lied sometimes and I am sure he did too. I just knew him like that.

I had never thought of my mother or sisters as sexual beings, but after my encounter with Bonnie, I began to look differently at them. I became protective and very suspicious of my sisters' boyfriends. As to my mother, I knew where babies came from and vaguely how they were made. But I just could not get myself to imagine her having intercourse with my father. In my twelve-year-old head, she had to be above that.

Even though I was grateful to Bonnie, sex was all I wanted her for and I thought more and more of her only as source of pleasure. It was just too easy. The next summer, when I tried to pick up where we had left off, she was no longer interested. It turned out that the reason she had picked Larry and me was that she thought we could not impregnate her. Now that we were thirteen, she was not willing to take the risk. Larry told me she had cut him off too. Perhaps she had found some other twelve-year-old. We tried to figure out who he might be, and briefly considered making some inquiries, but abandoned the idea. How would we have gone about it? Would we seek him out and ask directly? Would the lucky boy confess? Why would he? No, that summer had been our time, our place in Bonnie's embrace, and now it was someone else's turn. We would have to look elsewhere for an agent of release.

Part II

Leaving the security of the neighborhood

Chapter 4

Webster Junior high school

(1)

fter graduating from the sixth grade at Burnet Street Elementary School, I entered Webster Junior High School at the age of thirteen — a proud, brand new teenager. Webster would prove to be a dichotomous experience for me — a source of promise and pain. Personally, it gave me a chance to ditch the name Hugo. At Burnet, I had had about all of the taunting and teasing I could stand over that name and Webster gave me a chance to start anew. I would be David, henceforth.

I would never feel the sense of physical security at Webster that I had felt at Burnet. First, Burnet was only a quarter-mile or so from the Baxter Terrace Apartments — a predominantly colored development. Second, at Burnet, though colored kids were a minority, they were about one-third of the student body. Moreover, the white kids were not just white as the colored kids saw them; they thought of themselves in terms of their own particular ethnicities: Polish, Italian, Irish, etc. These groups had among them their own contradictions and they sometimes found themselves in conflict with each other. When there was a fight between a white and colored boy, it rarely had anything to do with race. Each boy had friends among the various groups cheering him on. Friendship trumped ethnicity.

I believe these two factors — a heavy colored presence and the diversity among white ethnics -- mitigated any significant acts of racial hostility.

The dynamics at Webster were completely different from those at Burnet. The school was ensconced just inside Little Italy, about a mile northwest of my tenement. The anxiety I had about going to a school in a neighborhood that had been the source of terror for me was somewhat reduced by its being relatively close to home. Unlike Burnet, Webster was overwhelmingly Italian; the colored students were in a small minority. Until I started attending Webster, I had come in contact with Italians only when I had to go to the swimming pool or Boys Club. But now I had to be rubbing elbows with them and be taught by a faculty that also was largely Italian. One was even named Mrs. Italiano!

My physical education teachers added to my discomfort. During my very first gym class, my classmates and I were lectured to by two first-year physical education teachers, Mr. Lombardi and Mr. Godfrey. They were explaining why the Negro and the Italian were best suited for certain sports. "The Negro, because he is tall, athletic and of slender build, makes the better basketball player. On the other hand, the Italian makes the better football player because he has a stocky build necessary for a game of strength." I reflected on these remarks, wondering about the other sports. It seemed to me that speed could be a competitive advantage in football. *No matter how strong and stocky you were, if you couldn't catch the man with the ball, what good were these attributes? Why hadn't they discussed other sports? Who was best suited for track, baseball or tennis? I was not slender or tall. What sport should I participate in?* These were the thoughts racing through my head as they spoke. I wondered what my classmates were thinking. I also wondered about the non-Italian white people and where they fit in all this race categorization.

The Italian intimidation factor, combined with the newness of the junior high school experience — a different teacher for each subject; having to change classes and walking through the halls, unsupervised, to reach them; and using lockers (with locks whose combinations I had to memorize (8-18-0) to store my books and personal property; girls who wore makeup, popped chewing gum and bled from between their legs — would force me to grow up in ways that I had not imagined.

Among the colored and Italian students, there seemed to be an unspoken agreement that they could get along as long as they all respected the others' space. The problem was the Italians were the ones who defined the space. It seemed that the cafeteria was one of their spaces, because few if any of the colored kids ate there. On the first day of school, I ate in the cafeteria where the only colored kids I saw were seventh-graders like me. This assessment was easy to make because the students sat in sections according to grade. I asked one of the eighth-grade girls who lived on Clay Street where she ate and she told me about Pop's, a store on the corner of Crane and High streets and directly across the street from Webster. At Pop's they served pizza, meatball sandwiches, and a variety of cold cut sandwiches as well. The most popular sandwich was the Italian hot dog. The hot dog was placed in a deep-pocket roll and smothered with onions and thick French fries all bathed in ketchup. For this nutritious treat and a bottle of soda, I paid fifty cents.

Eating lunch off school grounds was not new to me. We sometimes ate at Maxie's when I was at Burnet. But Pop's had a jukebox. It featured music by R&B artists such as Fats Domino, the Clovers, Coasters, Heartbeats (who later changed their name to Shep and the Limelites), Cleftones, Five Satins, Nutmegs, and Frankie Lymon and the Teenagers. Mixed in among these colored artists were Frank Sinatra, Tony Bennett, Pat Boone, Elvis Presley, and some lesser-known white artists.

I liked Sinatra, but I would not dare play one of his records in this environment. My friends would have ridiculed me. I got my dose of Sinatra on weekends in the privacy of my apartment.

A popular DJ named William B. Williams often used to play him on his Saturday morning show, "the Make-Believe Ballroom" on WNEW am. I listened to William B., as he called himself, when I could no longer stand the insulting, dumbed-down commercials on Newark's WNJR, which seemed to blast the commercials with greater frequency on Saturdays than on any other day of the week. Williams is credited with giving Sinatra the nickname, "Chairman of the Board." He also referred, respectively, to Duke Ellington and Count Basie as the Duke of Ellington and the Count of Basie. He was a suave man who had high regard for the intelligence of his audience and his approach to disc jockeying seemed to elevate it to an art form; indeed, I once heard him refer to himself as "no mere disk jockey but a radio personality."

When Lena Horne and Peggy Lee became grandmothers, he would occasionally inform the audience that we were now going to hear from the grandmother of (grandchild's name). I didn't have the vocabulary then to describe what he was doing by presenting us with these seemingly contradictory images of grandmother and sultry songstress, but I got it. I learned the word "obligatory" while listening to Guillermo B. Guillermos, the Spanish translation of his name, that he was fond of using. Like Symphony Sid, a jazz disc jockey on WLIB am, and a fixture at Birdland, whom I was to discover after I entered high school, William B. was not only cool, he was sophisticated.

Kids crowded into Pop's, ate their lunch and tried to dance in the tiny space. The Italians made their way to the back of the store and sat at tables to eat their lunch and watch the colored kids dance. The lunch-time crowd sometimes tried to dance but the grind was all we would do.

It required no particular skill. The couple faced each other, the boy would position one leg between the legs of the girl and with groins pressed tightly against each other they would move their hips in a circular motion. There was no room at Pop's to do any other kind of dance— not even the two-step — because we were packed in like sardines, which, ironically, made the brief, lunch-time gathering more exciting. Most respectable girls would grind at parties under the dim glow of a blue light, but never in the middle of the day in broad daylight. A vulgar variation of this dance was called the sandwich, in which the girl represented the meat and the boys the bread. One boy faced the girl and the other embraced her from behind. I had known only one girl who would do this dance. I met her at a party in the Dayton Street housing projects, where she showed her stuff. Boys stood in line to dance with her.

(2)

None of my friends from my neighborhood was in any of my classes. What was worse, I was the only colored person in them. That is until second semester when a girl named Delores, a transfer from somewhere down South, was placed in my science class. "Now we have a girl for Barrett," I overheard from a classmate named Sal (he became a Newark detective), while Dolores was checking in with the teacher. Dolores was a big-boned, tall, deep chocolate-complexioned girl and average looking. I had not yet grown out of my intra-group color consciousness — prevalent among colored people, but only quietly spoken of — and considered her too dark for me. Seeing her brought to my mind a popular song at the time whose first line was "I don't want her; you can have her. She's too fat for me." I would substitute the word "dark" for "fat". I didn't know it at the time, of course, but I had internalized a mocking disdain for dark-skinned colored girls for consideration as girlfriends. I had friends of both genders who came in all hues; but a friend was one thing and a girlfriend quite another. In this attitude, I was not alone. Most of the other cats were right there with me. "I want a girl with long hair and light skin because I don't want no dark-skin kids." This was the sentiment, or some version of it, I had been hearing in my neighborhood for years and seen reinforced with images in *Ebony* magazine, in the movies and on television …. "If you white, you alright; if you yellow, you mellow; if you brown, hang around; if you black, stay back." It also explained why I had been infatuated with Olivia for so many of my elementary school years, suffering silently and not even looking at anyone else. It never occurred to me that she might have thought I was too dark for her.

It did not take me long to adjust to Webster. I had begun to make some friends among the colored students and I got along with my other classmates. One of them was a first-generation Italian boy named Aldo who had come to this country from Sicily. Aldo spoke no English, so my English teacher, Mr. Tamphany, assigned me to help Aldo with his school work. I wondered why Mr. Tamphany had selected me. Virtually every other kid in the class was Italian, so it seemed to me one of them would have been more effective. It never occurred to met that I was selected because I was simply smarter than my classmates. My father suggested that Sicilians and Italians (he pronounced it "eye-talians") did not get along because the dark-skinned Sicilians were considered the "niggers" of Italy. The Italians had never forgiven the Sicilians for being overrun by Hannibal and letting his soldiers impregnate their women. "They left a lot of black babies in Sicily," he said. This made no sense to me because, as I figured, since they were all white, what could be the basis for the intra-group hostility?

I got along so well with all of my classmates, that on one occasion I forgot who I was. We had a substitute for art class one day, a short, rotund, bald man who was probably about fifty years old named Mr. Milano. He had a raspy voice that did not project well and was difficult to hear. When he raised his voice, it sounded as if he was straining and to my thirteen-year-old way of thinking, it was amusing. Well, my classmates began to act all wild, constantly talking, walking around the room and ignoring everything Milano told them to do. They weren't going to learn anything about art that day if it killed them. I had never before witnessed such a display of disrespect. But that didn't keep me from joining the crowd. The antics escalated to such a point that I got up the nerve to do something I would not have done under any other circumstances.

Mr. Milano had a straw hat that he had placed on top of the file cabinet, out of harm's way. I got a bottle of red paint, walked casually to the file cabinet, turned his hat upside down and poured some of the paint into it. While everyone else thought it was funny, Gus, the tallest one in the class, came over to my seat in the midst of all the confusion and told me "David, you shouldn't have done that. We're supposed to be just having a little fun and that should not include destroying his property." Gus was by far the most mature of any of us all. He had already decided what he wanted to be when he grew up. "I want to be a dancer," he shared with the class during the second week of school. This pronouncement met with some snickers. Who had ever heard of somebody dancing for a living anyway? Moreover, any boy who wanted to be a dancer was suspect. Gus had always been nice to me and I respected him, so much so that such criticism coming from him hurt my feelings and I felt ashamed of what I had done. It affected me so much that I never misbehaved again when I had a substitute because the image of me pouring the paint into Mr. Milano's hat would linger over me like the shadow from my past that it was. In fact, from that time forward, I would take the unpopular stance of being an aggressive advocate for showing respect to our substitutes and more often than not, my classmates listened.

When I became a teacher in the Newark school system myself some ten years later, I told my classes that if I should ever be absent and they were disrespectful to my substitute, there would be consequences they would never forget. On the two occasions I was absent, the subs left me notes praising the behavior of my classes.

My time at Webster came to a premature end as a result of a misunderstanding I had with an eighth-grade boy. One day when I was on my way to Mrs. Grasso's science class, walking alone as usual, a kid brushed by me and tapped the shoulder of a stocky boy, who was walking just in front of me, and quickly ducked out of sight, into the boys' bathroom. Naturally, the boy who had been tapped turned around to see who had done the tapping. He looked at me and loudly demanded, "Did you touch me, man?" I resented his belligerent tone and responded in kind, "No, I didn't touch you. I don't even know you." He glared menacingly at me and ordered me to "move on then." "I'll move when I'm ready," I forcefully responded. I figured I had to say something because since I was already headed in that direction, I did not want it to appear as though I was moving because I had been ordered to do so. A small crowd had begun to gather to see if anything was going to go down — I imagine there were some even hoping so. The belligerent boy dramatically gave his books to his pal and balled up his hands into fists, as he began to move counterclockwise in a small circle while saying, "Oh you wanna tro some hands, you wanna knuckle samich?" "I'll stuff your knuckle sandwich down your throat if you take one step in my direction you blockhead mothahfuckah," was my defiant reply as I dropped my books and prepared to defend myself.

The boy was holding his hands waist-high and I thought he was going to try a roundhouse. I was prepared to block it and respond with a left hook to his nose (my father's advice again). I was willing to take the chance and let him swing first because I didn't want to be the one named as the starter of the fight, but he seemed to be stalling as he just kept circling, trying to sell me a wolf ticket (an empty threat) and not even acting as if he even wanted to throw a punch. In the interim, Mrs. Grasso, my science teacher, who was on hall duty, noticed all the commotion and came running to the scene. Recognizing me, she shouted, "David, David, what's going on?" And stepped between us. She grabbed me by my hand and pulled me into her classroom, all the while shouting, "what are you doing, what are you doing? I'm surprised at you." While this was going on, my adversary shouted, "After school, Sambo." I thought, *How could she be surprised before she even knew what had happened? Was she automatically blaming me? Didn't she hear what he had just said?* I remonstrated, "I wasn't doing anything. He accused me of touching him. I didn't do it. Some other kid ran up behind him and then ducked into the bathroom." She told me to sit down while she went to get my books, but one of my classmates, who apparently had witnessed the incident, had already picked them up and, books in hand, met Mrs. Grasso at the door. It took Mrs. Grasso a while to settle the class, as they were all a-buzz with what had just happened. From the looks on their faces, they seemed amused that I had almost gotten into a fight, my Clark Kent image shed. I felt a sense of pride rush through my body. That pride was to turn into abject fear before the day was over.

During the next period, one of my classmates motioned to me to look at the doorway. I turned to look and saw a group of Italian boys directing menacing stares at me and shaking their fists. I thought of Emmett Till and the legend about a nameless Newark colored boy who had fallen on his head and died after he was shaken from Webster's playground fence by a group of angry Italian boys and men. I feared for my life. For the rest of the day, I kept looking over my shoulder thinking I might be attacked from behind. I knew these cats did not fight fair. There was no way they would let me and the other boy fight without somebody jumping in. I went to the library during lunch period. Going to Pop's would have been too risky. I knew they would be looking for me there. I searched my memory for a helpful lesson I had studied in my Christian Science Sunday school classes — one that would not only give me the courage to face my enemies but, also, to prevail in battle just like in the movies and in the story of David and Goliath in the Bible. The Twenty-third Psalm came to mind: "Though I walk through the valley of the shadow of death, I shall fear no evil ...." I was a Christian Scientist and they were Roman Catholic (as opposed to regular Catholic — I didn't know the difference.) If God could deliver the Jews from the grip of the Egyptians, surely, he could, if he would, deliver me, the David of Clay Street from the Italians. When I finally made it to homeroom for dismissal, I began to wonder how I was going to get home. Then, as fate would have it, the class started to get unruly and the teacher gave us detention! *I'm dead*, I thought. Just then, my friend, Larry, appeared at the door. I read his lips as he motioned that "they" were waiting for me on the High Street side of the building. They had apparently thought I lived on Stone Street, a little colored island ensconced in the middle of Little Italy, just west of High Street, where a number of colored families lived. I thought this was so stupid. Why didn't they cover all three exits? I concluded it was probably because they didn't have enough guys to form a gang large enough at each door to ensure victory. After all, I had not backed down and had even called the boy a motherfucker. They probably didn't want to take any chances, thinking, apparently, I was badder than I was.

I was grateful for Larry's warning. I knew that was the best he could do. I did not expect any of my friends to help me fight. The stakes were too high.

When the class was dismissed, at last, I went stealthily down the staircase on the Webster Street side of the building. I slowly opened the door to the street, looking north and south. Once I was convinced the coast was clear, I took off running toward Seventh Avenue, turning left when I reached it and right onto Broadway, not even stopping for the traffic lights. I did not stop running even when I reached the relative security of Clay Street. When I reached my building, I took the stairs of the stoop by twos and ran up to my apartment door where I paused to catch my breath before entering. Gasping for breath, I told my mother what had happened. I could see the concern registering on her face as she listened intently. When I finished my story, she asked me what I wanted to do. I told her I did not want to go back. "They'll kill me like they did that other boy, Mom." She must have seen the terror in my face because she took only a few seconds before she said, "All right, I'll walk with you to school tomorrow and we'll get you a transfer."

Serendipitously, around this time, Burnet had added two grades — seventh and eighth — after I graduated. My mother had decided I would transfer to Burnet. I thought, *Oh no, I'll have to be Hugo again*. But I also thought that was the least of my worries at that point.

The next day, my mother and I showed up at the school about 9 a.m. She had earlier called the school to request a meeting with Mr. Servin, the principal. We had not been waiting very long when a secretary announced that Mr. Servin was ready for us. My mother led the way into his office and he offered us seats. Calm and deliberate, my mother wasted no time recounting my story and letting him know she wanted her "son out of this school right now." Servin seemed taken aback by her directness. He pulled out what turned out to be my school record.

White-haired and ruddy-complexioned, Servin rubbed his broad chin, grunted, then said, "Your son is a very good student. We hate to lose good students. Are you sure you don't want to reconsider? His friends might think he is a coward if he should run away from his battles." "If I thought for one minute it would be he and the other boy fighting, just them, I wouldn't be worried. But I know the minute David gets the better of him, and I know he will, they will gang up on him. They'll kill him for sure. I'd rather have a live coward than a dead hero." Her referring to me as David sounded strange. I had always been Hugo to her. She had locked eyes with Servin during his little speech and continued her fixed gaze when she responded. I was proud of her. I had witnessed her speak so forcefully to a white man only once before.

(3)

Melvin and I witnessed my mother's previous stand of pushing back against a white man. It occurred in a butcher shop on Mulberry Street in downtown Newark. The store was one my father had introduced her to during one of her weekly trips to meet him for the grocery money. The only way she could be assured we would get money for food for the week was for her to meet my father on payday at the Novelty Bar and Grill on Market Street. Otherwise, he just might have spent it all buying rounds of drinks for his drinking friends and playing poker. Since we were downtown anyway and the butcher shops on Mulberry Street offered a wider selection of meats than the shops on Broadway in our neighborhood, my mother had taken to buying our meats there. She bought the rest of the groceries at the Acme or A & P.

My father seemed to take great pride in being on a first-name basis with white people, even those with whom he had only casual association, including the butcher. My mother, on the other hand, was very formal with everyone except her closest friends. Moreover, she thought that white people who took the liberty of calling her by her first name without her permission were being disrespectful. Black people never took such liberties. But it was more than just that. She told me on more than one occasion that white people think colored people are not worthy of having a handle in front of their names and it hurts them to have to use one. She recalled that in the South, they would call you uncle or "auntie" rather than "mister "or "miss." If she could command respect, she was going to demand it.

When we entered the crowded butcher shop with its sawdust-covered floor, I could tell by the expression on his face that one of the butchers had recognized my mother.

When it was our turn, he addressed her. "What can I do for you today, Ann?" My mother crossed her arms and stared right into his eyes. Glaring at the man firmly, she stated, "You can start by calling me Mrs. Barrett." He seemed startled for a moment, but recovered quickly as he realized she was not going to say any more until he corrected himself. "Yes, Mrs. Barrett, how can I help you?" I had watched this exchange with keen interest, and some trepidation. Though I was only about eleven at the time, I had the sense that white people were in charge of everything and that they didn't have to do anything they didn't want to when it came to colored people. It was for this reason that I considered of particular significance my mother's display of dignity and resolve in the face of this representative of the omnipotent white race. After all, she was "only" a powerless colored woman and could not possibly have conveyed with her tone that she might cause him harm in some way, if he did not do as she had demanded.

Over time, as I reflected on what had just happened, I came to the conclusion that colored people didn't have to take shit from white people. We just had to be dignified, unrelenting, and serious when we took a stand and willing to face the consequences whatever they might be.

Many years later, when my mother held firm against Mr. Servin at Webster to request my transfer, he could see she was dead serious. He promised to process the paperwork for the transfer and assured my mother, since there was only one week of school remaining, I could go home with her and there would be no penalty.

Having gotten the outcome she desired, my mother lifted herself from the chair and I instinctively followed her lead. She extended her hand to shake his, revealing for the first time her oversized extremity — a permanent reminder of the visible side effect from her mastectomy, years earlier. Mr. Servin rose too and he extended his hand to meet hers.

"Thank you for understanding. I could tell you were a good man the minute I laid eyes on you." She smiled as she spoke. Servin grinned and thanked her for coming in.

On the way home, I asked her how she could tell that Mr. Servin was a good man. She said, "Sometimes you have to say things to make people feel good about what they have done, even when they should have done it anyway. Cooperation should never be taken for granted even if it is forced out of someone."

That summer went very fast and about all I could recall of it is wondering how it would feel to return to the school from which I had already graduated. How different would it be? Would I be reunited with any of my fellow alumni? What stories would they have to tell about their hiatus from Burnet?

(4)

As I had moved on from Burnet to Webster, some of my former classmates had gone to McKinley Junior High and some of them too returned to Burnet. I did not know why and never even questioned it. I was back, why shouldn't they be too? Everyone seemed to have gotten so much bigger. The boy's voices had changed and the girls had gotten breasts and hips. I heard talk among them about something called a period. There was a sprinkling of new kids too — at least I did not recognize them from my first six years at Burnet. Things were going to be different.

And different they were, especially for me. In the one year I spent at Webster, I had been transformed from one ridiculed to one who was popular. I couldn't keep the girls away and the boys seemed to look to me for leadership. I would find myself looking in the mirror trying to discover what had changed. I still wore the Coke-bottle eyeglasses. I was Hugo again, but my dimples were deeper or maybe I just imagined they were when I failed to identify anything else that could explain this new-found popularity. Olivia, on whom I had had a not-so-secret crush, was now unabashedly competing for my attention. In the meantime, I became interested in Ianthe, whose parents were from Jamaica. By then I had learned where the West Indies were and that its people, while not considered colored, were just as brown as I, being they got there from West Africa the same way my ancestors got to America, but nobody liked to talk about slavery. We were ashamed of having been slaves — like we did it to ourselves or something.

Unlike Olivia, Ianthe was brown just like me. She had both an older and a younger brother and a younger sister who wound up being Melvin's girlfriend shortly after Ianthe and I hooked up. Her parents, who owned their own home, were very strict and would have had a fit if they had found out she had a boyfriend, which they never did, even though her younger brother would threaten to drop a dime to her parents whenever he got angry with Ianthe.

For Christmas she gave me an identification bracelet with my name inscribed on it. A flip of the cover revealed a photograph of her bright, smiling face and slightly visible ponytail. I looked at it every night before going to bed and even for a while after we broke up, three months later. She had started to act weird around me, complaining that my kisses (suddenly) were too wet and that she had a hard time keeping up with me on the rare occasions I would chance walking her halfway home. I think she was hoping I would get tired of the shit and quit her, but I was too dense to see what was going on, so she had to do the dastardly deed herself.

Though I shed my share of tears over the breakup, it didn't hurt as much as I thought it would. Besides, there were other girls just waiting for something like this to happen, maybe even counting on it. Unfortunately, I did not like any of them, not even Olivia anymore. I did, however, fool around with some of them to give Ianthe the impression that she had not been a big thing with me. Truth is I do not think she even noticed. But later in high school, I tried again to hit on her and she rebuffed me, claiming she did not want to be part of my harem. That word sent me to the dictionary. I was flattered when I read the definition.

My eighth-grade teacher was Mr. Laventer. Bespectacled and of medium build, he stood about five feet seven inches and appeared to be about forty-five (or sixty-five for all I knew -- I had really found difficulty estimating the ages of adult white people) years old. His eyeglasses magnified his blue eyes so as to give them a look of great intensity. But I liked him because he was fair and had complete control of the class, and that helped to create an environment that was conducive to learning.

I wrote my first paper ever in Mr. Laventer's class. It was on the Lewis and Clark expedition. I remember getting an A+ but; I do not remember anything about the paper except I had fun researching it as I learned about things I had never even imagined had happened. I did not understand why Lewis and Clark had the need to explore land that already had inhabitants. I figured they could have asked them whatever they wanted to know.

My best friends in eighth grade were Alan Lockhart (Alley Cat); Donald Green (Duck) Nathaniel Beck (Beck) and Richard Copeland (Cope). We were as different as any five peers could be — maybe that was the secret to our friendship. Duck and Beck were natural comedians; Alley Cat was quiet and slow to get angry, but deadly when he did; and Cope was a talented artist who drew caricatures and wordless comic strips featuring anybody he felt like fucking with at any given time. His most cutting strip was about a boy named Ronnie, a classmate who had been in and out of reform school. Cope's cartoon consisted of three panels. The first featured an elderly man sitting on a park bench while feeding pigeons bread crumbs from a brown paper bag. In the second, panel we saw Ronnie, a big stick in hand, scoping out the scene from behind a tree. The third panel showed pigeon feathers scattered all over the ground; the old man, apparently unconscious, lying on the ground and Ronnie, looking content, sitting where the man had been sitting, eating the bread crumbs from the bag with his stick resting easily across his lap. Cope, who sat behind me, passed it to me and I passed to the Beck. Eventually, the strip made its way to anyone who expressed an interest. Of course, Ronnie, who sat behind Cope, was not supposed to see the strip, but there was no way to keep it from him; and once he saw it, he was ready to kill Cope. He would have done so had it not been for the fact that Cope was tight with Beck, Duck, Alley, and me. We made Cope apologize and tear up the strip. That settled the matter. All of us at one time or another fell victim to Cope's cutting drawings; if you did not have a sense of humor, you would not remain friends with Cope for very long.

Not so easily settled was the trouble this same quintet got into for feeling up on Charity. Though no one explicitly said so, we thought because she was so countrified, she did not merit the respect we routinely showed other girls. When it came to Charity, we believed we could do with impunity whatever we wanted. I had such low regard for her, I never imagined she would tell Mr. Laventer on us, but she did. I knew something was up when one day Mr. Laventer began to call my friends, one by one, to his desk for a conference. *Maybe*, I thought, *just maybe he wouldn't call me.* I began to concoct a defense that I hoped I could sincerely mount, but I knew the gig was up for me when I heard: "David Hugo Barrett, come up here, please." Mr. Laventer had called me by all of my names. I started shaking in my shoes, as I tried to remain outwardly calm and appear bewildered at being called. "Yes sir, Mr. Laventer," I managed to say, once I reached his desk. "Sit down. Your name has been mentioned in connection with a very serious matter. Charity has reported that you and some other boys molested her. Do you know what I mean by molest?" His voice dropped to near whisper each time he used the word "molest." "Yes, sir," I firmly said. I got the sense he wanted to believe me innocent, a suspicion that was confirmed for me as he began to launch into character assassinations of my friends. He described two as not having the sense they were born with, and the third of having an IQ of a blade of grass. He was insulting my friends, but somehow, that did not seem all that important now. Fixing a cold gaze on me from behind his horn-rimmed glasses, he then asked, directly, if I had been involved. Looking and sounding as sincere as I could, I said, "No, sir, I wasn't." He said, "I didn't think you were. But you should be careful who you choose as your friends because somebody who doesn't know you would think you are the same as they, and I don't think you would want to be identified with this bunch."

Even though I knew I had gotten away with it, my heart was still in my throat. The whole time I was thinking, *I would never reveal this to my* mother.

For the remainder of the school year, I avoided eye contact with Charity and slowly broke off my relationship with the other three boys and never discussed the matter with them.

Not all of my eighth-grade adventures occurred within the school walls. I played hooky a few times too. I first played hooky in the eighth grade. Most of the time, I escaped alone, but occasionally Alley Cat and I would go together to spend the day at a dive of a movie theater, on Market Street near Mulberry, called the Rialto. It was frequented by bums (homeless men) who sought comfort there in hot and very cold weather. Once when Alley and I were there, a man sat down next to Alley, who was seated to my right. We thought this odd since the theater was practically empty. But we didn't focus on it too much until we noticed that whenever he laughed, he found some reason to lean on Alley. Alley told me what had been happening. I leaned over and looked at the man with as menacing a look as I could muster. He responded by raising the forefinger of one hand to his lips while making a shhhhh sound and, simultaneously, making a fist with his other hand. Well, that was enough for us. We got our asses out of those seats and headed to the balcony, which had been roped off. We didn't care; we figured if he was bad enough to follow us up there, we were bad enough to throw his ass off the balcony.

The next time I got an invitation to play hooky, I declined, not because of the incident at the Rialto, but because it would have been too risky. Some genius had planned a day of mass hooky-playing with half the eighth-grade boys from Burnet teaming up with former classmates who were now at Webster. The meeting place was to be Branch Brook Park by the swings. Alley was the one who told me about the plan; I told him Laventer would know something was up when he noticed so many boys absent, but Alley was determined to go.

They all got busted by three truant officers who had caught them shortly after they arrived. Alley said someone must have told on them. I reminded him of my warning and told him no one needed to tell on them — they had told on themselves. I told him that kids going to a public park in the middle of a school day were simply begging to be caught and that it served them right.

Mom and Dad
Camp Street, 1960.

Christmas 1955, Clay Street
Top Left to right: Me, Bobby Carter, Melvin (my younger brother), Pedro Carter.

My mother in Portsmouth, VA, 1934, with my three sisters: Rose Marie (held), Hilda, and Barbara.

Me in the middle with Phillip Parker (left) and Ianthe De Geneste, 1960.

Me (second from right rear) Central High School English Honor Society, 1961.

Me at age 9 standing on the corner of Clay and Spring streets.

Me (right) standing on stoop at 67 Clay Street with my brother Melvin, Clay Street 1952.

Me at age 8 on Spring Street in front of the steel foundry. 1954

Central High School track & field team, 1960.

My High School graduation photo, 1961 Central High School.

My brother James Jr., 1944.

Part III

Outside Interventions

Chapter 5

Learning the hard way

(1)

Before one of my friends told me you needed to have 20-20 vision to fly an airplane, what I really wanted to do was join the Airforce and become a fighter pilot. I had seen enough war movies to appreciate what a glorious job it could be and I wanted some of that glory. Not bothering to verify my friend's claim, I reconsidered and decided that I would do what I thought was the next best thing. I would become a jet airplane engine mechanic. My older sister's husband had been in the Air Force and learned to repair diesel engines during his service. Following his discharge, he got a job maintaining and repairing locomotive engines. I suspect both my idea of joining the Airforce and becoming a mechanic were influenced by him. So, while at Burnet, I decided to attend Bloomfield Vocational and Technical High School.

Newark had its own Vocational and Technical High School, called VoTech for short, but it did not measure up to the reputation of Bloomfield Tech. Moreover, my older brother, James, had gone to Bloomfield and done well, graduating near the top of his class and getting a job as a draftsman directly out of high school. But after only one year of drafting in the trade, he announced to our mother, "I cannot see myself bent over a drafting table for the rest of my life. I'm going to go to college." This decision confused me because he had always been so sure of himself. How could he have been so wrong about something as important as a career decision?

Though I concealed it behind a curtain of sibling rivalry, I admired my older brother. It seemed he could do anything he set his mind to, including building and repairing stuff. He built an end table for my mother and repaired my bicycle numerous times until I learned to do it myself. He learned how to drive and got a job working in the used car lot, Bruno's, across the street from our building; he bought a car and hired his own piano teacher, who taught him to read music and to play the piano, all by the time he was sixteen. The most courageous thing I recall him doing was take summer job working in the steel foundry around the corner on Spring Street. Temperatures soared as high as 120 degrees as the furnaces did their job heating the solid iron ore thick liquid that when cooled would present itself as the steel we are more familiar with.

As a young boy, however, he was a terror, at least according to my older sisters, who were in charge of everything when our parents were at work. The way they told it, James was particularly bad one day and they simply could do nothing to get him to behave. One of them got the idea to persuade him to play a game of cops and robbers. They convinced him he would make a very good robber because he was naturally bad anyway. He was flattered and agreed to the arrangement. Setting him up, they told him to make believe he had committed some terrible crime and they had captured him and had to tie him up while they questioned him about it. Binding his arms and feet, they tied him to a kitchen chair with some old clothesline rope. And there he remained for two or three hours, mad as hell, and off and on screaming his lungs out about having been tricked by the girls until my mother came home. What happened after that depends on whom you wanted to believe — James or my sisters. My mother claimed only a vague recollection of the incident.

At any rate, Melvin and I both hated and loved him at the same time and for the same reasons. He just had more talent than we had put together and as a big brother — he was seven years my senior — he did the usual terrible things a big brother does to his unfortunate younger brothers. He tormented us to no end. I remember his pinning me down on our bed once and dangling menacingly a long string of saliva from his mouth, and at the last possible moment, slurping it back into his mouth, only to repeat the process. On one of these terrifying occasions, gravity prevailed, rendering him unable to slurp his liquid bomb back into his mouth. I screamed at the top of my lungs as I watched helplessly the wet missile coming in slow motion towards my face and finally drop into my eye. "Let me up, let me up. I'll kill you; I'll kill you," I exclaimed. He started laughing and simultaneously apologizing through his laughter while he continued to hold me down. Then he suddenly pushed himself from me and fled out the back door. I ran to the kitchen sink and began to wash my face, still screaming as if I had suffered some great physical injury.

I reported him to our mother when she returned home from work. I never found out what, if anything, she did to punish him; but he never tormented me like that again, although he did continue to tease me about one thing or another. At one point, out of great frustration over whatever teasing James was doing at the time, Melvin and I threatened that we were going to wait until he was old and, in a wheelchair, then we would throw him down a flight of stairs — an empty threat, of course, but it felt good to make it. Naive, we did not consider that we would be aging right along with him, not to mention we would not be able to hold a grudge for so long. We never considered that death would intervene; but Melvin died of lung cancer at age 55.

(2)

Like most effective parents, my mother could be both my advocate, as she was with James, and my adversary when she denied me my cravings. As a child, I had a craving for cake and ice cream — so much so that my mother had to place restrictions on how much I could eat. I recall going for my third piece of chocolate cake one Sunday after dinner (the only time we had dessert. Other times, I would create my own dessert by spreading grape jelly on a biscuit). She kept the cake dish on top of the refrigerator, and as I reached for the dish, my mother asked, "What are you doing, Hugo" I replied, "Getting some more cake," in a what-does-it-look-like? tone. "Didn't you already have two slices?" "Yes," I said. "Well, you get no more tonight, do you hear me?" She fixed a gaze on me that demanded compliance. I sat down hard in my chair and mumbled, "I'll be glad when I grow up and get a job. I'm going to eat a whole cake every day and you won't be able to stop me." She burst out laughing. "You're not but ten now, but when that time comes, I hope we both remember this conversation, because I am telling you now, that will not be the case. We are poor people and unable to afford to expose you to a lot of things that would put cake-eating way in the back of your mind. By the time you get to college, and for sure after you graduate, you will have different priorities."

I didn't know what she was talking about. How could my appetite for cake ever diminish? Unable to fathom how this could possibly be, I dismissed her predictions. What I was not able to dismiss, however, was her calling us "poor" and saying that I was going to college. She had never discussed my going to college. How on earth would we be able to afford it? And poor? I knew we weren't rich, but I surely did not think we were poor. I had schoolmates who were poor. Many of them lived in storefronts and three-room apartments with four or five siblings. The Carter family even had nine children. Their clothes were frequently dirty and they seemed to never have any money. When they came to my house, they were frequently hungry and never turned down an offer of food. Though I never believed that being poor was justification for shoplifting, I did allow myself to fall under the influence of two of my friends.

The summer before I was to enroll at Tech, I went downtown to shoplift with Larry and his cousin Alfred. I had money, but I reasoned if I could steal what I wanted, I could save the money for something else. We decided to go to Klein's department store (S. Klein's on the Square was their slogan) because they were having a big sale and we figured we would be invisible among the throngs of adults. Klein's was known for having sales for which people began lining up two hours before opening time and rushing in like stampeding cattle when the doors opened.

We walked the eight blocks, stopping one block from Klein's in front of the Loew's Theatre to discuss our plan. Should we split up or stay together? I voted for splitting up because I thought we would be less conspicuous. But Larry and Alfred wanted the security that staying together afforded. I said that was fine with me and they could stay together. I would go by myself. I offered that we would just have to figure out where we gonna meet and at what t time.

The strategy was to steal only one or two things that we could easily conceal under our jackets without making a bulge. We would meet in the women's underwear department at 1 p.m., then leave together. We synchronized our watches like they always did in the movies. If for some reason any of us did not score, we would decide what to do at that time. Nobody could be late, that was not negotiable. We came together, we leave together.

I had decided to lift a belt or two. I would fasten them under my jacket, high on my waist above where my own belt was. When I got to the men's accessories, I tried to look really serious as I deliberated the many choices. I even held my money in my hand, occasionally brushing my face with it so everybody interested could see I had some and, therefore, could not possibly be a shoplifter. I took down one belt and examined it carefully. As I started to make my move, I felt uneasy about something and decided to just hold it while I walked around. I couldn't find a window of opportunity to slip the belt under my jacket, so I aborted my mission and bailed out. I walked around just to kill time and went to the meeting place to wait for Larry and Alfred. I had been waiting only a few minutes when I saw them approaching me, each carrying a brown, paper shopping bag. I thought immediately, *this does not look good. This is not what we agreed to. These bastards done got greedy.* They were grinning from ear-to-ear as they approached. I wondered if they could read the expression on my face, how stupid I thought they were. They shuffled past me and I reluctantly joined them as we headed out of the store. We had just made it to the sidewalk when we heard a deep voice behind us, "Okay, punks, just keep walking to the corner and turn right. If you try to make a run for it, I'll put a bullet in your ass. Give me those goddamn shopping bags."

The voice was coming from a white man of medium build who reached his pale, hairy, hand down and took both bags from Larry and Alfred. My heart jumped from my chest and settled in my throat as my hands started sweating; I was one scared soul. I was not afraid of being accused of stealing because I had not stolen anything; that was not my fear. I was afraid of getting shot for something I didn't do. I wondered what my accomplices were thinking. *Were they as scared as I? What defense were they going to muster? Would we stick together or would it be every man for himself.* We had seen enough movies to know that if one person were caught, he should not drop a dime on the others. But what if everyone is caught — with the goods no less? What was the rule then? Our gruff guide directed us to a side door Cedar Street side of the Klein's building. The door opened to a long concrete stairway that led to the basement. We did not say a word, but "Billy Goat Gruff "(I had nicknamed him to myself) talked almost continuously, telling us that he picks up punks like us every day and sends them all to jail and he would do all he could to see that we met the same fate. He was talking so much; he must have been as afraid of us as we were of the possible consequences of our actions. I wondered if Jesus would save me this time too, this one last time.

When we reached the basement, we had to follow a labyrinth of corridors to reach our destination. It was a small office with drab green walls and furnished with three full-length mirrors; four or five wooden chairs; two large pole-mounted fans, forcefully blowing warm air at each other; and a large brown desk behind which sat the biggest, most nefarious-looking woman I had ever seen. In the center of the desk was a thick wooden name plate—a block really — into which "Mary O'Hara" had been carved in a fancy cursive. Wearing a floral, short-sleeved dress, she had what must have been a size forty bust. The under sides of her upper arms shook like Jell-o with the slightest movement of any part of her body. She had brown hair through which snaked thin streaks of gray and she wore glasses that magnified her eyes so much that she looked like a fish peering out from a fish bowl. She must have had three chins. And this last detail -- the chins -- reminded me of the only teacher who had ever laid a hand on me.

I was in sixth grade and she was a substitute who had given us directions on the in-class lesson we were to embark upon and had directed us not to begin writing until she gave the word. I guess I hadn't heard the last part, or maybe, I was just eager to get started, but I began writing my name at the top of the paper. I was so absorbed in my task, I never heard her coming. The next thing I knew, slap, bam, my head slammed into the top of my desk. The woman had hit me! "I told you not to write until I said so," she screamed. Tears began to stream from my eyes, more from embarrassment than from pain, as my classmates snickered.

Memories of this incident flashed before my mind's eye as I gazed at O'Hara. In short, this was one intimidating woman who had put fear into me before she spoke even one word.

"What do we have here, Frank, some more punks who think they are smarter than we are?" *Ain't nobody trying to outsmart your ugly, fat ass,* I thought. Was she going to try to act as though what we had done had something to do with her and her crew? Nothing could have been farther from the truth, and I figured she was just putting together a ploy to personalize our actions so she could feel justified doing to us whatever they had in mind before they called the police. Before Frank could answer, she barked, "Sit down over there," pointing to three chairs that, oddly enough, had been placed side-by-side facing the mirrors to her right. The chairs were arranged in such a way that we had to turn our heads to our right side in order to look at her; we could see each other's faces only if we looked in the mirrors we faced. This was a slick move on their part because this arrangement made it impossible for us to send any kind of facial signals to each other once the interrogation began.

O'Hara ordered us to empty the contents of our pockets onto her desk, a request with which we, one at time, obediently complied. I was sitting in the chair nearest her, so I assumed I should go first. I thought about the business card a detective had given me a few years back. I was fearful she might call him if she found it. Fortunately, I had not transferred it to my new wallet. I did think about the condom I had been carrying for months; I was sure that if she saw it; she would have one more thing to crack on me. Alfred was next and Larry followed next. O'Hara went through their wallets, apparently in search of identification. We had, early in the eighth grade, bought wallets that contained cards with a place for you to write identifying information. In some juvenile display of fantasy, we had all written fake names on these cards. Mine was Darnez

Barretto, Larry had named himself Ringo Jones and Alfred was Rocky Johnson.

"Who's Ringo Jones?" demanded O'Hara. Larry said, "I am, ma'am." I was surprised at how humble he sounded in his response. "But that's not my real name. I just use that to be fooling around." "Well don't fool around with me, you jerk. What's your real name?" Larry gave his real name ever so meekly. "Do you think you're some kind of tough guy Lawrence? Do you know what we do with guys like you? We send them to Jamesburg [a reformatory for juveniles] where they become the girlfriends of the really tough guys. You may go in as Ringo Jones, but you come out as Rita Jones, if you come out at all." Larry remained silent.

"What's your story, Darnez?" she said, glaring at me. "I have no story. I didn't do nothin'," I replied with a certain amount of defiance. "I didn't do nothin'." She mimicked me, "I didn't do nothin', I didn't do nothin'. Nobody ever does anything. That's why you keep us so busy down here. That's why we have jobs, you goddamn jerk." I was struck by her casual use of profanity — she was a little bit too comfortable using profanity for someone who was supposed to be a lady! The only adults who had ever cussed me up to that point were white men. One was a policeman who picked me up as a suspect in an assault case. The other two were workers at the Bell Telephone Company on Broad Street, right around the corner from Clay.

In the latter incidents, I was riding my bicycle the wrong way on Eighth Avenue, a one-way street a block from my apartment and parallel to Clay Street. I was on the driver's side of an approaching car. Suddenly, the driver stuck his hand out of the car and slapped me in my face, yelling, "Get out of the street, you black bastard!" My glasses went flying from my face as I followed them and my bike to the ground, skinning my knee and the palms of my hands.

In the second incident, I was riding on the sidewalk, again on Eighth Avenue. As I approached the intersection of Eighth Avenue and Broad Street, I turned north onto Broad at the same time two white men were walking south. One of them grabbed the handlebars of my bike and, calling me a black bastard as well, hurled bike and me into the noontime traffic. Fortunately, the light was red for Broad Street traffic and there was no traffic turning onto Broad from the east-bound lane of Eighth Avenue. My bike hit the fire hydrant on the corner and I spilled head-first into the street. I sat there briefly, bewildered, tears streaming from my eyes, and looked at the men as they continued walking, never even looking back. Though the sidewalk was teeming with other workers, not a single one came to my aid.

Both times I told my mother what had happened. The first time, she reminded me that I was not supposed to be riding in the street anyway. "That should teach you a lesson." This second time, I asked her why white people felt they can do anything they want to us, even in our own neighborhood, and nothing happens to them? I reminded her that I had been riding on the sidewalk as she had instructed me. "Some white people are just mean to the bone and the man who did that to you was not a man at all, but a coward. Any man who would treat an innocent child that way should burn in hell." That was the first time I remembered hearing my mother curse. I knew she had to be very angry. I asked if we could tell Dad so he can beat him up. "Your father is at work when these people come into our neighborhood to their telephone company jobs." That answer satisfied me because I read into it that if Dad had been at home during the day, he would have beaten up the man.

The emotional scars from these two incidents would be reopened many times well into my adulthood. I had made a solemn promise that if I ever had children and a white man put his hands on them, I would try my best to kill him with my bare hands — a promise I had occasion to keep three times.

Today, I cannot help but wonder how many black men have similar stories to tell. How many are carrying around deep, emotional wounds from such experiences — wounds that explode at the least provocation — explode in the faces of neighbors, fellow employees, supervisors and authority figures because of these unresolved, deeply buried feelings of hostility toward white men? How many should be in therapy; but don't know it? I wonder too, about the two white men who assaulted me. *What must have been their mental state? What were they angry about? What were they teaching their children? Did they even know they were angry? Were they the rule or the exception to it?*

Formidable proof of the discrimination rule was sitting at her desk in the basement of S. Klein's, ready to launch the inquisition on three teenage boys from Clay Street. O'Hara glared at Alfred, who looked as though he was about to cry. "And I suppose you didn't do nothin' either, right Rocky? Is that your name? Rocky?" "No, ma'am, my name is Alfred and I didn't steal nothin'. I wouldn't lie. I go to church." I couldn't believe my ears. Alfred was copping out and they had not even begun to get tough with us. I felt sorry for him and Larry too because Alfred was Larry's first cousin, oldest child of his mother's younger sister. If it got back to the neighborhood that he had broken down before the going even got tough, he would never live it down and would truly be thought of as a punk. And who would want a punk for a cousin? On the other hand, since Larry would not tell anyone of Alfred's shameful, unexpected behavior; the only way anyone would find out was if I told and I wasn't going to do that. I had nothing to gain by doing so. I just decided right then and there; I would not let Alfred hang with me the next time we contemplated doing something on the other side of the law.

O'Hara asked Frank to give us a clipboard to which a form was attached. She directed us to write our real names, addresses, and telephone numbers on the form. When we finished, Frank took the clipboard and left the room. "What school do you attend?" She was looking at me so I answered, I told her I just graduated from Burnet Street and was going to Bloomfield Tech in September. "Don't you have to take some kind of test to get into Bloomfield?" I replied that I did and I passed. "Well, Mr. Darnez, you just blew your chance to go to Tech. When we pass on to them what you have done, they will not want you." *Oh, shit,* I said to myself. Then I said aloud, "You mean I can't go to Tech because of this?" I reminded her that I had already told her that I didn't steal anything. I was innocent. I didn't have a bag and that she could search me! Then I demanded of her again to search me! "Have you ever heard of the word accessory, Darnez?" I was the only one whose real name she had not requested and she had not looked at the clipboard so she apparently thought my fantasy name was close enough to be real. I thought for a while about an episode of the TV crime show, Dragnet, in which Sergeant Friday (Jack Webb) was explaining to a suspect that she was an accessory after-the-fact. It was the first time I had heard the word. I told O'Hara that I thought it meant that you help somebody do something bad. "Well, you're not as dumb as you look. You almost got it right. You don't actually have to do anything. You just have to be with the guys who do, or in some way, be involved with what they did after they have done it. You do not even have to have been there. That's called accessory after the fact. Well, whether you took anything or not, you were with these two fools, so that makes you as guilty as them. Do you understand that, wise guy?" She was beginning to get on my nerves as I gazed in the mirror at my cohorts and thought how pitiful they were.

The ringing of O'Hara's phone interrupted my thoughts. She turned her back and spoke quietly and briefly into the phone. She hung up and rolled her chair away from her desk. The she lifted her oak-tree mass, navigated herself around her desk and waddled out of the office. After she left the room, Larry said, "The cops must be here. What are we gonna do? What are we gonna do? I can't go to Jamesburg." I said, "We will soon find out, amigos."

After a few minutes, Frank and O'Hara returned. She was carrying a file folder that she waved conspicuously as she fell into her chair. She slowly opened the folder and pensively, stroked the lower of her three chins. "Okay, let's see what we have here. Well, none of you has a record and that's in your favor. The total value of everything you stole is less than $10. So, here is the deal. You get your asses out of here and don't ever set foot in this store again. If you do, we will bust you and send you straight to Jamesburg. You got that?" Then I asked her if she was going to report me to Bloomfield Tech. She answered my question with a smirk.

I sweated the whole summer, fully expecting a letter from Tech rescinding my admission. But it never came. Ironically, following my freshman year in college, I got a summer job working at Klein's. Before I applied to Klein's, I had been turned away by three other employers. They told me that they had no need for summer help. I had thought that my year of college would be an asset! I was too naïve to suspect there might be interviewers who, lacking a college education themselves, might be resentful of me, a colored boy, pursuing a college degree and might exercise what little power they did have to reject me. Frustrated over my bad luck, I told my mother that the prospects did not look good. "I've always told you and you have learned in Sunday school that lying is wrong. 'Thou shall not bear false witness.' Being a college student seems to be getting in the way of your finding a job. So, maybe if you were going to be an evening student at Rutgers instead of a fulltime student, someone might hire you."

When I completed my application at Klein's, I entered "first year college" in the column labeled "highest grade completed." I added a footnote in which I stated "not returning due to lack of funds." I got the job.

Chapter 6

Bloomfield Technical High School

(1)

Newark had a student transportation system that serviced, by and large, only students with disabilities. Most students walked to school. Others could buy a book of 20 bus tickets that were sold at a substantially discounted price by the state public transportation company (now called New Jersey Transit). For those who needed to ride the bus, this arrangement was a godsend. There were, of course, restrictions: You could not use the student tickets after 5 p.m. on school days and not at all on weekends. Also, you were supposed to tear the ticket from the book in front of the driver, otherwise, at his discretion, he could refuse it. The reason for this policy was to discourage students from selling their tickets. Athletes and others engaged in extracurricular activities that took them beyond the 5 o'clock cut-off time were apparently on the honor system. At least, I do not recall having any kind of pass to show the bus driver to prove I had a legitimate reason for being late. During track season, I frequently left practice after 5 p.m. I would have my duffle bag and track shoes slung over my shoulder and if there was a problem, I would simply announce the obvious — that I was on the track team.

To get to Bloomfield Tech, I had to walk one block from home to take the Number 29 Bloomfield or 60 Montclair bus for the thirty-minute ride to school. The bus would go up Broad Street, turn left on Bloomfield Place (home of Peskin's appliance store), and finally, it made a right turn onto Bloomfield Avenue. From there, it was a straight shot to the township of Bloomfield, where I got off just this side of the Newark line. If I hadn't exited the bus before the city limits, it would have cost another bus ticket. After I got off the bus, I walked the four blocks through a neat residential area that was sprinkled with single family houses with neatly manicured lawns and two-car garages. These TV houses were in marked contrast to the tenements on Clay Street. I used to wonder what the people who lived in them were like and what they did for a living. I had learned from the movies and my mother that Negroes simply did not live in such neighborhoods (passing rows of single-family houses on Sunday drives through unexplored Newark neighborhoods, whenever we had the opportunity to ride in a visitor's car, she would observe, "white people must live here.") How she was able to reconcile this belief with the hard fact that her parents owned the house in which she was raised and that all of her brothers had bought new houses in and around Portsmouth, I don't know. Had it not been for the fact that her father's three sisters (who had fled the South as soon as they had saved enough money, and eventually bought houses — big brownstones in Brooklyn on Green Street near Flatbush Avenue) owned houses, I would have thought she was thinking only about northern Negroes. I think now though that she did not give literal meaning to this observation of hers, and what she really meant was she had low expectations of what Negroes outside of her family could accomplish.

It was rare that I ever saw any residents as I made my way through this immaculate Bloomfield neighborhood but; those I saw were white and I found myself averting my eyes as they approached, walking their dogs. I had a deep sense of being an outsider, an interloper. That feeling seemed to intensify on the occasions I came face-to-face with them. I was sure my face showed it and I didn't want them to see how intimidated I was just walking through their space. Walking through this neighborhood made me think of how thoroughly my own neighborhood contrasted with it, and I felt a deep sense of shame and inadequacy.

Other than in the movies or on television, before my commute to Tech, I do not think I had ever seen anyone walking a dog. By the time I was in ninth grade, my family had had three dogs (Rocky, Teddy and Fluffy) and we never walked any of them. We just "let out the dog" whenever he went to the door, scratched his paws against it and whined. When he wanted to come in, he did the same routine, but from the other side of the door. In a song titled "Yakety Yak," the R&B group ,The Coasters, in the voice of an unreasonably demanding parent, instructed the overworked child, who had already completed several chores, "and when you finish doing that; bring in the dog and put out the cat," and also admonished the child not to talk back. That line validated, for me, that letting our house pets roam freely was not an aberration, but the norm — at least to the audience their song addressed.

The lyrics of many an R&B song spoke to me. It was as if the songs understood my thoughts, aspirations and feelings, because they mirrored them. It seemed I was naturally attracted to the harmonies, rhythms, and chord changes that these songs embodied. The adult themes of romance, conflict, reconciliation, and occasional betrayal seemed to reflect life as I observed it in my community. "Treasure of Love" by Clyde McPhatter, the first lead singer for the Drifters, and "Life is But a Dream," by Willie Winfield and The Harptones were representative of romance themes that were prevalent in my world of the fifties and early sixties. At the same time, I still clung to the lyrics and melodies of non-R&B songs, including such tunes as "How Much Is That Doggie in the Window?", by Patti Page; "Hey There (You With The Stars in Your Eyes), by Rosemary Clooney; any songs of the Mills Brothers; Frankie Laine's "Mule Train" (he also recorded "Rawhide," the theme song for the popular TV show of the same title); and anything by Frank Sinatra or Nat King Cole. When I first heard Sinatra sing "One More for the Road," I imagined my father sitting at a bar. The song seemed to have been written for him.

I was uncomfortable with many of the straight-out blues songs because of their strong innuendoes about sex, as exemplified by Hank Ballard and The Midnighters. Maybe it was because for a long time we had only one radio and I became embarrassed if my mother was within hearing range when one of these songs was playing.

Bloomfield Technical High School, which was all-male when I attended, shared the crest of a hill with the adjacent Bloomfield Junior High School. The proximity of the junior high school was an incentive for me to get to school early so I could hang out in front and check out the Negro girls who went there. Talking to one or two of them was about all I ever expected to do. Going with one of them was not practical. I figured since they were attending that school, they must be Bloomfield residents and the logistics of getting from Newark to wherever they might live in Bloomfield would have been simply impractical. However, there was actually one girl to whom I had been so attracted that I forgot about things practical. We would rendezvous mornings before school and talk on the telephone weekday evenings and weekends, but it never got past those conversations. Eventually, she stopped showing up for the morning meetings and was always busy when I called, promising to call "right back." She never did.

With a student body of about 700, Tech was a small and well-run school -- at least there were never any serious disciplinary problems, either in or out of the classroom that I experienced. Maybe that was attributable to the administration's no-nonsense attitude toward behavioral problems. One major offence or three lesser offences of any degree over the four years you were there and you were out.

The only class of mine in which there were behavioral problems was science. We had a Negro (the only one) science teacher who was new to the school -- Jackson was his name — whom the students did not respect. The kids pretty much paid attention only when it suited them.

Talking to each other during his lectures, they just ignored him when he asked for their attention. I thought they were doing it because he was a Negro and I resented it for that reason.

On one particular day, they were really out of control, throwing paper airplanes across the room and in other ways acting like jerks. His was our last class of the day and he threatened to give us detention if we didn't settle down. They just ignored him. After a few minutes of this shit, I stood up and angrily shouted, "Shut up. Shut up. I want to go home. What's wrong with you cats?" They all looked at me with amusement, quieting down for only a moment. Then the muttering began. "Oh Barrett's mad. Look at him." "You damn right I'm mad. You cats gonna make me miss my bus." As a fellow Negro, I somehow felt an obligation to defend the teacher, and I hated him for it. The class finally did respond to my demands, I think out of respect for me, more than fear that I might be inclined to punch someone, which I wasn't.

Tech afforded me the opportunity to meet and interact with a white student body much more ethnically diverse than that of Webster, although most of them were Italian. At Tech, I was among a handful of Negro boys who sought each other out for company and security. We would meet in the cafeteria and sit at the same table. There were so few of us that we needed only three tables. However, the Negro upperclassmen sat at their own tables. Negro or not, we all understood it was a privilege to be an upperclassman and we freshman accepted our status, knowing in a year, we would be where they were.

I was the only Negro in my academic classes the entire year I was there. One other Negro kid, Maurice, a talented sketch artist and jazz enthusiast who wanted to be a draftsman, joined me in one of my shop classes. He ultimately became my best friend and was to follow me to my next school. Being in the minute minority reminded me of Webster Junior High, where I had also spent only one year. I kept to myself for the most part, making friends with some of the kids who sat near me and ignoring the rest.

A big difference between Burnet and Webster and Tech was the teachers' practice of calling students by their last names — Barrett, Monar, Thorpe, Marino, etc. The students picked up on this and addressed each other the same way. I suppose for those students who had not attended junior high school, having to change classes for each subject took some adjusting as well, but my Webster experience eased that transition for me.

Classes were very easy for me; general math, phys ed./health, English, United States history, science and general shop was my load. The latter was designed to expose freshmen to a variety of trades over the course of a year so we could be more certain of what we wanted to do. You could not begin to specialize until tenth grade. I took carpentry and radio the first semester and airplane mechanics and electrical shop the second.

We had a boring, but respected, teacher for health class that met only once a week; Mr. Bonsack taught a unit on etiquette and dating. The only thing I remember about that lecture was his advice on how to treat girls. He told us it didn't matter if the girl "was as ugly as sin, to her parents she's the queen of Sheba; and we had better treat her as if she is." At the time, I thought his statement about being ugly as sin was funny; I had not heard that expression before. But in time, I came to understand the importance of his advice.

(2)

It seemed the older I got, the more consciously aware I became of white people's behavior. I learned a lot about them at Bloomfield. Their behaviors, habits, dress, and way of cussing, talking, walking, and even standing were a curiosity to me. I had had some exposure to them on my jaunts through Little Italy and at Webster, but now that I was older, the differences seemed now more pronounced than when they were younger. There were things that they thought were funny that did not even bring a smile to my face. They called each other names such as jerk off, son-of-bitch, wop and guinea (Italians referred to the sleeveless tee shirt as a "guinea tee." They wore them as an outer shirt). And told each other to fuck off — all in apparent jest. They would also issue provocative and offensive directives, usually in a dismissive manner. The most common among these were "eat me, kid," "blow me," and "jerk me off." The ultimate insult, however, was when a kid would spit on someone, especially in the face. This would be grounds for a fight or time to "tro' some hands," as they would put it.

To express affirmation, they sometimes used the term, "fuckin' a," as in, "did you pass the test?" "Fuckin' a, man," (meaning yes). I think it was an abbreviation for "you bet your fuckin' ass," though I am not sure. The Negro boys' equivalent of this was "you damn real," or the shortened version, "damn real."

Their idea of "cool" was also very different from that of the Negro boys. At Tech, the Italians seemed to set the standard for cool for the other white boys. I've already mentioned the guinea tee, but there was also the sleeved tee shirt whose sleeves they would roll up to create a cuff in which they would tuck their cigarette packages. Black leather motorcycle jackets, like in the Marlon Brando movie *Blackboard Jungle* were popular. Narrow-legged Levis and Wranglers were the dungarees of choice, always cuffed and worn two or three inches below the navel to create a baggy pants look. The pants were held up with a wide, studded belt — studded because its secondary purpose was to be used as a weapon. The coolest of the cool hunched over as they walked on thick-soled shoes whose heels were reinforced with metal heel plates that announced their approach from yards away as they scraped their heels for effect.

Negro boys would insert the word "man" at implicitly understood spots in our speech. We found it amusing to hear the white boys attempting to imitate us, always placing the word in the wrong part of the sentence or using the wrong emphasis. Since we invented this particular use of the word, we felt justified and qualified judging when it was being correctly used. Ironically, one of the ways in which a white boy would show his contempt for a Negro would be to address one of us directly, starting the sentence with "man," followed by some remark in which he expressed his displeasure about something you were supposed to have done or said. It was akin to being called out.

Our music tastes had also taken root. Among their favorites were Elvis, Bill Haley, Jerry Lee Lewis and the whole cast of the film *Rock around the Clock,* as well as a local group, one of whose members attended Tech and was tragically killed in a fire. They recorded the song, "Hey Now, Miss Annie." However, Maurice and I liked R&B groups such as The Moonglows, The Drifters, The Heartbeats (later Shep and the Limelites), Smokey Robinson and the Miracles, Frankie Lymon and the Teenagers and The Cleftones. We Negroes also had our own local group, The Monotones, who lived in the Baxter Terrace housing project and recorded "Who Wrote the Book of Love?" We resented white singers who copied the songs of colored artists, and if not the straight-out songs, then their style. Pat Boone's selling more recordings of "Tutti Frutti" than Little Richard and Georgia Gibbs doing the same with LaVern Baker's "Tweedle Dee" were often at the core of many a barbershop complaint about white artists who were making a living "stealing our music." I wondered what they would be singing if it weren't for Negro artists. "Them crackers like our music but won't buy our records. They have to wait until one of their people records the song, bad as it sounds, and Lord knows they sure do sound bad, and **then** they'll buy it. It's like a third-rate cracker is better than a first-rate nigger, even when the nigger's the one who created the music in the first place," or words to that effect, were the kinds of remarks commonly heard during such discussions.

This same mindset extended to sports in which colored players were involved. There was the fanaticism the white boys displayed over the New York Yankees. This behavior was led by the Italians who worshiped Joe DiMaggio and Babe Ruth. They seemed to have a need after every Yankees' game to discuss the performance of the team, and these two men in particular. They knew statistics such as batting averages, runs batted in, and season and all-time homeruns. You name it, someone in the discussion knew it.

I liked the Dodgers, as did the majority of colored people I knew, for one reason: Jackie Robinson played for them. I despised the Yankees because they had no Negro players and because they were such a dominant team. When the Dodgers and Yankees played each other in the World Series, tension grew high between Negroes and whites in school and at work (according to my father and the Negro men in the neighborhood who also reported the barbershops were filled with vitriolic references to the damn Yankees.) Negro and white boys at Tech never spoke to each other about the two teams, though both groups could be heard in the cafeteria carrying on conversations among each other loud enough for the others to hear. Two boys nearly came to blows when a white kid, unable to stand the celebratory antics of a colored kid, who was loudly praising Jackie Robinson's base-stealing, shouted "Jackie Robinson ain't shit!" The other boy responded, "Jackie may not be but your mama sure is." "What? What you say? I'll kick your shit ass," and he charged the colored kid, but before he could get to him, he was restrained by his friends. He had unwittingly become a victim of the dozens.

Clearly there was no way the Italian boy could have understood this tradition. He did not have the cultural grounding to appreciate that he was being challenged to a verbal sparring, so he reacted the way his own cultural grounding dictated.

Akin to the dozens was a nameless posturing exercise that was practiced in the third person when the subject was not present. It was designed to make it clear who was the toughest. If word got back to one boy that another was gunning for him, he would respond to the carrier of the news, "That mothafuckah rather walk through hell wearing kerosene-soaked drawers than fuck with me." Or "…. would rather run through the whole Sahara wearing five fur coats and eating a peanut butter sandwich than …"

Years later, Spike Lee would capture the essence of this smoke-blowing in his film *Do the Right Thing*, when he showed the character of the late Robin Harris and some of his buddies sitting in kitchen chairs neatly placed on the sidewalk. The Harris character was trying to impress anyone who would listen how much badder than Mike Tyson he was, as the others looked on and dismissed Harris for the absurdity of his claims. Since a contest to establish who was the better fighter would never occur, it was just academic and for the men's mutual entertainment. But that did not stop the other men from participating in the give and take as if it were serious discourse.

So, if Tech did nothing else for me, it made me see close up just how different were our cultural frames of reference. We may have shared the same space from 7:45 to 3 but we had little else in common and were satisfied to leave it that way.

One of the one few things we did have in common, in contrast to the TV white people, was our meaning when we used the word "fight." TV white people used it to mean to have an argument: "I had a big fight with my dad." But for the Italians and us, fight had only one meaning -- exchanging blows. When I reached college and heard one of my white classmates say she had had a fight with so-and-so, . . . it gave me pause.

(3)

Three weeks into the semester, my mother and I rode the bus to Tech's back-to-school night. We had completed one marking cycle and I had just missed making the honor roll, having gotten one C. My mother was an attractive, brown-skinned woman who looked ten years younger than she was. Curiously, the only people I had ever heard articulate how young she looked were white adults once they had learned the ages of her children, a subject that never failed to come up. I had always been pleased to have my mother come to visit my schools because I was encouraged by the interest she took in my academics and it also gave me a chance to hear my teachers say things about me to her that I would never hear otherwise.

On this particular evening, the pattern would continue. As we walked from classroom to classroom so she could meet my teachers, it came out somewhere along the way that James was my brother. I think it was Mr. Howell, my English teacher, who made the discovery. "You mean this is Jim's brother? Well, yes, now that you mention it, I do see the resemblance. You don't have any more like him at home, do you?" My mother told him "I'm afraid not." I was puzzled by her answer. I thought, *What about Melvin? He was only one grade behind me.* On the way home I asked her about her answer. She reminded me that Howell had asked if there were any more at home like me. She said that Melvin was not like me when it came to school work, so in a nuanced sense, she was being truthful.

By the end of the week, all of my teachers, even one who had not known James, let me know they knew he was my brother. Mr. Loftus, my math teacher, said, "Barrett, I understand you're Jim Barrett's brother. I didn't have him in any of my classes, but I have heard of him. At least I'm glad I got you." The next marking period and everyone thereafter, I got nothing but A's in all of my courses.

The only extracurricular activities in which I got involved were the track team and glee club. The decision to join the latter was a mistake. After being an alto through sixth grade and a baritone in eighth, I was now being asked to sing tenor. I hated singing the part because it strained my vocal cords and hurt my throat. I tried in vain to get the teacher, Mr. Clark, to switch me to the bass part, but he refused, asserting, "We need you in the tenor section because we have plenty of basses and not enough tenors." "But it hurts my throat," I told him. "You are blessed to have such vocal range and you should want to share your gift with as many people as possible and at every opportunity." I saw I was not going to change his mind, so I accepted my fate.

I had considered quitting, but singing was something I enjoyed too much to abandon, even though the Tech glee club was the most mediocre singing group with which I had ever affiliated. Only two or three members could sing harmony naturally, you know, hearing the melody and then just figuring out the harmony. No sheet music, just you and your ear. But the other cats, man, they were hurting. I discovered this problem one day while waiting for glee club rehearsal to begin. A quartet or quintet of them attempted to sing some of the songs popular among white kids at the time: one favorite was "Little Darlin'" by The Gladiolas. But this song did not become a hit until it was covered by the white group, The Diamonds, who to their credit also recorded an original, "Twinkle, Twinkle, Little Star." Both The Diamonds' and The Gladiolas' versions were played on the black radio stations. But the white stations played only the versions by The Diamonds. Yet, every note, chord, nuance, grunt and doo-wop of The Gladiolas was copied by The Diamonds exactly as The Gladiolas had recorded.

As far as my fellow glee clubbers were concerned, I could not believe how badly off-key they were. I wondered why they couldn't hear themselves and what they actually did hear when we were not singing the glee club stuff with the sheet music under our noses. Take away the sheet music and they were lost. And the glee club song selections, well, they simply were not challenging to me. Not only that, but also, most of the songs tended to have a patriotic theme. "Comrades in Arms" was a standard. When we sang that song, I would think about stories I had heard from my uncles about how during WWII, German prisoners of war, who because they were white, were treated better than American Negro soldiers. While being transported by train to prison camps, the German prisoners would eat with the white GIs and after the German prisoners had eaten, the Negro GIs would eat. In the eyes of the American military, a white enemy had had more status than their Negro American comrades in arms. I recall some of the lyrics:

> Lis't give ear, listen comrades in arms
> Lis't give ear listen comrades in arms
> When the call for honor and glory
> Be true and brave and win the fight
> Vow then to meet the foe before ye
> Be true and brave and win the fight

I did not know where the old brigade boys had gone, but I wished that those who had died had gone to hell and those who had not would eventually find their way there.

On one occasion, Mr. Clark scheduled the glee club to perform at what turned out to be the only off-campus concert we would perform that year. He didn't give many details other than the address of the site and the names of the songs we would sing. He said we would not need permission slips because technically, it wasn't a field trip since we were not all going together. He also said we would get extra credit.

When I saw the address on Sixth Avenue, I realized it was in, of all places, Little Italy. Once again, I had to put myself at risk by walking through Little Italy, at night no less. The venue turned out to be the Sixth avenue campaign office of councilman-at-large, Ralph Villani, where a re-election rally was being held on his behalf and that of the northward councilman. I was shocked when I realized what was going on and that I had risked my ass for this bogus event and I still had to get home afterwards. I thought it would be a bitch if I were to be beaten to a pulp after singing at an event for one of the sons of Italy. We had been asked to come to this place at our own expense and on our own time. But it was too late to do anything about it at that point. I was on the set. I didn't know much about politics at the time, but I did not believe it was kosher for an official organ of the school to be associated with a partisan political event.

We sang "America the Beautiful" to open the event and closed with "The Brigade" after the campaign speeches had been given. I saw the candidates' mouths moving as they spoke; but I could not hear either of them. The longer I stayed the more fearful I became; I just wanted to get out and go home and prayed like hell I would not get jumped in the darkness as I made my way. Intuitively, I believed the teacher had to have arranged our appearance without the knowledge of school officials. My mother confirmed my suspicions when I told her what I had been party to. She threatened to call the principal; but I told her not to bother since I was transferring anyway. I made up my mind that I wouldn't sing in any more concerts that are not in the school building. My time in Tech's glee club caused me to reflect on my singing experiences at Burnet.

In stark contrast to Tech, at Burnet I had been used to singing with kids who had been harmonizing as far back as fifth grade, singing two parts, with boys taking alto and girls singing soprano. By eighth grade, my voice had gotten deep enough for me to sing baritone. We had a music teacher who roamed from school to school. We had no choir, so she would teach songs to the entire class as part of our music education. Among the songs we had to learn was "Go Down, Moses," a song for which Alley Cat and I had created a variation on the baritone part, which we thought made the song sound richer. During one of our sessions, I noticed the teacher kept walking around, brow furrowed and looking otherwise puzzled. She was trying to determine who was singing the unfamiliar part. Having tracked us down when we had finished the song, she asked me how we knew to sing that particular part. "It's not the part that's in the book," she said. I just hunched my shoulders and told her that I just do and that I could simply hear it. I added that I did it all the time when I heard songs on the radio. I just make up my own harmony to fill in for the part that is missing. She flattered me: "You boys are gifted to be able to do that, when it's not written down." Alley and I joked about it later, puzzled that someone who called herself a music teacher didn't know that people could sing harmony without reading the parts on a page.

She appeared not to know that like poetry and storytelling, music comes from within, and then it is written down. I didn't see it as such a big deal since so many of my friends could do the same thing. In fact, by eighth grade, inspired by the popular group, Frankie Lymon and the Teenagers, Alley and I had already formed several singing groups — one even auditioned for the Ted Mack Amateur Hour show in New York — and none of us could read a single note.

In my second semester at Tech, I took as an omen an event that caused me to change my mind about continuing there. During aviation shop, I had been assigned to tool crib duty, during which I was responsible for dispensing tools to my classmates for two class periods. The tool crib measured about 20 by 8 feet, enclosed by a steel gauge chain link wire fence like those used for playgrounds, so you could see through it. I managed the tool borrowing; students had to sign tools out. No one else was allowed in the tool crib except the teacher, Mr. Greene, and any student to whom he gave permission, which was rare.

During a lull in tool crib activity, Mr. Greene sent me on an errand; I returned to a demolished tool crib. Someone had failed to securely bolt down the propeller of an airplane engine and when the engine was fired up, the propeller launched itself and flew across the room where it came to rest right where I would likely have been sitting. Clearly, it had happened just moments before, because Mr. Greene was still lecturing the class on the importance of following all safety rules. His back was turned to me as I approached, but I could see the remorseful faces of the students. "That damn thing could have killed any one of you. Am I making myself clear? Is that what you need to happen before you take the shop rules seriously?"

Rather than take a place with the class, I sat on the perimeter of the shop and from there listened to Mr. Greene while I stared at the crushed cage. I remember thinking, *That's it for me. I'm getting the hell out of this place. These dumb suckers are not going to kill me. I'm going to college.*

(4)

During that same semester, a family from North Carolina, the Brewers, moved to a third-floor apartment in my building. It had been vacated by the Wilsons, a family that had moved to East Orange after ten years on Clay Street. I envied them. Mrs. Wilson was one of only two neighborhood mothers with whom my mother socialized. And Mr. Wilson was the only father who had a new car, a shiny black 1955 Mercury with whitewall tires, that he kept across the street in a rented garage on property owned by Bruno, the used car dealer. Mr. Wilson drove the car only on weekends, to get groceries and to attend church.

Mr. Brewer was a construction worker and was married to the mother of two children. He had no children of his own. Also, living with them was Mrs. Brewer's adult brother, J. R. He was the first person I had ever heard of whose name was just initials. The oldest of the children was a girl named Barbara. Though countrified, she was one foxy girl with an engaging smile; she got my attention right away. I was going with her two or three weeks after her family moved in. I had not known any children who had moved from the South to the North, so in that respect, she was an anomaly for me. I could understand everything she said because I had gotten used to Southern accents because of visits with my grandparents in Portsmouth and Franklin where the people talked like Barbara. Ironically, the kids in Franklin had the nerve to say I talked funny. Once during a summer visit to my paternal grandparents', some of the boys in the neighborhood would get Melvin and me to entertain the other kids by asking us to "say somp'm" to the group. When our words, cloaked in our Northern accent, exited our mouths, the kids fell into boisterous laughter. Melvin and I weren't offended; on the contrary, we laughed right along with them, though not for the same reason. We associated the Southern accent with ignorance and thought, arrogantly, how pitiful it was that these country bumpkins didn't know they were country bumpkins.

Now we had a country bumpkin in Newark who was like a fish out of water and it just sounded so strange to hear that kind of accent in my city. Pronouncing "nunh-hin" for nothing and "y'all" for you, second person plural, just pricked my ears. But coming from Barbara's lips, to me, they sounded cute and she would giggle when I teased her about it.

Country bumpkin or not, Barbara was my first real girlfriend in the sense that I could openly court her and everybody knew we were an item. I was really proud that she liked me back and she was not bashful about expressing her feelings. For example, when during our courtship, Sam Cook had a hit song called "You Send Me," she concluded a letter to me with those words, adding the second line of the chorus, "honest you do." I remember so clearly how this declaration brought a broad smile to my face and a sense of warmth to my body. I felt as though our fates had been sealed forever because she had written these words.

When I visited her, we would sit in the room right next to the kitchen that served as the TV / sitting room. From there I could smell some pork dish that was emitting an offensive odor. It reminded me of chitlins, but was not quite as foul. Chitins smelled so bad that I had to leave the apartment when my mother cooked them. My siblings thought I was exaggerating; but the damn things brought on a serious attack of nausea. I didn't ask Mrs. Brewer what she was cooking, because I was afraid she would offer me some of whatever it was. I was also afraid my tone of voice would give away my true feelings. This strategy was to no avail because out of nowhere, Mrs. Brewer called out to me, "David, do you want some hog nuts?" I couldn't believe my ears. She was cooking hog testicles and was actually going to eat them. Not only that, but I was also embarrassed that she used the term "nuts." That was a street term for my boys and me and not for polite, sophisticated adults. I believed anybody from the South was, by definition, country (except my relatives, of course) and this just proved it for me. I told her no thank you because I had eaten just before I came up. I was lying through my teeth, but it seemed a small price to pay to avoid eating an animal's balls, and from a nasty pig too. Elijah Muhammad's Muslims had been growing in influence and getting their message out with the sales of their newspaper, *Muhammad Speaks*, and they had been warning us of "the dangers of eating swine." I had not yet given up pork; but I had never eaten chitlins, pig feet, hog maws, or neck bones. All of that shit smelled, well, like shit, with the chits being the most odiferous of the group. They offended my olfactory system even more than the camels at the Bronx Zoo. Mrs. Brewer said she could wrap something up for me to eat later or take to my mother. I politely declined, saying our refrigerator was full (a lie, though I wish it were true) and my mother wouldn't be hungry anyway since she had just eaten too. Barbara, knowing I had been lying, just chuckled through the dialogue and plucked me in the head.

(5)

Barbara may have been from the country but she knew a few things this city slicker didn't. We were on our way to a matinee movie one Saturday; I led the way as we descended the stairs. When we got to the last flight of stairs, I turned and kissed her. I was standing one step below, so we were at that moment about the same height. As our lips met, she thrust her tongue into my mouth. I went into a state of shock, frozen into inaction as I tried to figure out what I should do. I felt myself getting nauseated as I imagined her saliva flowing into my mouth. I began to lose my balance and started falling backward. Our bodies and, more importantly, our lips, came apart and I caught myself by holding onto the banister. She burst out laughing, calling me silly and shit. I was shocked and embarrassed. Shocked because I was afraid of germs, and embarrassed because I was supposed to be the hip, city boy and here I was getting a lesson from this country girl. "Haven't you ever French-kissed before?" "Ah, yeah. You just caught me off guard, that's all. I'm hip to French-kissing. What do you think I am anyway, some kind of square?" I sensed she knew I was lying, but was just too kind to challenge me. Besides, I'm sure she took pride in teaching me something. Eventually I grew to like and expect it. Turns out it was but a prelude to the kissing experience I would have with a girl in my junior of college.

By the end of my freshman year, Barbara had moved back to North Carolina. When I wrote her a letter, I addressed the envelope to "Derm, North Carolina." That was how she pronounced the word, or at least that's what my ear heard. When she answered my letter, she wrote that I had spelled Durham wrong. Country!

Near the close of the school year, I went to Tech's guidance office to announce that I wanted to transfer to Central High School and to find out how to go about doing it. My first choice had been Barringer High School because it was where my sisters had gone. In a meeting with Barringer's principal that my mother attended with me, I learned, to my dismay, that I did not live in Barringer's district; instead, I was in the district that Central High served and the only way I could attend Barringer was if I wanted to study subjects or a curriculum not offered at Central. I retorted that Central was a commercial and technical high school and I wanted to go to college and would need a college preparatory (CP) curriculum. The principal responded that central had just introduced a CP program. I then argued that my sisters had gone to Barringer; so why was it now that we are no longer in the district? They said the boundary lines had been re-drawn to accommodate population shifts.

At that time, 1958, Barringer, situated in the northwest edge of Little Italy, had a predominantly Italian student body. When I was in elementary school, I had had more than my share of near-death experiences with nigger-hating Italian boys, but I was not concerned with any recurrence of these events because my sisters had attended without incident. Little did I know it was because they were girls that they were not subjected to the harassment colored boys were. Italian boys back then actually liked colored girls — at least they acted like it. It was just the colored boys they despised.

When I went to the Tech guidance office to announce my intentions, I was told they would have to send to Central a copy of my transcript once all of my grades were in. After Central received my grades, they would be in touch to let me know when and where to report the next school year. In the interim, I would have to take a withdrawal form to all of my teachers. The form contained information about my plans to transfer and requested that they get my grades to the guidance office a week earlier than scheduled. All but one of my teachers asked me why I was transferring and when I told them, they wished me luck. The one exception was my history teacher and track coach, Mr. Branagan. I walked into his class and found him seated at his desk while the class was taking a test. Wearing one of his two seersucker suits, this one light blue, he greeted me as I gave him the form. When he realized what it was, a puzzled look came across his face as he asked, "What about the track team?" I had not expected this reaction from him and I was speechless for only a moment. I told him that I was going to college and that I couldn't get the courses I need to get into college if I stayed here. Besides, I continued, I could run track where I'm going. I knew I sounded terse, but that's exactly how I wanted to sound. I had been an honor roll student, getting straight A's in his classes and the first thing that came to his mind was my future with Tech's track team! I thought the remark was selfish and I hoped he saw the indignant look on my face.

    I shared this story with my mother when I got home. Reminiscent of her response when I told her what my Sunday school teacher, Mr. Pedersen had said about Negro spirituals and blind faith she said, "He doesn't care anything about you, boy, only with you being on the track team. Don't even worry about it. You're doing what's right for you." She told me she had not wanted me to go to "that school anyway." She reminded me of James' experience, stating, "James Junior spent four years there, worked one year as a draftsman and then decided he didn't want to be bent over a drafting table for the rest of his life. So, he had to go to Newark prep to take the math and science courses he needed to get into college." I was surprised to hear that she had not been in support of my going to Tech. Why hadn't she tried to dissuade me from attending? I asked her about this issue the day of my graduation from Central High School. She said that there are some things I needed to find out on my own and that picking a high school was one of them and there would be many more before it's all over.

On my last day of school, as I left to walk through the TV-perfect neighborhood one last time, I knew I had made the right decision and never looked back.

Part IV

Central High School and Beyond

Chapter 7
Ernie

(1)

Central high school started in the tenth grade. The four-story, red building sat high on a hill on High Street a few blocks west of downtown Newark (the first line of the alma mater is "High above the busy city, far beyond all touch of ill ... .") and right across the street from the Newark College of Engineering (now the New Jersey Institute of Technology). The majority of Central's 1,200 students were female, probably because it used to be a commercial school. Its original name was Central Commercial and Technical High School. Most girls I knew at Central were enrolled in bookkeeping, stenography, shorthand, typing, or accounting. They were being prepared for careers in the business world. Girls made up less than twenty percent of my college preparatory classes, but were usually among the top performers, especially in English, Spanish and biology.

What I found most encouraging about Central was for the first time, the majority of my classmates were Negroes, as more and more of us had begun to call ourselves. By then (thanks to the Civil Rights movement), and we had three Negro teachers. By the time of my senior year, Central had had four Negro teachers and Negro football and track coaches (the history teacher doubled as the track coach). This ratio was in stark contrast to my days at Burnet, Webster, and Tech, where I had two, none, and one teacher, respectively, although a Negro science teacher, Mr. Jackson, did join Tech's faculty at mid-year.

I joined Central's mixed chorus, the Choristers, right away. I found it refreshing to be in a chorus whose members could actually sing, and who sang even when they were not at rehearsal. It was common to hear all kinds of harmonizing in the halls as students changed classes. Teachers turned their heads the other way, I suspect, because they enjoyed it and also because it was a minor problem in comparison to what could have been going on between classes.

During my sophomore year, there was a popular product on the market called the Flavor-Straw. Drinking milk through a Flavor-Straw was more pleasant, because the milk absorbed the flavor of the straw as it passed through on its way to the young consumer's mouth. One of the Choristers, known for clownish ways, wrote a one-line song that combined the Flavor-Straw and oral sex. The song opened with a pronounced bass part — bo ba ba ba, bo ba ba ba, followed by four-part harmony of "eat me raw, suck me through a Flavor-Straw." The line was repeated over and over again, but with improvisations on the melody. This ditty, of course, the teachers tried to suppress, but with little luck since we usually waited until no teacher was in sight before launching into the song. The boldest of us would sometimes amuse our classmates right under the nose of an unsuspecting teacher, by running the bass line right in class; just softly enough so the teacher would not hear it, but loud enough to be heard by classmates in close proximity. I suspect it was the tension of anticipating that someone just might be bold enough to start singing the lyrics that made this funny. No one ever did.

My time at Central was rich. My homeroom, 519, was in one of the towers that made up a kind of fragmented fifth floor. The towers were located at each of the four corners of the building. One of the towers was the home of the board of education's radio station, WBGO-FM, where I appeared as a contestant in a spelling bee while I was at Burnet. I was eliminated in the second round. No longer affiliated with the school system, and broadcasting from the Robert Treat Hotel, WBGO-FM Jazz 88 became one of the pre-eminent jazz radio stations in the world.

My pregnant, freckled-faced, homeroom teacher was Mrs. Weiss. She was what I later learned was called a strawberry blonde. This designation made no sense to me at all as it sounded like an oxymoron. Her skin reminded me of Miss Matoronna's — smooth and kind of a milky white. Pregnant or not, Weiss was the foxiest teacher in the school. I never got a chance to check out her body in its non-pregnant state because she was gone by December and did not return — at least not by the time I graduated.

The homeroom period lasted about fifteen minutes, but during this daily short period of time, it wasn't long before I had made friends with three people who sat in my immediate area. One of them, Patton Russ, was in the college prep program and he was in all of my classes. He was a brown-skinned, very thin, curly-haired boy who had a deep voice and would have been an excellent addition to the Choristers if he had known how to sing. Sitting right behind me, he was the only one of my close friends who smoked. Sitting next to Patton was James Younger, a slick, fast-talking, fine-dressing, super-cool dude who had the most engaging eyes of any boy I knew. When he laughed, they blew up like a blowfish. He worked after school and from the way he dressed, he must have spent most of his income on clothes. I am talking custom-made waffle-weave pants, kangaroo-skin shoes and expensive Italian knit sweater shirts from Joe Fishman's men's shop on Branford Place. He did not participate in any extracurricular activities and his whole conversation with me was about girls and clothes. He lived in a pretty rough area of the Central Ward called the Hill, that the most infamous of Negro gangs — Dukes, Outlaws, Nomads, and Conquistadors — called home. Such gangs were very much in the news in the mid-to-late 1950s. They had gang fights in which their members were stabbed, cut, or shot with zip guns. Such gangs had begun to die out by the 1960s because their leaders were either dead or in jail, and their little brothers had discovered heroin, so there was no one to whom to pass the gang legacy.

Mrs. Weiss distributed report cards during homeroom after each marking period. She had a ritual of passing them out in achievement order. CHS had two honor roll categories: super, which required a student to have all A's and no more than one grade of B, and standard honor roll, with no grade less than B. She would first call out the names of those students falling into these two groups, and then she would start calling everyone else, in no particular order — or maybe there was an order, I can't say for sure, because after I received my report card, I did not pay attention to who followed me. I cared only about those called before me; they were my competition. When Mrs. Weiss called my name as part of the super honor roll group, I stood up to get my report card; but as I left my seat, I heard someone exclaim "What?" It sounded like James's voice. As I returned to my seat, he was gazing at me with a look of utter disbelief. After I sat down, he tapped me on my shoulder and said, "Man, I didn't know you was into the books like that. What do you think you doin'?" I said, "I'm doing the best I can. Isn't that why we are all here?" He replied, indignantly, "Oh yeah, well, we'll see how much good dem A's and B's gonna do you in the streets." I paused for a moment trying to decide if I really wanted to articulate what I was thinking. Concluding that our friendship, such as it was, was probably over anyway, I decided to be blunt. I said, "James, I'm not going to be in the streets."

That conversation marked the beginning of the end of our friendship. By January, James had dropped out of school, headed, I supposed, to the streets, and with no marketable skills, to a life of poverty, crime or both. I never again saw or heard anything about what had become of him.

My third homeroom buddy was Ernestine, who sat in the chair to my immediate left. She was the most sophisticated-looking and acting fifteen-year-old I had ever laid eyes on. Up-to-the-minute in the latest fashions, she wore her considerable wardrobe of skirts and dresses an inch or two above her knees that were attached to perfectly sculptured, sepia legs. Once I had figured out what time she arrived at homeroom, I made it a point to be seated when she arrived so I could scope her out as she glided through the door and sat gingerly in her seat. I would take it all in — the walk, her intoxicatingly sweet perfume, green eyeshadow, clothes matching the eye shadow, the beautiful, smooth, brown skin, the meticulously groomed hair, a little too much makeup — she was a work of living art. "Hey, Ernie." "Good morning, David." We might say a little more if it was report-card time or bad weather, but for the most part, that was the ritual for the entire first semester. But that was soon to change.

While passing through the cafeteria one morning on my way to homeroom, I noticed her sitting at one of the tables with Patton and some other students. They were circulating a piece of paper and laughing, as one person would pass it to the next. I knew most everyone there, so I felt comfortable going over and asking what was so funny. The person who was holding the paper at that moment made a gesture to give it to me. Ernie protested vociferously. Her reaction made everyone's antennae go up. "Why can't David see it?" someone demanded. At this point, I had concluded it must have belonged to her and this realization made me more determined to read it. So, over her protestations, I did just that. It was a lengthy joke; I don't remember the details, but I do recall it concluded with a reference to "that fishy smell," referring to the vagina. I was taken aback, even crestfallen, by the fact that Ernie had not only owned this piece of paper, but she also had brought it to school and was sharing it in mixed company. I remember thinking, *this could not be the Ernie I had become enamored with these months.* My image of her had taken on a serious stain. Little did I know it would be only a blot compared to what was in store.

One Friday in January 1958, during homeroom, she asked me what I was doing on Saturday night. I told her I had no plans and asked her why she had asked. She told me about a party in the South Ward on Clinton Avenue and said I should come check it out. She gave me the address and the name of the girl who was giving it. She was a student at perennial rival, South Side (now Malcolm X) High School. I asked if I could bring one of my friends. I had never gone alone to a party before. It was prudent to have at least one person with you — more for security than anything else. She told me the hostess had given her permission to invite only one person. Then, jokingly, she said if I brought someone, then I might not be able to get in.

I left home on a Saturday night about 8 o'clock to walk the half block to the bus stop on Broad Street, about fifty yards northeast of Eighth Avenue. I leaned into the unmerciful wind as I quickened my pace. A blue-black cold gripped the night and teamed up with my father's Old Spice aftershave lotion to envelop me as I stood the ten minutes or so waiting for the bus. I liked Old Spice as much for its fragrance as I did the jingle, I would hear them pitching it so often on the radio. "Old Spice means quality, said the captain to the coxswain ... ." I didn't even know what a coxswain was; but that didn't stop me from singing the song whenever I splashed myself with the cologne. I was wearing a double-breasted, belted, beige trench coat — not warm enough for the weather but it was the coat of choice for the hip; and it was worth being cold if it meant you could be cool. I wore my best black wool pants and burgundy loafers I had bought from one of my brother's friends who worked for Florsheim, a men's shoe store on Market Street. I had polished them with liquid Esquire. I fortified myself against the bitter cold with a white turtleneck sweater over which I wore a black cardigan sweater of the style Sam Snead, the golfer, made popular, and wool burgundy scarf. I covered my head with a black beret, pulled to the right, so it covered the upper part of my ear the way I had seen in photographs of some jazz musicians, in particular Dizzy Gillespie. To complete the ensemble, I wore a pair of black fur-lined leather gloves. I wanted to be the hippest-looking thing at the party; more importantly I wanted to impress Ernie.

Finally, my ride arrived. I climbed aboard the Number 13 Clinton Avenue bus and dropped my twenty-five cents in the glass, cylindrically shaped coin-collecting receptacle. There were plenty of seats available, but I took one in the rear, a habit that I had gotten into when I was younger and had mischief on my mind. I eased my shivering body into the brown vinyl seat and leaned to my left as the bus kicked into second gear and headed for the set.

It was a fifteen-minute ride to the apartment building just above Jelliff Avenue in a pretty nice section of town. Among the first Negroes to move into the neighborhood five years earlier, my sister and her husband had bought a house on Ridgewood Avenue only four blocks away. So I felt relatively safe. Nevertheless, when I got off the bus to cross the street, I made sure I put on my do-not-mess-with-me bad walk I had adopted during my thug days. I wasn't taking any chances.

I entered the building and walked up to the third floor. As I reached the landing, I could hear Smokey Robinson's velvety, smooth voice singing "Bad Girl" drifting from the apartment. *A slow song*, I thought. It was rare that the hosts played a fast number, and when they did, it was usually girls who danced with each other. Slow was the boys' preferred speed so we could do the grind. Some girls had graduated to the two-step and would not grind with boys they didn't know. Unfortunately for them, some boys had never learned to do anything except grind, so there was sometimes a short, awkward exchange of words on the dance floor when the boy started moving his hips and the girl started moving her feet. I used to watch these contests, making a silent bet with myself on the one I thought would "win."

I knocked on the door and waited a bit before someone answered. A soft, "hello" sailed from the mouth of a girl who looked almost as good as Ernie. I told her my name and that Ernie had invited me. She beckoned for me to come in; she called out to Ernie, announcing that "a friend of yours is here." *Damn*, I thought, *why don't you tell the whole world?* I stepped into the apartment, taking off my gloves, scarf, coat, and beret as I sauntered across the room. The part of the apartment where the guests had gathered was illuminated by a blue light bulb and it made it hard to see peoples' faces. Ernie had not responded, so I decided to look around to see if I knew anyone else. Just then, the girl who had opened the door, and turned out to be the hostess, said "I'll take your coat and hat. My name is Della. This is my party." I thought, *You're a little late with that information*, while I tucked my gloves, beret and scarf into the right sleeve of my coat, the way my mother had taught me when I was in kindergarten. I then gave her my coat, and moved to join the party. Most of the fifteen to twenty people were either sitting or leaning against the wall checking out the action. The party area spanned two rooms — a dining room whose teak table had been pushed against a wall to turn part of the room into a dance floor, and a living room. Both rooms were bathed in blue light that reflected oddly off the freshly polished hardwood floor. I moved to the table on which the refreshments had been placed, picked up a paper cup and poured some punch into it. As I raised the cup to my lips, I saw Ernie out of the corner of my right eye coming in my direction. I tried to be cool — even insouciant — and acted as if I hadn't seen her. When she saw me, she seemed surprised that I had made it (*Was she acting too?* I wondered.) She said she didn't think I would come. I asked her why she would think that. She hunched her shoulders and said I had acted like I wasn't all that interested when she told me about the set.

Sensing there was a game going on, I told her if she hadn't been the one to invite me, I didn't think I would have made it. I wanted to say that I would have gone to the end of the earth to meet her, but what I really said was I had faced not only the hawk, but also the hawk and his entire family to make it to the party. It seemed so natural to refer to the cold wind as the hawk. I had been using the term ever since I could remember. I don't recall when or where I had first heard it, but all the Negroes I knew used it as casually as I did. A few years later, singer Lou Rawls would take the term beyond the boundaries of the Negro communities of the North in his recording "Dead End Street." At the beginning of the song, Rawls performs a monologue about the treacherous, merciless, "all-mighty hawk" in the windy city of Chicago where the hawk is cruelest, and as legend has it, the nickname was also born.

I said, It's cold as a motha out there, girl. Calling me by my first and last names, she asked if I was so cold, why I was drinking that cold punch, then? *Why was she calling me by my first and last names? Was there some significance to it?* "You should be dancing with someone to warm yourself up." She was playing with me, and I didn't know the game; but I was determined to learn it before night's end. *Was it flirtation or just teasing? Where would it lead? Suppose I was misreading her? Oh shit,* I thought, *I knew she was bad. Would I be able to hang? She must be getting these lines from one of those romance novels she's reading all the time.* A fresh record had just dropped and Shep and the Limelites started singing "You're a Thousand Miles Away." I thought, damn, this is too good to be true — Shep and the Limelites and Ernie too. I had to be smooth in this situation, I did not want to blow my cool by misunderstanding her. Not to be outdone, I reached down deep and came up with, you look like the warmest thing in here so I guess I should be dancing with you. I studied her face to see how she would react. I was rubbing my fingers up and down my chin, the way I had seen some of the older boys do when they were blowing smoke or trying to hit on a girl. I emphasized "should" so as to create a sense of mutual obligation, since she had opened the door by telling me I should be dancing with someone to warm myself. "Then why aren't you?" she said, reached for my cup and, taking it from my hand, gently placed it on the dining room table without even looking. Her eyes were locked into mine as she placed her arms on my shoulders and gracefully, even calculatingly — or maybe I just hoped it was calculated — moved her body towards mine. Instinctively, I started to move my hips to begin the grind. She told me she thought I was too sophisticated to be grinding, and she just stopped moving. Embarrassed, I instantly changed up and started doing the two-step, while stating, "I was just testing you to see where you were coming from." *I'm always coming from the same place. You'll find that out when you get to know me,* I thought, *Now what the hell is that supposed to mean? Can't she speak straight? Why do I have to interpret everything?* She reminded me of my mother when at fourteen, I was about to leave the apartment to go on my first real date.

Her name was Joanne and she lived in north Newark on North Fifth Street, a few blocks north of Bloomfield Avenue. It was a Sunday afternoon and we were going to the movies. Just as I reached the door to leave, my mother called to me. "Son, it's nice to be nice." "Okay," I said and left, pondering what kind of nice she was referencing.

Now here was Ernie trying to be my mother. Maybe that was how older people and girls like Ernie talked. But I hadn't known any girls like Ernie. She was the unique girl throughout my high school years.

We eased into the dance.

You're a thousand miles away-ay
But I still have your love to remember you by

I was oblivious to everything but her as we turned a small, clockwise circumference that defined our world at that moment. I could smell her perfume and another smell that must have been her makeup. She felt soft as velvet as I held her in my arms. She moved her hands from my shoulders to the back of my neck and I felt myself getting hard. *Oh shit, please johnson, don't do this to me, not with Ernie. I have got to be cool; please don't embarrass me. Don't do this to me. Could she feel this thing?* It was no use. I could not control it. Shep continued to enhance the mood as he sang:

> *Oh, my dar-ar-arling, dry your eyes*
> *Rata tat tat tu*
> *Daddy's coming home soon oo oo oo oo oon*

Now she rested her head on my left shoulder. Was she feeling what I was or was she just playing with me?

> *On my knees every day-a*
> *All I do is pray, baby, just for you, for you*
> *Hope you'll a-a-a-always want me too. Me too*
> *Daddy's coming home soon soo oo oo oo oon*

I not only did not want this night to end; I also didn't want the record to end. I wanted Shep to keep singing it. Sing to us until our bodies melted right into each other.

> *It may be on a Sunday morning.*
> *Ouu-ouu-ouu*
> *It may be on a Tuesday afternoon.*
> *Ouu-ouu-ouu*

"You're a good dancer." I heard a voice seeming to come from nowhere and everywhere at the same time. "What?" "I said you're a good dancer, silly. What's the matter are you in a trance or something?" I replied that it was not that. I just liked that song. I said, "Shep is bad. I wish they hadn't changed their name from The Heartbeats." "Yeah, me too," she replied in a suggestive whisper.

But no matter what the day is,
I'm going to make it, doowop, my business, doowop,
to come home soon
Lala la lala la lala lala

I asked her if she remembered their first song, "Crazy for You". I added that I wanted to dance with her to that song and asked if she knew if Della had it.

"That song's pretty old now. If they do, it's probably scratched to death. I know my copy is." Staying on topic, I told her that mine was too, and added; "Well, I guess it ain't gonna happen."

"What?"

"You and me dancing to it."

"You mean you and I, don't you?"

"You bet I do."

"There you go getting smart. I was correcting your grammar, silly; and you trying to take it to another place."

"And what place would that be?"

You're a thousand miles away
But I still have your love to remember you by—you by
Oh, my dar-ar-ar-arling, dry your eyes—your eyes
Daddy's coming home soon
So-ou-ou-ou-ou-ou-ounn. Sou-ou-onn.
Oo we oou oou.

We held onto each other for a moment or two after the song ended. I was hoping another good one would drop while we were still (at least I was) floating on air. But Ernie said she needed something to drink. She probably wanted to wait the next one out while my johnson returned to its resting state. That was okay with me. I guess I needed the break too.

I poured her and myself some punch and we went to stand in a corner where, eyes aglow, we looked at each other while drinking from our cups. Neither of us said a word for it seemed like hours, though it probably was no longer than a minute. A boy who came over to ask Ernie for a dance interrupted the deep silence between us. He was tall, athletic, probably a couple of years older than I and really bagged down in gray, sharkskin pants and a black, Italian knit sweater shirt. He was as cleaner than the Board of Health and a Kansas City chitlin, combined. She turned her head slowly toward him and said, "I'm doing just fine right here. Thank you for asking." She had dismissed him, but ever so politely.

Got damn. This is one smooth chick. I looked at the dude, poker-faced for just a moment. *I guess she told you, you jive-ass suckah*, I thought. "Maybe later, then," he said. "Yes, maybe later," she replied, as she reached for me at the start of the next record. "Hey, we haven't finished drinking our punch," I reminded her. Then she pulled away slowly and placed her cup to my lips and gently raised it while we danced. "Umm, why does yours taste so much better than mine?" "I don't know. Let me taste yours." I returned the gesture, placing my cup to her lips, trying to be as gentle with her as she had been with me. I managed to spill a little, but caught it with my free hand as unruly punch ran down the right side of her mouth. "Umm, your finger is adding some extra kick to this punch," she said. This girl was too much for me. She was a master teacher who was taking me to school. I had never engaged in repartee at this level with a girl; with this quality of nuanced give and take, though, I daresay, I was taking more than I was giving. "Girl, if I didn't know better, I'd think you were trying to get fresh with me." "Getting fresh? Since when is being honest being fresh?" "Okay, okay, Ernie, you win." "Win? Win?" She sang the words in a question. "Are we in a contest or something?" "No Ernie, no contest, no contest. I'm sorry. I take it all back."

I had met my match. We spoke no more during that dance; but as we continued to dance, I thought I could feel the smile on her face radiating right through her body, and I looked at her to see if I was right. I was. "Why are you looking at me?" "I love your smile because when I take it in, it pushes everything else out of my mind." "Then I'll have to be careful not to smile at you in school. You won't be able to concentrate and learn anything and you won't be able to get into college with an empty head." "How did you know I had plans to go to college?" "Boy like you has to go to college. You have no choice."

"What time is it?" she asked. "11 o'clock."

"I'll have to be going soon or I'll miss my bus." "What time does it come?" "11:45." "Do you mind if I accompany you (I was going to say "take you home," but under the circumstances, I thought I would continue my coolness.) "It's kind of late." "No, I was hoping you would ask." *Finally, a straight answer.*

At 11:30, we announced to Della that we were leaving and asked for our coats. She led us to the bedroom where the coats were placed. We had to pass through the kitchen, where her parents were sitting monitoring things, to reach the bedroom where we found our coats neatly stacked along with everyone else's. I spoke to her parents, who seemed surprised at the greeting, while I helped Ernie on with her coat. I overheard one of them whisper, "He seems like a nice young man." Ernie seemed to expect help with her coat and behaved as if it was something she was accustomed to. I put on my own coat, pausing when I felt something in my sleeve. I had forgotten I had placed my gloves, scarf, and beret there to guard against losing them. My mother taught me to do this after I had lost three pairs of gloves while in kindergarten.

As we exited the bedroom, Della's father said, "Good night, young man." "Good night," I said. Ernie echoed,

"Good night." When we reached the door, she paused to finish buttoning her lime green coat. She adjusted her scarf and looked at me wide-eyed, signaling she was ready. I put on my beret, made the necessary fashion adjustments and opened the door. She brushed against me as she walked into the hall. I stepped in front of her to lead the way down the two flights of stairs. When we reached the door, I said, "Okay, it's time to meet the hawk," and I took her arm, hunching my shoulders and leaning forward, as we headed into the cold.

She locked her arm in mine as if it were the most natural thing to do and we turned left up Clinton, headed to Bergen Street to catch the number 3 Bergen Street bus. The street was relatively empty for a Saturday night, a fact I attributed to the cold weather. I was witness to and participant in many discussions in the barbershop about Negroes' hatred of cold weather. This aversion to cold would be the basis of all explanations as to why there were no Negroes playing winter sports "like them white folks," an informed barbershop patron once shared with anyone who would listen. I did my best to recall the most recent of those discussions. "Ice skating, hockey, skiing, they white folks' sports. You don't see no Negroes doing that shit. No, sir, I don't know why we don't all move to Florida." Then providing his own response, he stated, "Yes I do too. It's because of the hurricanes. We are more afraid of them than we are of the hawk. Now, a hurricane can kill your ass but you can dress to protect yourself from the hawk. The only way to protect yourself from a hurricane is to hide in a cave or something. But then a tree might fall in the doorway, trapping you inside and nobody would know you was in there and then you would starve to death. Now, I would rather freeze to death than starve because starvation hurts. At least with freezing, you eventually go numb and then pass out so it's like dying in your sleep. If you ever been really hungry, then you might have an idea of what it's like to starve. Well, I have, and I don't want no parts of it." His tale was but one of several stories I had heard told about Negroes' disdain for cold weather.

I reached into my pocket to see how much money I had. The single dollar I felt would be enough to get us to her place, but not enough to get me home from there. I'll just have to hoof it, I thought. When the bus finally came, we suspended our conversation while I paid our fares. We found a seat in the back of the nearly empty bus and she expressed amusement at my improvised barbershop tale.

"Did anybody join in to challenge him?" she asked, her ivory teeth gleaming. "Yes, one of the barbers, but what he had to say wasn't all that much deeper."

He said, "You know the real reason we can't stand the cold, don't you?" Without waiting for an answer, he offered, "It's because we're from Africa and we're used to the heat. Even though we've been over here for 300 years, the love of heat is still in our bones and it will always be there." Another patron added, "That's why the Negroes here are meaner than the ones in Cuba, Jamaica and all of South America." Someone interrupted him and admonished him that he had better not let a Cuban hear him call a Cuban a Negro. The storyteller shouted back, "You know I hate an ignorant nigger like you. Don't you know that Negro is the word for black in Spanish and ain't most Cubans black just like some Negroes in America is light, bright and damn near white, you dumbass? And the same goes for South Americans, Dominicans, Jamaicans and all the other islanders in the Caribbean." The interrupter seemed perplexed, as if he was hashing over a complex thought. The storyteller's face glowed because he knew he had silenced the interrupter, at least for a while. He continued, "We still mad because our ancestors was dropped off here instead of in one of them warmer places."

"That's absurd," chuckled Ernie. "Yeah, I know; but I'm not finished." A third cat shouts out "Africa? Africa? I ain't from no Africa. What you talkin' about, man? You must be outta your mind. My people come up here from Georgia." "Oh, yeah, right, and where were they before that?" asked the barber. "Nowhere, they always been in Georgia." Ernie laughed again, this time more loudly. I studied the small mole on her face. I never thought a mole could be beautiful. I noticed the bus driver glancing in his rear-view mirror at us. I could tell she was enjoying the story, so I continued, telling her the barber said, "Would somebody show this ignorant niggah the door?"

Hearing the word "nigger" a second time was enough for Ernie. "Oh, I hate that word. David, are you sure you aren't making up that story?" I was, of course, but only the details. I had heard conversations like this one often enough that I felt I had earned a license to repeat my own version of it. I told her that I wish I were making it up; you can hear some really way out stuff in a barbershop. I continued, saying If I had the talent, I would write some short stories based on the weird stuff I hear there, like Langston Hughes does with his Jesse B. Semple character. "Why don't you?" I told her that I didn't have the talent though I could write okay, but not well enough to do that. I sensed she wanted to say more; but she apparently thought better of it and just leaned into my shoulder, sighing as she did.

"By now I sensed we should be getting close to her neighborhood so, I asked where do we get off? "At Fifteenth Avenue. I'm not going home. I'm going to my aunt's house. She wants me to go to church with her because she's in the choir and they're singing tomorrow; she's doing a solo." "Can you sing, Ernie?" "Just a little." "What about you?" she asked.

"You know I can sing, girl, I'm in the Choristers and the Madrigals and the Bell Chords too." "Oh yeah, I forgot," she said. "How could you forget that?" I asked, pretending to be slightly hurt. "Maybe it's because I can't hear your individual voice when you are singing in a group. Yeah, that's it." She seemed relieved she had found a logical explanation, hoping it would assuage my pain, or so I wished to believe. "The next stop is ours." She reached up and pulled the cord, signaling to the driver to stop at the next bus stop.

I was first to step into the waiting cold and instinctively reached for her hand across the space between us and stepped once again into the bitter night. She locked her gloved hand into mine. Notwithstanding the cold, we walked slowly down Fifteenth Avenue, realizing together that the night was drawing to a close. We both grew quiet and did not speak for the remaining two blocks. "Here it is," she said as we approached a two-family dwelling. We stopped at the bottom of the stairs for a moment and then turned to ascend them. She reached into her purse to get her keys. Quickly finding them, she inserted a key in the outer door that swung inward from the force of her hand. It opened to a vestibule from which one could enter the first or second floor apartment through separate doors. Once we were in the vestibule, she turned to me and said, "I guess this is it. Thanks for bringing me home." "You're welcome. I had a good time and thanks for inviting me."

The next thing I knew we were kissing, first, tentatively, then with more force, determination, and passion, a scene I had seen many times on the silver screen, though not involving Negroes. I could not believe this was happening. My dream girl, my sophisticated lady (my father had taught me about Duke), here melting in my arms and I in hers. Who would believe me? This fine brown thing actually liked me and was proving it right now on this cold-ass night. She seemed softer now than when we danced and I noticed her hips beginning to move. I thought about my other sexual encounters. None of them was like this. They were just pure meat hunts, lust. But this was different. I actually felt something for this girl and it had nothing to do with sex. We escalated our passion, pressing our bodies harder into each other, each responding to the other in some evolving ritual, maybe; I didn't know. But the next thing I did even shocked me. I started pulling up her skirt, then her slip, slowly and gently, willing to stop if she had asked, but hoping she wouldn't. Finally, I got her slip to join her skirt up past her groin, so that I was then rubbing directly against her panties — her stockings were being held up with a garter belt, so there was nothing else, no girdle, nothing, to negotiate. If things went that far, would I be able to pull her panties aside at the right time. I reached for my zipper, pulled it down and took out my throbbing penis. I don't know how long we were locked in each other's embrace, before suddenly, Ernie stopped — stopped just like that and pulling her body away from me, pulled down her skirt. "What's wrong?" I asked. "I didn't know you were like that," she responded.

"You didn't know I was like that? What are you talking about? We were both doing it." She said nothing as she bowed her head. I couldn't figure it out. There's no way I was the first, so that couldn't have been it. "I'm sorry, Ernie. I thought you wanted it too." "That's not it. I did, but not like this. Not in a hallway, up against a damn wall, for goodness sake." The force with which she made this statement caught me off guard. "Well, I'm sorry. It's just that once I started kissing you, stuff came up from within me that I did not know was there, and I couldn't stop myself." She started crying, lightly kissed me on the cheek and turned to put the key in the door. She opened it and turned to look at me once more and said "good night" before closing the door.

It was a twelve-block walk to Clay Street, but as cold as it was, I was feeling none of it. I even defiantly cussed the hawk. "You can't fuck with me now; Ernie has set me on fire." I was both exhilarated and perplexed. She was one complicated girl.

When I got home, everyone was asleep. I got undressed and climbed into bed and placed my cold feet against James' warm legs. I know I slept with a smile on my face.

The next day I wanted to call Ernie, but I didn't have her telephone number and she would not have been home anyway. I thought, *you dummy, you just took her to her aunt's house.* I began to wonder what I would say to her, what would she say to me in school on Monday? *Should I try to act as though nothing had happened? If I did would she think that night had met nothing to me? Man, was my mind messed up.* To make matters worse, I had no one in whom I could confide, whose advice I could seek. Those in whom I could confide wouldn't understand my concerns. In fact, they wouldn't even know why I was concerned. "You should be glad you almost got some," I could hear them saying. Then I remembered. Ernie and Patton were good friends. I could ask him. He would understand and maybe even be able to tell me how to handle myself; how to overcome my awkwardness, my embarrassment.

The next day, I went straight to homeroom after I got my books out of my locker. I didn't take the shortcut through the cafeteria because I did not want to risk seeing her there. I wanted our next meeting to be in the classroom where it would be less public if we made a scene or something. I took my seat and opened a book to read. After a while I realized I had been on the same page for quite a while and had no recollection what I had read. Most of my classmates had arrived; but I had been unaware of their arrival. Ernie was not among them. She did not come to school that day. Now I was really worried. I thought she might be angry with me because we had gone too far. But if that were so, shouldn't she be angry at herself as well? I couldn't think of any other reason that she would be absent. She had had perfect attendance so far. Why would she be out now?

The day after, she did come to school. She walked right by my seat and gave me an envelope. She had written "David" on it. I opened it slowly and began to read it. She told me that she had thought a lot about Saturday night, a whole lot. My heart started pounding. That she did not mean to hurt me. And if she had, she was truly sorry. Now I felt certain wetness in my armpits.

Then the bell rang for first period classes as if on cue to signal the end of a scene. I turned to say something to her but she looked straight ahead, doing her best to avoid eye contact. In an instant she had gone, but I was determined to talk to her. I could not let another day pass without doing so. We had to return to homeroom for dismissal after the last period, so that would be my shot.

If there ever was a time, I spent a whole day in school and not know a thing more than I did at the end of the day than I did at its start, this had to have been that day. I didn't think the eighth period would ever get here. But, of course, it did. When the bell signaling its end finally sounded, I headed directly for 519. Ernie had already arrived and taken her seat. James was absent so I sat in his chair, which was right next to hers. "May I talk with you, Ernie?" "What about? "About what I may want to say, are you interested in that?" There was a pregnant pause. Then she opened her notebook, wrote something on a piece of paper, tore it out and gave it to me. "Call me tonight after 7." The bell sounded and she got up and split, glancing over her left shoulder as she glided out the door.

That night I called her. "Hello, may I please speak to Ernestine?" "Who's calling please?" "David Barrett." "This is Ernie. Why did you ask for Ernestine? You've never called me that." "I don't know. I guess it was because I didn't recognize your voice and didn't know if your mother called you Ernie or not. And I didn't want to mess up again." She laughed softly. "That wouldn't have been a mess-up. Lots of my friends call me Ernie." "Well since I don't know any of your friends except Patton there's no way, I could have known that. But next time, if there is a next time, I'll know better." "Why wouldn't there be a next time?" "Come on Ernie, don't mess with me. This is not the time."

I did my best to explain why I was feeling guilty about Saturday night. Even though I was sincere, I didn't sound convincing, even to myself. After considerable back and forth, she said she believed me, but that the best we could be was friends. She told me that she hadn't been totally honest with me: She had a boyfriend. They had an agreement that they could both date other people, but that was as far as it would go and she had violated that trust. She said that she was the one who messed up. "I'm the one who invited you to the party because I wanted to be alone with you, outside of school, to see what you were like without a book in your hands. And I guess I found out. David, I like you — a lot —but I've been going with Brett for two years. He's seventeen and very nice to me." *Seventeen,* I thought, *that's ancient.* She continued, "Do you understand? So, I'm just gonna forget about all of this and we can just be friends, okay?" "What does that mean, friends? Can I call you, can I still you?" "Why not?" she acquiesced.

A month later, Ernie's family moved to East Orange and she transferred to East Orange High. I rode the bus to E.O. a number of times to visit her and we even went out to see *Porgy and Bess* at the Adams Theatre in Newark. I remember suggesting we go to a matinee, to which she said, "Ohh, why are we going so early?" I had up to that point never gone to anything other than a matinee, but I surmised that if I was going to associate with girls of Ernie's sophistication, I had better up my game. We continued our relationship for the rest of the school year and part of the summer.

It would be eleven years before I would see her again. By that time, we both would be married and I would have had my first child, a boy.

Chapter 8

The Bell Chords

(1)

Mr. Lundy was the music teacher who directed the Choristers, the school chorus. Tall, with wire frame eyeglasses and a Friar Tuck balding head, he was an easy-going man who set very high standards for us. I think he knew he had a group of talented singers; they just needed to be challenged and taught a little discipline so he could help us leverage our talent. Because he was so easy-going, he had trouble controlling his classes when we became unruly. The only way he could get control was to yell at the top of his lungs. ("People, please be quiet and pay attention.") That would make me feel sorry for him, and move me (the new kid) to admonish the class, "Come on you cats, you heard Mr. Lundy. Quiet down!" And they (we) would settle down.

Boys and girls rehearsed separately, so that Mr. Lundy could focus on two-part harmony in each separate rehearsal; boys singing bass and tenor and girls their alto and soprano parts. This arrangement also helped to rule out disruption due to boys' showing off "in front of the girls."

While waiting for class to begin, it had become pretty much standard for some of the boys to entertain themselves by singing parts of their favorite R&B songs to show off their harmonizing skills. Anybody could join in to sing a part that had not been covered or to replace someone, who, in the newcomer's view, was not doing a respectable job. After singing bass in all of the groups of my earlier, years, I had discovered I had a decent falsetto and could sing first tenor. One day, after a class in which I had been participating in one of these singing sessions, one of the older boys, Isaac, approached me and told me he and a couple other cats were trying to put together a singing group and wanted to know if I was interested. Flattered because I had heard him sing and I liked what I had heard, I figured if he was with some other cats, they could probably sing too. I also wondered how it was decided that Isaac would be the one to approach me. We agreed to meet after school in the boys' bathroom on the Summit Street side of the building to try it out.

I was so excited that I told some of my friends about the invitation I had received. A few wanted to know if they could come along to listen; but I didn't think it was a good idea because I did not want to run the risk of being embarrassed if should be rejected. For the rest of the school day, all I could think about was the coming audition.

Finally, the bell for the last period rang. I headed to homeroom to wait the five minutes there for dismissal before rushing to the meeting place for what was to be my "audition." I entered the bathroom to find Isaac (whom I later learned was called Iz—pronounced "eyes" for short) and three other boys waiting for me. Isaac introduced me to Charles Knox, whose nickname was Pop; William Huffington (Huff) and Mike Slayton (Big Mike). Isaac was a baritone, Pop and Huff were second tenors and Mike was the bass. All of them had excellent lead voices and stage personalities (my father called this "showmanship") to match.

Pop appeared to be the leader. He was all business and wanted to hit a tune right away. We decided on "Crazy for You" by The Heartbeats. Everyone knew the song and was free to improvise in any way and anywhere he saw fit. Singing an already-recorded song was a way of measuring a performance against a common, well regarded R&B

standard. It was also a test of just how deeply we dug R&B. Any ballad by The Heartbeats would have sufficed.

I was surprised at how easily we felt each other as we moved into the song. Standing in a circle so we could read each other, we smiled alternately when we heard something that moved us. The way one of us responded to a particular improvised note the another had sung would cause both parties to acknowledge each other approvingly. The give and take reminded me of the way jazz musicians interact with each other, always pushing the envelope, searching for a way that was more creative, not just different, to present a song. It was in sharp contrast to what we were being taught in the Choristers, that is, to "sing only the notes in front of you." I thought of my eighth-grade music teacher who was baffled that my friend Alley Cat and I could improvise on "Go Down Moses." My inspiration had its roots in jazz.

I discovered jazz when I was thirteen and babysitting my two-year-old niece at my sister's house on Ridgewood Avenue in the summer of 1955. Bored after a few days of child care, I began to look around for something, anything to do. I found some 33 1/3 long playing records (lp's) and randomly began to play them. Among them were records by J. J. Johnson and Kai Winding (*J and K*) and Coleman Hawkins, Charlie Parker and Lester Young, *though I can't recall the names of their albums*. This experience put me on a musical path quite different from the R&B I had grown accustomed to.

By the time I was fifteen, I had in my jazz collection Miles Davis' *Kind of Blue* and *Sketches of Spain*; Ahmad Jamal's *At the Penthouse* and his classic *But Not for Me* and Art Blakey and the Jazz Messengers' *Cu-Bop*. Additionally, I had become enamored with the way these cats dressed — bebop sunglasses (at the time, I didn't know bebop was a style of jazz from which the glasses got their name), and berets pulled over the left or right ear. I wanted to do with my voice the equivalent of what they did with their instruments.

I found I was inspired by the tightness of the four-part harmony that this new group I was to be a part of had achieved by having one background person singing essentially the same part as the lead while the rest of us sang in harmony with him. Mike kept time with his deep, smooth, bass voice that resonated off the bathroom walls and filled the room at the same time. When we finished that song, we all gave each other some skin. "Give me some skin, baby." Most times, however, one did not have to say anything because everybody sensed when something was laudable and one would just hold out a hand, palm **up** for someone to slap it, or alternately, hold one's hand palm **down** suspended in the air until someone brought his hand under, but within reach of yours to be slapped. It was considered an insult to "leave someone hanging", i.e. unslapped. This is yet another invention of jazz musician. The high five, which is now globally popular, is a variation of "give me five." Thanks to television, African American basketball players had introduced this cultural practice to the world. The fist bump, or pound, is a variation of "give me five" and a creation of the hip-hop generation. Notice how close the terms are to each other in rhythm – bebop, one word, and hip hop, two words, but the same rhythm and feeling.

Pop told me I wasn't bad for a "slopmore." Since Central started at the tenth grade, tenth-graders got the disrespect traditionally reserved for freshmen at other schools. Consequently, sophomores became slopmores. That was the extent of the harassment I would receive from upperclassmen. In the bathroom after school after school that first day, our group then polished off three more ballads. I was feeling more comfortable with each successive song. It was the best singing experience I had ever had. With all of the other groups I had been in, I had been the leader, the teacher giving the direction, setting rehearsal dates and deciding when we had rehearsed enough and co-writing songs with Melvin. Now I was with some boys who were older than I — they were all seniors — and knew so much more about music (and girls as well).

We named the group The Bell Chords.

I was proud to be associated with these older and, from my point of view, hipper, boys. I was fortunate too, because it elevated me to a level of popularity that I could not have achieved otherwise – especially in such a short time and in a totally new environment.

I wasn't yet on the track team; a rule in interscholastic athletics prohibited transfers from participating in sports for a full year. I wondered why there wasn't such a rule governing membership in the band or cheerleaders. I was, however, practicing with the track team so I could stay in shape. I had also begun to demonstrate my academic prowess, but only a small circle of folks, namely those who were in my classes, knew about my successes there. The other Bell Chords had been at CHS for more than two years and had become popular in their own circles. Pop, the only athlete besides me, was a star point guard on the basketball team. The other three members were well-dressed, well-mannered, average-to-good students, and each moved in his own circle. Through my association with them, some of the relationships they had transferred to me. And as fate would have it, right in the middle of all of this, word got out somehow (probably from one of the students who had been at Burnet with me) that my middle name was Hugo. When I became aware of this, I became anxious, anticipating a repeat teasing of my Burnet days. To my surprise, these more mature high school girls loved it; they thought it was cute. I was walking to class one day and a group of upper-class girls spoke to me, sing-songing in unison: "Good morning Hugo." I was taken by surprise and turned instinctively in the direction of the voices. Embarrassed, I smiled and waved to them as they giggled. I found their behavior a pleasant surprise after the hell I had to put up with in elementary school, where at Burnet my middle name had been an albatross. At Central, it was going to be currency.

(2)

The Bell Chords entertained the school at many an assembly. Some of the teachers told us we were the best they had ever heard in all their years of teaching at CHS. My history teacher, Mr. Schectman, even hired us to sing one Saturday night at the Jewish Community Center, in South Orange, the suburban town in which he lived.

By this time, someone had convinced us we needed a secretary and we recruited Gloria Henry, who years later, became a Playboy bunny and then a film actress under the name Hendry.

We were surprised to learn that these suburban white kids liked our music (we had begun to write our own songs) as well as the popular R&B songs. Mr. Schectman was ahead of his time by taking a chance that these young Jews would dig us. But dig us they did. I watched their faces as we delivered whatever he had promised – or so it seemed from the reaction of the audience of fifty or so. The girls reminded me of the girls on the TV program American Bandstand, hosted by Dick Clark.

Mr. Schectman paid us ten dollars for our trouble. We decided to split it six instead of five ways to accommodate Gloria. I cannot even say what value Gloria added to the group. One thing I was certain of is one of the cats had a crush on her. She was pretty, so I said to myself, *what the hell?* If nobody else objected, then why should I, a mere slopmore, protest.

When we reported to school the following Monday, nearly everyone we came in contact with wanted to know how it had gone with the suburban white kids. I answered, "We threw so much shit at them; they didn't know what to do with themselves." My statement was vague enough to ensure that none of the other Bell Chords could contradict me. And who would deny a compliment even if it weren't exactly true?

This one appearance outside the boundaries of Newark ensured that our rep had been legitimized. Our popularity spread across the city as we got to be known at all of the other high schools, at least among the Negro students.

We rehearsed regularly at Morton Street School. Other groups used the auditorium to practice and we always had an audience of young people who were there for recreational activities. One of the more popular groups that I believed were as good as we were, was a quartette called The Four Most. They did an up-tempo interpretation of "The Breeze and I" and a slow, romantic version of "Weeping Willow Tree" that used to leave girls in the audience crying, no matter how many times they had heard it. The lead singer was a cat named Bobby Moore, who had an incredibly wide range and a falsetto that even I envied. Talented as they were, they had all been students at Montgomery Street School, a school for slow learners, like my neighbor on Clay Street, Bobby Carter. I remember asking one of them if they spelled their name f-o-u-r or f-o-r-e. After puzzling for a moment, he said, "yes." I decided the spelling wasn't really important anyway and dropped it.

Sometime before I graduated, I heard The Four Most on the radio station WNJR singing "The Breeze and I." These dudes had beaten us to the recording studio.

At Morton Street, there were more girls in our audiences than boys. One of them approached me when I showed up for rehearsal a few minutes early one night. Her name was Sarah and she had a reputation for being a little loose and generous with her stuff. She walked right up to me and introduced herself. She told me she had been checking me out and had decided to give me some. Just like that. I was taken off guard and all I could say was "Now?" "No, silly, you got to practice now. I mean the next time you come or after practice tonight if you think you'll be done before they close up." I remembered that I had no condoms and I did not even want to go near this girl without protection, so I said, "H

ow about next week? I'll come at 6 instead of 7. That will give us an hour. Where are we gonna do it?" "You let me worry about that," she said.

I showed up the next week as I had promised, and Sarah was right there waiting. She took me to an empty classroom and we did it on the floor after several attempts to do it standing up. She was much shorter than I and I could not navigate myself into the right position to penetrate her. "This is going to be difficult standing up. We're going to have to lie down on the floor." I told her that it was okay with me, and down we went.

(3)

I don't recall just how it happened; but somehow, a songwriter and Newark resident named Winfield Scott heard about the Bell Chords and contacted one of us about a possible record deal. I knew he had written or co-written the Laverne Baker hit, "Tweedle Dee." He invited us to his home in the Weequahic section of the South Ward. He lived on South Tenth Street and after hearing us sing a few numbers, he agreed we were good, but he could help make us better. He offered his home as the place we could rehearse and where he could record us to create a demo tape. He told us we could call him Robey, as that was what he was called by his friends

Married to a very warm and polite woman, Robey had all of the ostentatious trappings of a successful man — big, nicely furnished house, original African artwork, library stocked with books, new Cadillac Eldorado, fine clothes. He was instantly credible to us. Moreover, he showed us some sheet music that bore his name and some 45-rpm records where he was similarly credited. We were on our way! It was all I could do to contain my excitement.

Rehearsals at Robey's were demanding. Meeting at his house once a week, we learned some of the finer points of singing. These included breathing, articulation, and word bleeding, as he called it. This technique involves holding on to the end of one word and, without taking a breath, sliding smoothly right into the beginning of the next word. He explained that a song was much like a poem, in that you have to say a lot in a little bit of time and space. Therefore, every single word is important. Johnny Mathis, Sarah Vaughan, and Frank Sinatra were masters of all of these skills and he played some of their records to demonstrate. Robey also presented these vocalists as models of articulation and phrasing, something he said was sorely lacking in R&B.

He would not let us sit down while we were singing because, he said, we should rehearse in the same posture we would if we were performing. Moreover, he explained, sitting tends to make you want to relax a bit too much. "We can relax a little after you make it big, and I mean big."

After we had been with Robey a few months, he announced that he had been in discussions with ABC Paramount Records and had sent them a tape of one of our rehearsals and expected to hear from them within a couple of weeks. I was very excited to hear this news. It was something for which I had hoped, but never thought would come this soon. I wanted to tell friends at school; but thought better of it. Once again, I did not want to risk being embarrassed if our tape was rejected.

Finally, the call came: they wanted us to come in at 11 a.m. one Wednesday in March 1959. Our parents had to write letters asking that we be excused from school for part of that day so we could go to the ABC studios in New York City. It wasn't long before word was all over the school. Everyone I ran into was very excited for me and wished me luck. Some said I should not forget them when I became famous and rich. Some of my more serious friends advised me to make sure I still went to college.

The day of the audition, we showed up at school dressed to kill. I wore a blue blazer, gray slacks, burgundy loafers and navy-blue socks, a blue shirt, and a burgundy tie, consistent with the college-boy look I had been trying to cultivate. The other cats wore finely tailored three-button suits with waffle weave or shadow stripe patterns.

Over the intercom, the vice principal, Dr. Rectenwald, on behalf of the faculty and students, wished us "the best of luck." "Show them what Centralites are made of," he exhorted.

We were to meet Robey on the High Street side of the school at 9:30. When he arrived, the five of us, bursting with anxiety, piled into the Eldorado Caddy. We did not talk very much and did not sing at all. Becoming very introspective for the occasion, I knew what we had to do and was just going over it in my head again and again.

We were on our way to the Big Apple. Robey took the Jersey Turnpike to the exit for the Holland Tunnel that led to midtown Manhattan. After a short ride uptown, we pulled into the parking lot of ABC. I felt as though I needed to pinch myself to make sure I wasn't dreaming. I wondered if the other cats felt the same. I did notice they were all smiling. Robey let us out of the car, got out himself and took the ticket from the parking lot attendant. At the same time, he gave him a tip of at least one dollar — it was single bill, but I couldn't make out the denomination. *Must be insurance,* I thought. never having been with someone who parked his car in a parking lot, I had no idea what the protocol was.

We followed Robey's lead to the building and were stunned at the luxuriously appointed lobby. It was fancier than any building I had ever been in. We took the elevator to, I think, the 24th floor and walked toward a large set of double doors made of a dark wood. *Probably cherry, I* thought. Forming an arc, the name ABC Paramount was set in bronze letters. We stepped inside onto a hardwood floor that shone like glass. A cute, very pale-skinned, red-headed receptionist wearing a tight green sweater pleasantly greeted us. I liked the way the green complemented the flaming red hair. Gazing through her hazel eyes, she recognized Robey. "Good morning Mr. Scott. We have been expecting you." I noticed she had not used the contraction, "we've." "Good morning, Gloria, how are you today? Are they on schedule?" "Pretty much, maybe a few minutes behind. It shouldn't be long. I'll let them know you're here. Can I get you coffee or anything else to drink?" "No, I'm okay. What about you, boys?" We all declined.

"Won't you have a seat then?" We complied with her request and sat in the comfortable leather chairs that were neatly arranged along the deep blue wall, from which hung pictures of various artists on the ABC label. I recognized only Ray Charles. I began to leaf through some music magazine, imagining what it would feel like to read an article about us.

After a few minutes, Gloria's phone buzzed quietly. She answered softly, then directed us through the door on her left. We gathered ourselves and headed to the door. Robey seemed to know just where to go as we approached a door marked "studio." He opened it and stood aside as he beckoned for us to precede him. The people in the room, all white men, warmly greeted Robey. He, in turn, introduced us. "Gentlemen, I'd like you to meet the Bell Chords." He then individually introduced each of us. I smiled and nodded when he called my name. I hoped I did not appear awkward. Pop, who was always Mr. Cool and sported a Fu Manchu mustache, head cocked slightly back, simply nodded.

The room was furnished with two black leather couches and a Steinway grand piano. The white carpeting was so thick, my feet sunk into down to my ankles, or so it seemed. Robey explained that we were going to sing two original arrangements of standards — our upbeat interpretation of Nat Cole's "Walking My Baby Back Home" and the Flamingos' "Lovers Never Say Goodbye," and an original song, "Zing," patterned after the Coasters' "Zing Went the Strings of My Heart", and written by Mike, arranged by me and featuring Mike as lead. Robey directed us to a platform raised about six inches above the floor, our stage. We performed the numbers in the pre-arranged order. I tried to read the poker-cold faces of the four men as we glided through the songs; but nothing registered for me. I probably should have closed my eyes and pretended they were not even in the room; but I was only fifteen and had not developed that level of discipline. My armpits were wet.

When we finished all of the songs, Robey asked us to wait for him in the reception area. The redhead smiled approvingly at us. Robey came out in a few minutes and said, "Okay, let's get on back to Newark. But first we need to get some lunch. I know you men must be hungry ... there's a Horn & Hardart not too far from here. We can walk there and they have a nice selection of dishes." I was hoping he would tell us how he thought we had done without our having to ask. After we arrived at the restaurant, an automated place that featured a wide selection of hot meals in what was essentially a vending machine, Robey gave each of us a five-dollar bill to pay for our lunches. You put your money in, selected your meal, pressed the appropriate button and your plate fell into the chute. Dessert and drinks called for separate transactions. I was hoping that eating in this restaurant would not be a bad omen, because when I was in sixth grade, the group I led at the time had eaten there after we auditioned for the Ted Mack Amateur Hour. Afterwards, the judges told us with smiling faces, we would be hearing from them very soon. They lied.

Once we got our food, we joined Robey at the table he had selected for us. After we were all settled, he told us we had met his expectations and impressed the ABC guys. They would get back to him in a couple of weeks and he would call Pop as soon as he heard anything.

When I returned to school the next day, I filled in everybody who asked how we had done. Somehow, I was not optimistic. *Why did we have to wait so long? What was it they had to consider? They had heard us at our best. We had gone as deeply as we could and left nothing untapped. Why hadn't they scheduled a negotiating session?* These were the questions that were bouncing around in my fifteen-year-old head.

Finally, we got word from Robey. Pop informed us that while the ABC cats liked us, they were even more impressed with Mike. They wanted him as a solo act. Without consulting with us, Mike told them he could not do that. It was either all of us or none of us. At the time, I didn't know Mike had been married since the start of his senior year because his girlfriend had gotten pregnant and that they were living in an efficiency apartment on Clinton Avenue. After the ABC non-deal, we had occasion to rehearse at Mike's. I was appalled at his living conditions and recall telling myself that if I had been in Mike's shoes and had his kind of responsibility, there was no way I would have been loyal to the Bell Chords. I would have looked out for my family and hoped everyone would understand.

After that great disappointment, June could not get here fast enough. After graduation, Pop went to college on a basketball scholarship and after college, joined the

Newark police force, eventually rising to the rank of precinct captain in Newark's Central Ward. After he retired to the Poconos, he became an expert witness consultant, and later took a law degree from Seton Hall. He married his high school sweetheart, Sheila (who I learned ten years later, was a close friend of Carolyn Ryan, the wife of my good friend, S. George Reed Jr.). Isaac and Huff joined the Marines and Air Force, respectively. I heard two years later that Mike had died from a heroin overdose. Pop is the only one I ever saw again.

(4)

Aside from Ernie, and my time with the Bell Chords, the two defining experiences in my sophomore year were the Algebra 1 class taught by Mr. Tumin, and the popularity I gained through my membership in the Bell Chords. I was not surprised that I did well in algebra because with the exception of long division, I had liked math more than any other subject. However, I think the light went on for me when one of my elementary school teachers showed us how multiplication was shorthand addition and division had a similar relationship with subtraction, as well as being the opposite of multiplication. She used addition and subtraction, two subjects I thoroughly understood, to facilitate the teaching of multiplication and division. When she realized I was still struggling with long division, she showed me how to perform multiple subtractions until the number you were subtracting from was smaller than the number you were subtracting. The smaller number that was left was called the remainder. For example, to divide 45 by 10, you subtract 10 from 45 leaving 35; then subtract 10 from 35, leaving 25. Repeating this process twice more leaves you with a 5, since 10 is bigger than 5, 5 is the remainder. Count the number of times you had subtracted up to this point and that was how many 10s were in 45. I did scores of exercises using this approach to division before she introduced the "shortcut" division, as she called it. She introduced the formal terms; subtrahend, minuend and difference after I understood the process. Once I grasped the concept, division was easy. When I took theory of numbers in college, one topic we studied, modular arithmetic, drew from this concept I learned in sixth grade.

I later learned from my brother James that Mr. Tumin was an English teacher who had taken a minor in math. He stood about 5' 5", had a roly-poly frame and a swarthy complexion. His head was bald on top but encircled by a two-inch ring that looked like a sweatband made of hair. He was the first white man I had ever known who wore a mustache. He was very confident in his ability to teach algebra. "All I need from you is the desire and a commitment that you will try your best. You give me those two things and you will learn algebra in my class," he told us.

He had a way of placing his hands on his desk, wrists facing each other and leaning over it, scanning the room as he was trying to make a point. He always wore a suit and would place his carefully folded jacket on the right side of the desk. I noticed the labels in his suits and sport jackets and was impressed that the labels were always Browning and King (now defunct). Browning and King was a high-end men's store in downtown Newark into whose windows I would gaze longingly whenever I passed the store on Broad Street, just south of Raymond Boulevard. The suit of his I liked most was a three-button, drab olive model with a houndstooth pattern. Even though he had a wide girth, his belly did not hang over the front of his pants as I had seen with other, less meticulous big men. Instead, his pants were even at the waist all the way around. He was second only to my Uncle Hugo as a model of the well-dressed man, but Tumin was the reason I made up my mind to buy my clothes at B & K once I got out of college and started working.

Uncle Hugo and Frank Sinatra were the two reasons I started wearing "adult" hats and, like them, I always wore them angled to one side. I favored the right side and still do to this day.

I can't pinpoint exactly what it was about Tumin's teaching style that made him so effective, but I do recall he had the attitude that we all could learn; he set high expectations for us. One way he demonstrated this was his practice of assigning exercises for homework and telling us to "do as many as you can." Many of these assignments had as many as sixty exercises. I suppose one result of this approach was it allowed us to set our own limits. He didn't presuppose what would have been enough or reasonable for us. I found this approach refreshing. He believed we really could learn as much as we wanted, but that wasn't enough. We had to convince ourselves too.

I took this as a challenge and set out to do all of the exercises. When I got stuck, I would call upon James, who was in his senior year at Bloomfield College and majoring in math. With his help, I was able to complete every assignment Mr. Tumin gave us. Each day, he would start the class, asking if anyone had done all of the exercises. I would be the only one to raise his hand. He would then ask if anyone had any questions. If there were, he would invite me to put my solution on the board and after I had done so, he would ask me to "talk us through it." This approach satisfied at least three objectives: he got some assurance that I had actually done the work, it reinforced my confidence, and it rewarded me in front of my peers for my accomplishment. In my second career, 44 years from then, I too would teach algebra and would employ some of Tumin's pedagogical methods.

When he taught, it was clear he was enamored with the subject matter. He spoke of the balance in equations as if he were describing a beautiful painting, even smiling as he did so. He explained that an equation was like a sentence in that it made a statement. It was different from an English sentence in that it's absolutely either true or false. It does not permit ambiguity. As the song goes, "Don't mess with Mr. In Between." Tumin explained, "If you perform an operation on one side of the equation, you must perform the same operation on the other side to preserve the balance. You must always preserve the balance to preserve the beauty. Otherwise, you destroy the equation." His voice had a sad ring to it when he said, "destroy." He encouraged us to show every step as we worked our problems, so he could follow our logic. "Please don't do anything in your head, even if the computation is trivial. If you put everything on paper, I can see if the mistakes you make are due to a failure to understand the algebra or just careless arithmetic. Of course, I care about the latter, but it is the former I am teaching." This utterance was the first time I had ever heard the words "latter" and "former" used in this way, but from the context, I knew what he meant. So, I learned a little about English in his class too.

Mr. Tumin had passed on to me his love for mathematics, a love that would only grow stronger as a result of my discussions about math with James and some very good, though not inspiring, teachers the rest of the time I was in high school. It was a love that made summer school palatable.

I lost essentially a full year of high school when I went to Tech. The only courses I could use as units for college admission requirements were English and U.S. History. To graduate on time, I needed to attend summer school to take algebras II, III and IV, physics and biology. What I most appreciated about summer school was my experience of competing with students from some of the more strongly academic schools in the city and meeting a girl named Donna (whose father was a funeral director) from Arts High School. She was taking algebra II over again because she had gotten a grade of B during the regular school year. It was the teacher who revealed this secret, to the class much to Donna's embarrassment. Meanwhile, I had to *make up* for the time I had lost at Bloomfield Tech.

(When students registered for summer school, we had to fill in the "reason for attending" line. On the first day of class, the teacher had his copy of the forms in his hands as he called the roll. When he got to Donna's form he said, "Well I have seen a lot of different reasons for students going to summer school but this is the first instance I have seen of someone doing so to get an A to replace a B." *Me too,* I thought. I set my sights on her as the person I had to compete with. I figured she already had a leg up and if I could keep up, I would be one happy cat.

Summer school was fast-paced and the teacher was demanding, but Tumin had prepared me well for such rigor. Neither Donna nor I received a quiz score of less than 92% and we were always within a point or two of each other. I remember once getting a score of 99% when she got 100%. I went to the teacher to protest the loss of the percentage point, but lost the argument. I don't think I cared that much about the one point I lost. While I did not mind so much her getting a higher score, I could not stand her getting a perfect score while I had not.

On the whole, I found that students from the other high schools to be no better prepared for the classes I was taking than I. Many were repeating the course because they had failed it or gotten a D, so it was clear I wasn't matched against the best of each represented high school, but that didn't matter to me because I always sought out the best in my classes and went gunning for them. Central did not have the best reputation for academics, so I took great joy at the looks on some of my classmates' faces when they learned I was a Centralite. I was making a statement for the school as much as I was for myself and hoped like hell, they would take the word back to their respective schools. I think it was Mr. Tumin who helped bolster my confidence to the point I thought I could compete with anyone.

I carried this attitude with me to all of my summer school classes and did equally as well as I had done in algebras I and II. Some of my Clay Street friends called me crazy for taking "all those hard classes." They asked me what I would ever need physics and algebra for. The only answer I had was I needed them for college. My mother, her brothers and my older siblings had high expectations of me and I was not going to disappoint them, nor was I willing to put my chances of getting into college in jeopardy by getting mediocre grades or taking lightweight courses just to avoid peer criticism.

(6)

In my junior year, I rode my popularity into the vice presidency of the student council. I really wanted to run for president, but a new cat, a transfer from some school in Morristown, a suburb seven to eight miles west of Newark, caused me to change my plans. He was a handsome, light-skinned dude with sandy brown hair and hazel eyes. He dated girls regardless of their race or ethnicity and soon was dubbed "International Gary." Girls liked him because he was cute. Boys hung around him thinking they might attract at least some girls because of their association with him.

Before I could even announce my candidacy, Gary had posters plastered all over the place: "Swing with Swangin: Vote for Gary Swangin, student council president." There was no way I could make up the jump he had gotten on me, so I decided to run for the second slot. It turned out to be a smart move because I won by a two-to-one margin over my nearest opponent, the cute Penny Watson, on whom I had a crush until I learned she smoked cigarettes. Gary won by an even greater margin than I.

The most memorable event of the Swangin administration was the student talent show Gary conceived. (At least, I think it was Gary). Everyone was in favor of it. We formed the talent show committee, of which Gary was chairman and I was vice chairman. The committee was further divided into various functional subcommittees. My job was to oversee them while Gary had overall responsibility. The publicity committee placed an ad in *The Tangent*, the school newspaper, and also placed posters in strategic places around the school announcing the event, as well as the deadline for notifying the audition committee if they intended to audition. We had decided that if anyone were really bad (the dictionary definition), we would not reject him or her outright. Instead, we adopted a gentle policy. We would tell the aspirant we had already seen a much better act "just like yours" and it might be embarrassing on the day of the event if people had already seen acts that they thought were much better than his, or words to that effect. As fate would have it, some peoples' opinions of themselves were not grounded in reality, and thus, only one act dropped out as a result of the audition committee's advice.

In all, we had fifteen acts. They included vocal and instrumental soloists on piano, trumpet and saxophone; dancers; a jazz quintet; a vocal group, an African drummers and dancers group and a mime. The talent show was to be put on twice, once for each of the two assemblies. It was not to be competitive, but simply for the entertainment of the school. Gary was the master of ceremony and I was his back-up.

The program was scheduled to take place on a Wednesday, and beginning that Monday, it was announced over the intercom along with the other daily messages. I sensed more than the usual amount of electricity in the air as the appointed day approached. Or maybe it was just my own anticipation. I do know that it was reported that absenteeism was the lowest on that program's day than it had been all year.

Well, the show was a smashing success. I had deliberately stayed away from the auditions because I wanted to be surprised at the presentations. And I'm glad I did. I saw on that day, boys and girls with whom I had sung in the Choristers and heard playing in the school band transform themselves into brilliant musicians comfortable in their music of choice. And a few made complete fools of themselves.

On the other hand, there were three acts that stood head and shoulders above the others. One was the jazz quintet that played Benny Golson's "Blues March." All the cats in the band were in the school band as well, but as I listened to each of them launch into his solo, I could not believe how much different they sounded — simply electrifying — than when they played school band music. From that point on, I thought of them as musicians rather than just members of the school band. Sadly, none of them found a career in jazz; I say sadly because I believe that they were all talented and creative enough to have added to the long line of jazz artists (among them Grachan Moncur, T-Bone Washington and Reggie Workman) who came out of Newark. I was personally acquainted with Gerald Parker on drums, Leslie Walker on piano, and Nate Best on tenor sax.

The other jazz player was a cat named Carl Freeman (tragically killed one year after we graduated when a car jumped the curb in front of the apartment building on 301 Broad Street where he lived and crushed him against the wall.) Carl played a smooth, mellow version of "Harlem Nocturne" that had the girls screaming and the boys shouting "Blow, Carl, blow." After I started writing this memoir, I tried unsuccessfully to find a version of the song to recreate the haunting melody I had heard in 1960, more than 45 years ago. I wanted to recreate and write in the mood that enveloped me for the three minutes of Carl's solo. To solve this problem, I consulted my nephew, Jacques Burvick, a professional jazz pianist who played with Norman Connors. I asked him for some names of great blues sax men. He offered the names of Houston Person and Eddie "Lockjaw" Davis. I researched and bought their CDs, hoping I would find "Harlem Nocturne" among their selections.

I was crestfallen when, upon playing them, their renderings sounded unfamiliar. Neither of them could match what 18-year-old Carl had done. . Perhaps it was because Carl's was the very first version I had heard and my neurons just would not release it, rendering me biased toward the sound he created that day.

But the act that set the place on fire was the African drummers and dancers. They graced the stage dressed in their idea of West African clothes. A Nigerian national and member of the Yoruba ethnic group, Babatunde Michael Olatunji, had burst on the American scene the year before with his hit album *Drums of Passion,* so the high school group had an authentic Nigerian model, not only for the music, but also for their selection of clothing. Until then, my perception of everything African was rooted in the images I had internalized in my fragile, impressionable youth as a result of my exposure to Tarzan and Jungle Jim movies with their depictions of "wild natives."

This performance resonated so much with the students that year, it seemed as though every classroom desk and even the cafeteria tables would be transformed into djembe drums. At the drop of a hat, the polyrhythmic "Akiwowo" was the first song the ensemble performed, followed by "Odunde."

For several days afterwards, I could not walk the halls without someone commending me on the "great show the student council had put on." I was on cloud nine and proud of it. I even got praise from some teachers who said it was well organized and that they could not believe some of their very own students were so talented.

Lost in all of this adulation was the fact that Gary had the vision to conceive of such a show. Yet, because of my own popularity, I got more credit than I deserved. More than forty years later, I was in touch with Gary for the first time since we graduated and to our mutual surprise, we spoke of how each of us was in awe of the other. I quote in, part, an email he sent me:

> I have to confess that I was flattered by your comments. But I have to admit that I was envious of you during those days because I thought you were extremely smart. In some ways, I felt like a fraud because I appeared to be in control of things. When I was at Morristown H.S, I was considered a poor student with no

chance of going to college. That's because MHS had very high standards for the "white kids" and not us colored folks. Black kids in Morristown who enrolled in college prep were shot down before they had a chance of coming out of the starting gate.

Ironically, CHS [Central High School] proved that I could rise above my problems and be proud of myself. Here's something I think you should know. Two weeks after I had won the student council election, I nearly killed a man for attempting to rape my mother. In fact, I put a gun to his head and nearly pulled the trigger. Fortunately, I was talked out of it by my neighbors on Bleeker Street. It was then that I felt more comfortable being at Central than at any other place in the world.

Prior to going to Central, I attended Barringer with all of its racial tensions. I stayed there for one marking period and returned to Morristown. Admittedly, I hated Newark and its high schools, and hoped that I would never return to the area. What I heard about Central was even more alarming. To me it was a "blackboard jungle" — the mother of all bad schools in Newark. Little did I know that I would grow to love the school, the Centralites and its teachers.

Had he pulled that trigger in defense of his mother, Gary would have been yet another statistic at Rahway State Prison; instead, he is a father of two girls and a senior network engineer for a large holding company in New Jersey.

Many years later, I had the opportunity to teach Swahili at Rahway and met there many motivated, bright black men. Now I wonder how many of them might have been productive citizens like Gary had they taken the extra moment Gary had used to reconsider whatever act got them charged, tried, and convicted.

The absolutely worst act of the talent show was a tap dance routine performed by a girl whose body looked like a spider that was trying to accustom itself to just two legs. (Kafka's "*Metamorphosis*" in reverse?) And as evidence, she even slipped a few times. This same girl invited me two years later to attend a recital of a performing arts school from which she was graduating. I had not seen her since we graduated from Central and was surprised to run into her near the Rutgers campus where I had enrolled. She invited me to the school's recital to be held the next Sunday afternoon at a hotel on Hill Street just off Broad Street in downtown Newark.

It was a pleasantly warm sunny day and the hotel was a few blocks from my apartment, so I hoofed it to the program alone. It featured a performance by each of the graduating students. Marcella, the girl who had invited me, did the same tap-dance routine she did at the student council talent show three years earlier. I could not detect that she had improved at all. But what I do remember most was a male graduate who sang without a song. I had learned the importance of enunciation when I was in the Bell Chords and I had developed a very sensitive ear to a singer's diction. Well, this cat came to the stage and when the pianist played an introductory chorus, the first word out of his mouth was "wif." I could not believe my ears. This man had paid some sum of money in tuition for who-knows-how-many weeks of training and yet he could not say "with." This was his graduation and I can only assume he was presenting what he and his teacher thought was his best. I suffered through the song, all of the time thinking, I can't wait to get home and tell my mother about this. When I did, she said his teacher should have played some Roy Hamilton or Nat King Cole records for him.

(7)

Meanwhile, I had been on again and off again with a girl I had started seeing when I was at Tech. She was the best friend of the girlfriend of my best friend, Maurice, and quite a looker. Her name was Cassandra and, like Maurice and his girlfriend, Gloria, she lived in the Columbus Homes too. In fact, she lived in the same building as Gloria with her two brothers and two sisters. Her dad was a super hip, handsome cat whom she dearly loved — I thought a bit too much.

Cassandra was, by far, the most complex girl I had ever dated. She was moody, capricious, and whimsical. She had a habit of falling into long periods of silence and being unable or unwilling to articulate what she was thinking. Sometimes she made statements or did things inconsistent with the nature of our relationship. For example, she told me once that she was going to marry a doctor, knowing I had no plans to be one. Then she once let a senior named John walk her home while she and I were still dating. I found out and confronted her; she did not try to deny it. We were standing in the stairwell just outside her second-floor apartment. After a long, strained discussion about the incident, I decided I would try to smoke her out in case there was something she was omitting from the story. If a girl had let me take her home and the conditions were right, I thought about what I would do once we arrived at her door.

Remembering what had happened between Ernie and me, I asked, "Why did you have to kiss him?" Without thinking how I could possibly have known kissing had gone down, she blurted out, "I didn't kiss him. He kissed me." She had fallen for the psych. "Later for you, girl," I said and abruptly turned away and went down the stairs.

(8)

After I broke up with Cassandra, a new girl named Rosita moved to Newark from Charleston, (which, at the time, I thought was in North Carolina — I was thinking of Charlotte) South Carolina, to live with her brother. Rosita was a cute, self-assured, thin, chocolate-brown girl who was a straight-A student. I had noticed her in my Spanish class but since I was hooked up with Cassandra, I didn't bother her. Now that I was free, I decided I would take a shot. I approached her after class one day and asked, "Is it true you're from North Carolina?" She said she was not, that she was from South Carolina and asked me why I wanted to know. I said, "I once knew a girl from Durham and you don't talk anything like her. She was plain country." "Well, I'm from Charleston, South Carolina, born and raised — so far." The "so far" sounded like an afterthought, as if she realized she had not been fully raised. "I'm living with my older brother." "Are you going to stay here in Newark for good or are you going back soon?" "I don't know. We'll just have to see." "When is your lunch period? I have some more things to ask you." As it turned out her lunch period was the same as mine and we agreed to meet by the trophy case at the beginning of the period.

We had a wonderful time at lunch and shortly afterwards we were going together. Rosita was in a word, fascinating. She was insightful, very smart and knowledgeable about issues way beyond her years, and she liked to debate. I just liked being around her. I had recently bought Miles' *Kind of Blue* and *'Round Midnight* and Ahmad Jamal's *Jamal at the Penthouse* and *At the Pershing: But Not for Me* (the song "Poinciana" became a hit single even on the pop charts.) She was not hip to jazz and I enjoyed hipping her, almost evangelically, to the music. We were not good around other people because the topics of our conversations were way outside anything our peers were interested in and we did not like to dumb down our stuff just to fit in, so we steered clear of others when we were together.

Every so often, we would talk about our career plans. She said she wanted to be a dermatologist. I didn't even know what that was. She chuckled. "For somebody so smart, you certainly don't know a lot." "I know what I know. What I don't know, I have the good sense to ask about. That's a sign of wisdom." "So it is", she said, "so it is." I had never known anyone so young who was so focused on what career she wanted to pursue. She was the most serious student I had ever met. Her sense of purpose and direction inspired me. She was the first girl I could actually imagine myself being married to.

Given this sentiment, it was ironic that ours was strictly an in-school romance. Her brother, Ralph, (whom I was to meet seven years later and campaign for his shot at a councilman-at-large seat during the 1970 Newark election campaign to elect the first black mayor) would not allow her to have company. That was really tough.

Nine years later, I was visiting with him in his office when he was director of Action Now, an ombudsman's office established by the new mayor, Kenneth Gibson. Ralph had begun to tell me about his early days in Newark during which his younger sister, Rosita, had lived with him for a while. I realized that his last name was the same as hers and asked him if she had gone to Central. He said she had. I told him the whole story and he was so amused he picked up the telephone and called her. After they exchanged greetings, he told her he had a surprise for her and gave me the telephone. She was the first ex-girlfriend with whom I had spoken since I had gotten married so I felt a little awkward but I quickly got over that. She had not become a dermatologist after all, instead, she had married one. He was a Cuban immigrant. As for her career, she had gone into nursing.

In high school, we once chanced my walking her home, but she got cold feet and I had to abandon her at a corner, one block from her house. I felt really bad about having to sneak around as we did. But I was willing to put up with it since that was the only way we could see each other. We never talked about it, but I knew it had to be as tough on her as it was on me.

While I was seeing Rosita, the cheerleader sister of a senior star football player started paying attention to me. Alma was blessed with a nearly perfect body, smooth brown skin and a slight gap between her top two front teeth, which I thought was cute. She was warm, outgoing and friendly and had a way of placing her right hand on my left arm or shoulder when she was talking to me. She was one year ahead of me and very popular. Many boys had tried to hit on her only to be rebuffed. And as far as I knew, she did not have a boyfriend. Now here I was, a year younger than she was and a year behind to boot; but despite these shortcomings, she displayed some interest in me (or so I thought.) Word got out that I liked her but when Rosita confronted me with this, I said that Alma and I were only friends and that, "You are still my girl."

Alma extended an invitation to me to come and visit her at her crib on Springfield Avenue and I took her up on it one Saturday night. We sat around and talked a good three or four hours. She asked me about my plans for the future and about Rosita and me. I told her that Rosita was very nice but I didn't see us as a long-term item since I was sure she would probably head back to Charleston at some point. I also told her that I had been puzzling over something for a long time and that my heart was pulling me one way and my mind another and I was just stuck. She said, "I always follow my heart." I thought she knew what I had been alluding to when she said that. I left her place determined to set myself free of Rosita so I could be available for Alma. That Monday, I broke up with Rosita. She was shocked and I was heartless.

The following weekend I was at Alma's again — this time to announce that I was available. I was sitting next to her on the living room couch; I was so excited that I could hardly contain myself as I tried to figure out how I was going to tell her. Finally, I said, "Do you remember your advice last week about following your heart?" "Yes," she said. Upon hearing that "reinforcement," I learned over and kissed her. Mouth closed, she gently pushed me away. I don't know who was more shocked, she or I, but for a moment, we were both speechless. When I gathered myself, I quickly apologized? She said it was all right and asked me why I had tried to kiss her. I explained that I thought she knew what I was alluding to when we were talking last week and I reminded her of her advice to me to follow my heart. To be sure, I told her, "I asked you again tonight and you gave me the same answer." "Oh, Hugo, I'm afraid I misled you. I'm sorry. What about Rosita?" "I quit her Monday." She exclaimed, "You did what?" I was feeling smaller and smaller by the minute. I wanted to get out of there as fast as I could. Sweat was beginning to ooze from my armpits and down my rib cage. I felt like a "brand new fool," as my father would say.

Everything after that was a big blur for me. I don't recall saying goodbye to Alma; I just remember feeling like the weight of the world had just crushed me. Nor I do I recall sitting on the bus on my way home, wondering how I was going to face everyone at school on Monday. *Should I try to get Rosita back? Would she take me back? Did I deserve to be taken back?*

On Monday, as I was passing through the cafeteria on my way to homeroom, I saw Rosita sitting alone at a table, reading. Before I could retreat, she called out to me. Reluctantly, I went over to where she was sitting and stood over her. I didn't dare sit down and she didn't invite me to do so. She got straight to the point. "I heard you are going with Alma. Is that true?" "No, it isn't." "Then what's wrong with me?" "Nothing." My voice sounded juvenile. "Then why don't we get together again?" She sounded as if she knew I had to give an affirmative answer, as if she could not be rejected twice. She was right. "That's fine with me."

Just like that I was in again. She had forgiven me and was not too proud to seek reconciliation. My mother had told me a number of times about something she called strength of character. I thought I now understood what she meant. Rosita was its personification.

Rosita and I never discussed my brief hiatus. She just acted as though nothing had happened and was just as considerate and cheerful as she had always been. I wondered if Alma had called her, telling her what had happened and imploring her to give me another chance. Since Alma and I were the only ones who knew what had happened at her apartment that fateful night and I was too embarrassed to tell anyone myself, there is no other way Rosita could have found out. But I never asked her.

Getting back with Rosita turned out to be good for me beyond the direct benefits of the relationship. I had been getting little tidbits of information about some boy named John who was in Rosita's homeroom. The way I got it, he didn't like her and would say all kinds of insulting things to her to demonstrate it. I asked Rosita about it and she said it was nothing and that she simply ignored him. I decided to let it go. The last thing I wanted to do was fight over a girl who didn't think she needed defending. Not only that, but also, among the Clay Street gang, there was a stigma attached to a boy who would go so far as to fight over a girl. Even though I no longer palled around with them, the sentiment had become a part of me. However, after the umpty-ump time someone told me about John's continuing offensive behavior, I decided to say something to John. He must not know she's my girl, I reasoned. While I knew John by reputation (a very mean cat), I didn't know what he looked like, so I had to get someone who did to point him out to me. I told this same person to make sure John knew

I was looking for him. I had hoped if he got that word, he would consider it a warning, though not directly from me, and fearing a confrontation would just back off. That was a miscalculation on my part.

My emissary told me the next day that he had delivered my message but got no reaction from John. About a week later, I ran into John in the cafeteria. I told him who I was, and that Rosita was my girl. Then I asked him about the reports I had been getting about his behavior towards Rosita. He told me he didn't know what I was talking about. I disregarded his response and continued, "I would appreciate it if you would leave her alone. Anything you might have said or done to her up 'til now, I'm willing to let go because you didn't know she was my girl. But now you know." I walked away before he could respond. We were both alone so there was no one around we had to impress. But inside, I felt like the virtuous cowboy who had just confronted the town's bad man.

The next day, Rosita told me in Spanish class that John had approached her and berated her for telling me about him. This report weighed on me because this time it was Rosita herself giving the report. Moreover, it was clear from her demeanor that he had frightened her. I told her not to worry about it. "That's the last time that's going to happen," I assured her.

I knew which side of town he lived on and deduced what exit he would take to go home. I told my friend from Burnet, Alley Cat, that I might have to teach John a lesson about respect and asked him if he would come with me to talk to John. I knew I could depend on Alley to break up the fight if I started getting my ass kicked. I also knew that he would expand beyond the peacemaker role if the opportunity were to present itself. I had witnessed Alley in a fist fight at Burnet where, though he has small hands, he demonstrated superior boxing skills.

When school let out, I saw John coming out of the Summit Street entrance, which emptied into an alleyway between the north-west side of Central and a neighboring building of the Newark College of Engineering (now the New Jersey Institute of Technology, NJIT). He was easy to spot because he was so tall — about six feet. I did not wait for him to exit the alley.

Instead I walked toward him and reminded him of our conversation of the previous day. Then I told him what Rosita had told me about his most recent insult. Dramatically, he threw his arms up in the air and said, "Oh, man, I didn't say nuthin' to that bitch." "Oh, she's bitch now, mothafukah, she's a bitch now?" I came out of my coat and gave Al my glasses to hold. John jumped into his boxer's pose and started dancing around. He was holding his hands very high, leaving his midsection fully exposed — a big mistake for someone with such a height advantage. I slammed a left hook to his rib cage and followed it with a right cross to his temple as he grimaced in response to the rib blow. He grabbed me around my waist and tried to throw me down. Somehow, I managed to slip from his grip and get him in my deadly headlock, my left arm tightly wrapped around his neck while I pounded him on top of his head with my right fist. At some point, he slipped out of my grip and with my back to him, locked his arms around my waist.

The crowd that had gathered to watch had been yelling like crazy, but when John made this move, they let out a loud, collective groan -- indicating what I thought was concern. I was definitely concerned, and I used every muscle in my body to try to pry his hands apart. Inspired by the noise of the crowd, I succeeded and somehow managed to grab him by the back of his shirt collar, pulling his head down as I frantically delivered uppercut after stinging uppercut to whatever part of his face I could reach, until he held up his hands in surrender. I didn't want to stop, but Alan pulled me away as John, his nose bloodied, staggered backwards and steadied himself against the fence. Al ceremoniously gave me my glasses and coat. Putting on my glasses, I could see how badly John was bruised and bleeding. *Damn, I fucked him up for real,* I thought. I looked at my hands. My knuckles were on fire and glowing red. The policeman who was on duty at the school had begun to make his way in the direction of the commotion and Alan and I speedily left the scene as the crowd began to disperse. Other than the from-behind bear hug, John never laid a hand on me.

The next day, I woke up with throbbing knuckles on my right hand, the hand I used to deliver the uppercuts. They had swollen to nearly twice their natural size. I feared that should John want a rematch; I would not be able to respond because of the condition of my hands. But he did not show up for school that day, or the next or the next. As I walked through the halls on my way to classes, small groups of girls would approach and congratulate me for what I had done to John. They told me that he had been mean to all of the girls and that they all hated him, and they were "glad somebody had taught him a lesson." Rosita just said thank you.

I had intended to defend *only Rosita*, but as fate would have it, I had, by proxy, defended all of the girls. At Central I knew that John had a reputation for being one of the baddest cats on the hill, but I had no idea just how far it spread. At football games that season, strangers (boys and girls) would approach me and tell me they had heard about the hurt I had put on John. At another football game, I learned that John had transferred to South Side High -- the school at which I was to do my practice teaching seven years later, and where my brother, James, was to be vice principal in the late sixties.

The way things worked in Newark, the one way you could be guaranteed no one would provoke you into a fight was to get a rep at the expense of someone who was already going for bad. Unlike the fastest gun in the West, where the gunfighter was bound to have others eager to prove they were faster come after him, in Newark, having a bad rep served like an insurance policy and had the opposite effect. The only catch was you could not exploit your rep by flaunting it and going around picking fights. Instead, you had to be the kind of boy who would not fight except in self-defense or in defense of honor, as was the case with Rosita.

My rep as one of Newark's bad boys was not something I sought. I had given up the thug image and behavior after my shoplifting incident and after my transfer to Central; I took on the image of what we referred to as Joe College and Ivy League, (we were called Ivy Leaguers, but the name had more to do with an attitude than the schools), both of which encompassed a certain demeanor, haircut and way of dressing that said you were going to college. I had exchanged my lean-to-the left swagger for a straight-back, head-up look of someone very self-confident. I abandoned my Caesar haircut and let my widow's peak grow in while I instructed my mother (she was my barber and remained so until I left for college) to cut the sides closer than the top. For my clothes, it was heavy crew and boat neck sweaters. I had a couple of lightweight V-necks too, but they did not count as much as the others. To this I added high-water (touching just above the ankles) cuff less pants; and one pair each of black and burgundy shoes made of imitation cordovan leather; and over-the-calf, black (always black) socks. And no wardrobe was complete without the mandatory blue, three-button blazer. I wore it with a blue, Ivy League (meaning button-down collar) shirt, burgundy tie and gray slacks. The extra hip, which I considered myself to be, also had a black beret, a couple of Big Apple caps and at least one black hat.

The outer garment was either a duffel (sometimes called stadium) coat in the winter and a trench coat for days not so cold. I could not afford a duffel, so I bought a trench with a zip-out lining to make it (almost) hawk-proof.

This image and the new rep I had acquired were not consistent with each other. I mean, someone who was supposed to be bad was also supposed to look the part in Newark and the Ivy League look was not the one. Actually, the incompatibility of the thug rep and the college-boy image served me well. As in the movies, I was like the cowboy who did not smoke, cuss or drink liquor. Instead, he would order soda pop at the bar to the snickers of the uninitiated. Amused by this out-of-place character, one of the bad hombres would inevitably pick a fight with him and get the ass-kicking of his life. He established that he was not one to be messed with, his appearance notwithstanding. Whenever I went to a party off my turf, I would make sure I introduced myself as the David Barrett who goes to Central. I distinctly remember meeting one dude from Weequahic High who said he had heard of me but had somehow pictured me looking different. I lied and said, "Yeah, I get that reaction all of the time."

I was able to get through the rest of my time at Central without so much as a challenge, much less a fight. But John was to come back into my life again, albeit all so briefly.

Two months after the fight, Rosita told me she would be leaving to visit her family in Charleston for Christmas break. *It was just as well,* I thought, *because I would not have been able to see her anyway.* She might just as well have gone to the moon. The week before break, Rosita and I exchanged gifts. I gave her a bottle of perfume and she gave me a set of silver-plated cufflinks with gray stones. It was my first pair of cufflinks; unfortunately, I had no French cuff shirts. On the card she gave me, she wrote, "A boy like you deserves nothing but the best." I presumed she thought French cuff shirts fell into this category. Not wanting to seem unappreciative, the next week, I bought one.

(9)

A few weeks after Rosita left, I went alone one Saturday night to a dance at the Continental Ballroom on Broad Street in downtown Newark. The lead act was Teaneck's own Isley Brothers. Their hit recording "Twist and Shout" was still going strong and in person, they were better than the record. Dressed entirely in white, they made a lasting impression on me with their animated dance routines that accompanied their songs. I don't even recall who the other acts were, but I do know I enjoyed the whole show, so much so that I didn't even feel like dancing.

I was standing there checking out one of the other acts when someone tapped me from behind on my left shoulder. I turned around and found myself staring up into the eyes of John Jackson, the boy I had fought over Rosita! *Oh, shit,* I thought, *if I have to fight this cat again, I might not be so lucky this time. I have no one to hold my glasses. If they get broken, (and I was sure they would) how am I going to make it home?* I felt my pulse accelerate, but, surprisingly, John had a smile on his face as he extended his hand for me to shake. Seeing his approach, I recovered from my fright and extended mine, also with a smile. "How you doin', man?" he asked as our hands met. "I'm cool, baby," I replied. He continued, "I saw you standing there by yourself and thought I'd come over and speak." "I'm glad you did." Our hands were still locked, and I was steadily watching his eyes and his left hand, ready to defend myself against a cold cock. But none was to come. He released my hand and said, "Well, it was nice seeing you again. Later." "Yeah, me too. Be cool, baby."

He turned and went back wherever he had come from and I never saw him again. Why he did not walk up behind me and whack me upside my head was something about which I speculated for some time afterwards. Why did he speak at all? I thought of the courage he had to muster to approach me. Was it respect won the hard way?

When she returned to school after break, Rosita told me that she would be "moving back home" to Charleston after she completed the semester. Her announcement shocked me. I naively thought she was doing it to get even for what I had done to her with Alma. But I dismissed this idea as making no sense. I had known a few other kids who regularly had moved back and forth among relatives and between Southern cities and Newark. But they all presented themselves as being from unstable environments, judging from the number of schools some of them told me they had attended and their use of the verb "to stay." "I stay with my aunt," on Blank Street was the way they had of telling you where they lived, or "Who you stay with?" As opposed to "where do you *live*?" It was the temporariness of the word "stay" that resonated with me. But Rosita did not use the term. When we met, she told me she lived with her brother. I tried to imagine what it must be like to have to move so often, not you and your family, but just you, leaving old friends and making new ones and leaving them too. I had lived on Clay Street for sixteen years before I moved and then it was the whole family, not just me. My older brother and sisters had told me that before I was born, they had moved very often and even had to live with my grandparents for a while because they kept getting evicted. But these were only stories to me. I had not lived it any more than I had lived Rosita's experience.

Rosita and I exchanged letters for a few months and when it became apparent, she would not be returning, we just stopped the letter exchange. I figured she had taken up with her old boyfriend, Featon. These thoughts made me very sad and I shared my feelings with my mother. She "comforted" me by telling me I would have my heart broken many more times "before it's all over." Of course, at the time, I did not see how this could be. But it dawned on me some time afterwards that counting Barbara, she was the second girl I had lost to the Carolinas. The Carolinas and girls named Rose would appear in my life multiple times at seemingly random times. Two of the three died: my sister Rose Marie and my fifth-grade classmate Rose Urciolli.

I endured the remainder of the semester and the summer without having a girlfriend but compensated by reading a lot of fiction. It was during this period that I read and was deeply moved by W. Somerset Maugham's heart-wrenching story, *Of Human Bondage,* and then was excited about what the future might hold from reading H. G. Wells' *The Time Machine.* Though my fate was nothing like that of Maugham's Philip, the tragic protagonist, I still could identify with him, and *The Time Machine* just took me far, far away as no other book had before, during a time I needed to escape.

(10)

Having no prospects in the romance department, sometime during the fall semester of my junior year, I called Cassandra to see what was happening. She had heard about Rosita and seemed to expect my call. Cassandra and I became "just friends" for a short time and had spent only a few weeks together when I learned that a girl in my English class, this one named Sandra, had been checking me out. She sat right in front of me and while I thought she was cute, she did not seem like my type. But I figured if it was true that she liked me, I would not have to mount too heavy a rap to hook up with her. Her style of dressing reminded me of Ernie's. At about 5'2 and 102 pounds, she had a honey-brown complexion, a chip in one of her front teeth, short cut hair and she walked slightly slew-footed. She had a way of holding her head to one side while she walked as if she was trying to make out something in the distance.

One day after class, I followed her into the hall and asked if she would mind if I walked her to her next class. I repeated this routine for a couple of weeks and was soon going with her. My close friends were surprised to learn that

I was going with Sandra. She certainly did not fit the profile of any of my former girlfriends, except Cassandra. Like Cassandra, she was not in the college preparatory program and did not participate in any extracurricular activities except the Choristers, where she dazzled me with her beautiful alto voice.

She came off as somewhat of a bad girl compared to the other girls I had dated. Maurice used to tease me by singing Smokey Robinson and The Miracles' song, "Bad Girl," when he saw me with her. I don't think she ever caught on.

There were only two things I didn't like about Sandra: she kissed with a closed mouth and her conversation consisted mainly of short, monotone comments to whatever I would initiate. I mean she would even call me on the telephone and when I answered, she would say "hello" and wait for me to carry the rest of the conversation! "Don't you have anything to say, Sandra?" "Yes." "Then why don't you say something?" "I just called to see how you were doing." "Then why couldn't you have asked that after you said 'hello'?" "I don't know." We'd do that for a few minutes and then I would just have to work at continuing the conversation. I much preferred the in-person version of her.

Because she was so reticent, I usually took her to the movies or a party when we went out because neither of these activities required much talking. She came to my house one cold Wednesday night while my mother was at a Christian Science testimonial service. I had told her that Sandra was coming over and would likely be here when she returned. I knew no one would be at home and I didn't want my mother to think I had planned it that way, even though I had. I really had no idea of anybody else's schedule. I had, however, planned the evening -- Miles Davis' *Kind of Blue* album for music and, just in case, some R&B 45s, soda, potato chips and a blue light. I had gotten permission to light the oil stove so the living room would be comfortable. It was a special occasion.

We alternately sat on the couch and dry kissed or danced to the Miles album, speaking very little during its entire 45 minutes of playing. She especially *liked "Flamenco Sketches,"* a very slow, reflective ballad that seemed perfect for the occasion. She must have thought so too because she asked me to play that cut again. She had little knowledge of jazz and thought it was music older people listened to. She wanted to know what I was doing with so many jazz records. I laughed at the question out of a sense of flattery and embarrassment. I didn't want to appear too far out for her, so I downplayed my enthusiasm for the music and told her my sister had recommended the records.

The Miles album had set a very romantic atmosphere and at one point, while we were kissing, I had gotten enough nerve to run my hand up her skirt, but when it arrived at the sweet spot, she would break the kiss and I would retreat. I repeated this action a few times more. Not being encouraged to continue, I took it as a sign she wanted me to stop, though she never said so, or even tried to block my hand. I decided not to press the issue. I didn't have a condom anyway and I did not want to risk getting her pregnant.

When my mother came home, she made her way to the living room, calling me as she approached so as not to walk in on anything. "Where are the lights? How can you see anything? It's so dark in here," she said, chuckling. Sandra and I stood up to greet her. "Mom, this is Sandra Baskerville. Sandra, this is my mother." "Hello, Mrs. Barrett." "It's nice to meet you, Sandra. I guess you don't mind the blue light." "It's okay." "Hugo, is this all you're feeding her, chips and soda?" Before I could answer, Sandra said she wasn't very hungry and that she didn't eat that much anyway. "That's why I weigh only 102 pounds." She giggled as she said this. "I see. Well, I'm going to straighten up the kitchen. Hugo, don't you keep her out too late." "We're leaving in a few minutes, Mom. We were just waiting for you to arrive so she could meet you."

After only a few months, Sandra and I began to drift apart. I was a natural talker but during the time I spent with her, I was starved for conversation because she simply was not willing or able to participate meaningfully in it. During what was to be the last telephone conversation we would have as students, (Thirteen years later, I ran into her in a Newark bar while I was campaigning for a seat on the Board of Chosen Freeholders. She had become a nurse and had had one child. By that time, she might have been tipping the scales at 110 pounds.) I was trying to discuss a theoretical topic in a departure from the usual teenage blabber. I could feel her growing more irritated as the conversation wore on. I seem to recall that I was asking her if she could travel right through the center of the Earth, at what point did she think she would stop going downward and begin going upward. She did not appear to comprehend the question. "What do you mean? What are you talking about?" she asked. I tried again, this time rephrasing the question. When she still did not get it, I changed the subject to discuss the book, *Silas Marner*, we were reading in Mr. Pearlstein's English class. She didn't want to talk about it, she protested that she got enough of school in school. I realized I had messed up and tried to explain to her that what we were learning in school wasn't for school as such; rather, it was for life. And one way we could reinforce what we were learning was to talk about it outside of school and it was also to seek to identify in the outside world examples of what we were learning in school. I waited for her to respond, but all she could manage was a grunt. I knew I had totally lost her interest with that statement and her grunt confirmed it for me. *She's upset but why stop now?* I thought. I continued with my arrogance, "I like you a lot, Sandra, and I am trying my best to get you to my intellectual level. You can't expect me to come down to yours." Still she said nothing. "Sandra, are you still there?" I knew I had hurt her feelings and I was beginning to feel guilty about my cruel, arrogant statement. "I have to go," she said. "I'll see you in school tomorrow." And she hung up. Somehow, I knew it was over between us and I began to wonder what I would say when I saw her in class.

In English class the next day, we ignored each other and both seemed to be cool with that. When the bell rang, sounding the end of the period, I lingered in my seat and she rushed out, not even looking back as she had done before we hooked up. It was over and I think we were both relieved.

(11)

In the June of 1960, I was concluding my junior year at Central. The civil rights and black Muslim movements had begun to pick up momentum. Not a day would pass without a major story about a sit-in, boycott or other activity related to Negroes' pursuit of civil rights. Muslims were selling *Muhammad Speaks* on every street corner and telling us about the white devil and admonishing us to stop eating the poisonous swine. Internationally, African nations had begun to gain their independence and my mother and father remarked often about how good a thing it was that Negroes here and black people in Africa were getting things together. This era was also around the time I started thinking of myself as a Negro and stopped being colored. In spite of the Muslims' references to the black man, I had a hard time referring to myself as black. The word "black" was frequently followed by the word "nigger" thanks to the Italian boys in my neighborhood and at Webster Junior High. In college psychology classes I was to learn that this connection is what is known as word association. Evidence of this phenomenon is that I had no trouble recognizing continental Africans as black.

Jack Kennedy was running for president against Richard Nixon and there was lots of talk among the adults in my world and in the *Newark Star-Ledger* and *The New York Times*, which I subscribed to at school (mostly to admire the men's clothing and automobile ads), about whether America would elect an Irish Catholic president. I didn't even know he was Irish. How could one tell? And why should his religion matter? Were Italians Irish Catholic? Was there such thing as Italian Catholic? My mother said the criticisms had something to do with the Pope possibly influencing him. Who were the Americans who would not vote for him for these reasons? Certainly no one I knew. These concurrent events — the Muslims, Kennedy's ethnicity issues — forced me to engage in a lot of introspection about my own identity. Midway through my junior year, I did not think I would graduate from Central because we had moved from the North Ward to 52 Camp Street in the East Ward, about one block east of Lincoln Park and around the corner from the Essex House Hotel and the federal building. My mother had found an apartment on the second floor of a three-family house. I don't recall there even being any discussion about moving. I knew my parents had been looking, but I didn't know how serious it was. Then one day, my mother announced that we were moving to an apartment that had steam heat! The rent was $90 a month (we were paying $ 70 on Clay Street) and it was in a three-family house — not a tenement. My mother was going to buy twin beds for Melvin and me and we would have our own room to share.

I don't know what possessed me to do so, but I reported to the school officials that we were moving out of district and asked if I would have to transfer. (No, I do know. My mother told me to do it. "It's the right thing to do.") Dr. Rectenwald, the vice principal, told me, "We never want our good students to leave us prematurely, David. We will be proud to have you as an alumnus of Central. If you were a troublemaker, we would show you the door. But clearly, this is not the case." I was so relieved. A transfer would have meant I could not run track any longer because of the one-year-sit-out rule I had to abide by when I left Tech for Central. It would also have meant I would have to start all over again in the popularity game and in a new school, it would have been impossible for me to reach the level of popularity I had reached at Central. At this point, I wanted to run for president of the senior class.

I was already vice president of the student council, president of the English and Spanish honor societies; a member of the math club and destined to become president of the National Honor Society as well. I just had too much momentum going to change horses now.

When I told my Clay Street neighborhood friends we were moving, I was accused of thinking I was "too good for Clay Street." I had found a new group of friends at Central, so these remarks, intended to hurt, did not affect me the way they might have. All I had in common with them now was Clay Street, which wasn't even the same as it was even five years earlier when some of the old-timers had begun to move, only to be replaced by people with vastly different values.

We moved to the apartment at 52 Camp Street in downtown Newark. Our landlady, a widow named Mrs. Byrd, lived on the first floor. The apartment had three bedrooms; as my mother promised, Melvin and I shared one that was furnished with the Goodwill-bought twin beds and a chest of drawers. James, who had graduated from Bloomfield College in May and was to be married in December to his childhood sweetheart, Judith Roberts, had his own bedroom. We also had hot water all of the time and radiator-generated heat; we had truly moved up!

It was a quiet residential area whose residents were about one-third Puerto Rican. With the exception of Miss Muller, a pleasant, elderly white woman who lived in a house directly across from us, the rest were Negroes. Miss Muller had a house full of cats and apparently rarely emptied the litter boxes; the house had an absolutely debilitating stench. Standing in her doorway, no matter how briefly, while she held open the door, would leave one nauseated. Entering the house was out of the question. On the occasions she needed someone to run an errand, we had to draw straws to see who the victim would be.

Two houses west, there lived a Negro man who was married to a white or very light black woman, (no one was really sure). They owned a royal blue convertible Cadillac Eldorado with wide white-wall tires and were, among us boys, the envy of the neighborhood. Not being able to conceive of Negroes being able to afford a new Caddy, my father speculated (or maybe he knew): They must be in the numbers business.

Even though, by this time, I had had three years of Spanish (I took one year in summer school), I had not used it outside of school. Living on Camp Street, I could now change that. There was a bodega around the corner from our house that carried Goya products (I had never heard of the company before). And I would do my best to converse in Spanish with the store employees who showed their appreciation by patiently encouraging me as I grappled for the right words. I would also listen to the Spanish-speaking radio station out of New York and read the billboards advertising Schaefer Beer. "*La cervesa, me gusto mucho,*" read the billboards, from which beamed the face of a man the advertising people thought looked Latino enough.

During the five years I lived on Camp Street, I never experienced nor was I aware of any tension between Negroes and Puerto Ricans. After my experiences in Little Italy, I sort of expected that there would be a Puerto Rican parallel. Gladly, I was wrong. Had there been conflict, it certainly would not have been based on skin color, because there was as much range in hue among them as there was among Negroes. Our different styles of dress were about the only distinguishing physical characteristics between us. Puerto Ricans tended to wear clothes like those they wore in Puerto Rico — multicolored, short-sleeved shirts and brightly colored pants. During the colder months, they wore light jackets or none at all. Noting this fact and revealing her ignorance about geography at the same time, my mother used some upside-down logic to conclude that, "Puerto Rico must have a cold climate." It didn't dawn on me until years later that they just might not have had the money to buy coats.

My first summer on Camp Street, 1960, was the most memorable of my high school days. Ironically, I spent it in Portsmouth.

(12)

A company formed by two white men who were brothers-in-law, awarded my Uncle C. C., a successful and well-known builder, a contract to build some cheap houses for low-income Negroes. Uncle C. C. invited me down to Portsmouth, Virginia, to work for him as a carpenter's helper. I was excited about the opportunity because it meant I could earn some money and at the same time visit my other uncles and cousins. The arrangement was for me to stay at Uncle Hugo's on Green Street and C. C. would pick me up at 7:15 a.m. to take me to the work site. I was the only teenager on the site and I met some very interesting people who were to become my co-workers for the remainder of the summer. Up to this point, my contact with people on my visits to Portsmouth with my mother were limited to my relatives. My uncles and their wives were middle class, college-educated people who lived in neighborhoods of single-family homes that sat neatly on immaculately trimmed lawns. Uncle Oliver was a musician and composer; Uncle James was a Baptist minister and Uncle "if it's-a boy-name-him" Hugo was a dentist who in the 70s became Chesapeake's vice mayor. For the most part, they represented my models of the Southern colored man —

educated, independent, and successful. But the construction crew who were to be my co-workers contradicted that image.

Not counting me, there were a total of twelve crewmen, two of whom were white — the kind of white person I came to know later as "white trash" — a term, Uncle C. C. told me middle-class white folks had bestowed upon them. Even though the Southern accents of the men were challenging enough for me to understand, by their contexts, I could figure out the meaning of some of their idiomatic expressions. One example was when I was asked by one of the crew if he could borrow my hammer; when I said as soon as I was finished, he could, he said "just chuck it ch'heah when you readah." The hardest thing for me to adjust to was their use of language, in particular their grammar, syntax and use of verb tenses. It appeared to be completely outside of all the rules I had learned. "I be done went upside yo' head." I tried to imagine diagramming such a sentence. By summer's end, I had learned a good many of the idioms which were to serve me well during the year I later spent in Dover, Delaware.

A gifted carpenter and a veteran of WW II, Uncle C. C. was a tall, dark, joyful, practical, unpretentious man who hated his experience in the Army. It was he who first told me the story of the way Negro soldiers were treated relative to the German prisoners of war. He drove a blue Ford pickup truck that had removable wooden sides. When Melvin and I were younger, we enjoyed riding in the truck's bed, wind sucking our breaths away and blowing our eyes closed. He would refer to us as if we were a unit — HugoandMelvin.

But that was some years earlier. Now I was old enough to work for him and, not wanting any special attention, I was eager to prove myself. Uncle C. C. was very effective at treating me no differently than the other crew members. Somehow, I sensed they were watching my every move to see if C. C. would call me out if I made a mistake. I made my share and when he was aware of them, he would call them to my attention, punctuating the criticism with the term, "city boy."

On my first day at the site, when he announced it was lunch time, I asked where I could wash my hands. He paused for a moment and then, looking less than contemplative, casually responded, through a suppressed chuckle, "Anywhere you can." I was about to respond by asking where he washed his hands, but in the time, it took me to formulate the question, I realized the meaning of his response and caught myself.

On weekends, I spent time with Uncle Hugo and his family at their beach house in Virginia Beach, which they modestly named "Sea Hut." It was a house like none I had ever been in before, which admittedly, was not saying much. Since I had never been in a beach house, I had nothing to compare it to except the houses of his brothers and his parents; and with its four bedrooms, kitchen, dining room, family room and full basement, it was certainly bigger than any of theirs. I looked forward to the weekends because my welcoming cousins treated me like royalty, especially Paula, the oldest, and Patrice. Hugo Junior was pretty much indifferent and was content to watch his sisters indulge me. It seemed that all I needed to do was wish aloud for something — usually something to eat or drink — and one of them would ask me how much I wanted. When we sat on the couch to watch television, the girls sat on either side of me and smothered me with affection. They would not know until decades later what a boost to my self-esteem they gave me that summer and it was to be the only summer after which I did not look forward to returning to Newark.

Their attention and compassion would have the same effect on me when I visited Uncle Hugo and Aunt Helen some fourteen years later, following the breakup of my first marriage and my abrupt departure from my beloved city.

But return to Newark I did, only to realize that Camp Street placed me so far away from Central that walking to school was not an option as it had been when I lived on Clay Street. I had to take the number 13 bus to High Street and Clinton Avenue where I transferred to the number 46 High — a bus that, some Newarkers joked, ran every three hours — to school. Making the trek to the bus stop one morning, I noticed a handwritten sign on the porch of an apartment building on Camp just a few yards east of Broad Street. It read "Partment for rent." I sighed and shook my head in disbelief.

Now that I was a senior, I had things to do: take the SAT, have a good track year so I could nail down a scholarship, and have a good academic year so I would be maximally prepared for college. I had set some other goals too. I wanted to be president of the senior class read the billboards, from which beamed the face of a man the advertising people thought looked Latino enough. And graduate in the top ten. I mistakenly thought it would be the easiest year of all but Mr. Hasler's chemistry, Mr. Strasburg's solid and analytic geometry and calculus, and Mr. Franzblau's college prep English classes caused me, by the fourth week of school, to alter my thinking.

(13)

There were only thirteen students in Mr. Strasburg's class and we were all boys. I had taken what today would be called a very sexist attitude toward the only girl remaining in my trig class the previous year. Margo was an attractive, deep-brown-skinned, bohemian-dressing girl. She looked especially good when she wore one of her long, button-up sweaters that hit two or three inches above her knees. My favorite sweater was the burnt orange one that she wore with a dark brown, plaid, pleated skirt that fell just above her knee; so from behind, I could see an inch or two of skirt and her shapely figure.

Though Margo was in the college prep program, she had not yet academically distinguished herself, meaning she did not make the honor roll every marking period. She struggled with trig; so much so I once tried to intimidate her by predicting that trig would be her last stop in the math department. I added that she should skip solid (our abbreviation for solid geometry) if she knew what was good for her. She sat in the seat immediately in from of me, which gave me the opportunity to tease her about the trouble she was having, which I readily did. In spite of this surface antagonism, I think deep down inside, the other college prep boys and I respected and liked her because she toughed it out with the boys, as it were, in chemistry, physics and math.

Though she and I never clicked very strongly romantically (like Sandra, she was a dry kisser), Margo and I went out a couple of times and often on those occasions engaged in very enjoyable intellectual sparring. She was more opinionated than I and I appreciated the intellectual challenge she presented.

Thirty years after we graduated, I saw Margo at our class reunion in Newark. To my surprise, she had become "Dr. Margo King, clinical psychologist," as her business card read. She had one child and was living in New York. I joked with her about our experience in trig class and was disappointed that she did not remember. I offered her a belated apology nonetheless.

Margo was also in my college prep English class, taught by Mr. Franzblau, who was feared by all, which gave him great amusement. For me at least, the fear was due in part because he was so demanding and I did not want to be embarrassed by not knowing the answer when called upon or by getting a poor grade on a paper I did not take seriously or an exam for which I had not studied.

Many students at Central would use the plural form of a verb with a singular subject or omit the "is" form of the verb to be. ("Do he know what he talking about?" He talking too fast.) On one occasion, I was in the process of asking a question and my answer started with "do." Before I could get the rest of the sentence out of my mouth, frowning, Franzblau shouted "do???" in apparent anticipation of a singular subject following. I calmly and confidently said, "if you wait a minute, you'll hear a plural subject not far behind my plural verb." He couldn't hold back his laughter and neither could the class. It was rare that anyone could outwit him and for a minute I was "famous" for having "gotten" Mr. Franzblau.

Another speech characteristic of some Central students was the adoption of an aspect of Southern speech by omitting the letter *r* when it appeared after an *o* so that "whore" and "before" became "ho" and "befo'." I don't think it was a case of their not knowing how to pronounce the word — they would pronounce it while reading — as much as it was their way of not conforming, of being hip. We worked from a vocabulary book called *Word Wealth* and during a drill, ran across the word "potion." Even though the definition of the word was right there before our eyes, Franzblau found it necessary to point out to us that it was not "portion." So we would not miss the point, he held on to the "r" just a little longer than he normally would have. I think Franzblau believed that those of us in his class who spoke like that may not have been hearing ourselves and this citing this word was his chance to call it to our attention without singling out anyone in particular.

Not that he was above embarrassing anybody, -- he had no problem with that -- but if you did your job by coming to class prepared, you had no fear of embarrassment. He would conduct what amounted to a drill — we called it "the Gatling gun" — when he called upon someone who took longer to answer the question than Franzblau thought he should. The student would be abruptly passed over and the person sitting directly behind him would be quickly called upon next. Franzblau would continue in this fashion, responding to each failed attempt with a dismissive remark ("Don't give me that gobbledygook. We don't tolerate fuzzy thinking in my class. Don't waste my time, boy. Next.") until someone correctly answered the question.

Meanwhile, you could hear the sound of flipping pages of the books of the unprepared ones as they searched for the answer, hoping to find it before it was their turn. Franzblau would hear them too and sometimes remark, "anybody who doesn't know the answer by now can't turn the pages fast enough." Of course, the first few people called upon were at a disadvantage because if they didn't know the answer, well, there was really no time to look it up.

Like Mr. Tumin in algebra, Mr. Franzblau had high expectations for his students and detested academic mediocrity and, even more, those who settled for it. Following an assembly program during which we heard campaign speeches from students running for various offices of the senior class, he told us that he had been impressed with the quality and range of candidates: "They were a good bunch."

When I was giving a speech as a candidate for president of the senior class, I used as a prop at the end of the speech a bull's eye target, I had made just for the event. I had printed my name in the bull's eye and printed the words "my opponents" in the outer circles. At the end of my speech, I said, "If you are a marksman, you will shoot for and hit the bull's eye on election day." The next day, Franzblau recalled to us the times when the candidates were some of those "dese, dose, dem guys." Since I was one of the current group of candidates, I was pleased to hear, even by innuendo, that I had met his standards even outside of the class.

In 1967, two years after I'd gotten my degree in mathematics from Rutgers and entered the world of work, I returned to Central to visit only one teacher, Mr. Franzblau. Somehow, he did not seem so intimidating now. I was taller than he and I was six years older than I was when I last saw him, but he was still twisting his neck in customary fashion. He introduced me to the class and told them, accurately, where I used to sit. He asked me if I wanted to say anything to the class. I said only, "If you think Mr. Franzblau is tough, wait until you get to college."

(14)

During the first semester, I took a part-time job at a newspaper distributorship around the corner from my house. It was a small shop that had a Jewish readership in New Jersey and all of the boroughs of New York City. Since I had no experience, the owner, a short and short-tempered man in his early sixties, offered me the job for $.75 an hour, $ .25 below minimum wage. He said he shouldn't even hire me since I had no experience, but, if I worked out, he would give me a raise after 30 days. Since I was not running cross country that year, I worked on Saturdays from 8:30 a.m. to 3:30 p.m. My job was to operate a machine that pasted mailing labels on the papers as they made their way down the conveyor belt. I was supposed to stack the papers in a certain order as they came off the belt. In order for me to get the stacking right, I had to operate the belt at a speed a bit slower than the boss wanted. He would come to watch me every now and then and give me pointers on how I could work faster. As he left the room, he would matter-of-factly increase the speed of the belt, never even bothering to ask why I had slowed it down in the first place.

One particular Saturday in late October, he was more impatient than usual when he became displeased with my work and fired me. He led me over to Loretta, a plain-looking, brown-skinned woman about 35 or 36; who among other things, managed payroll. He directed her to pay me for the rest of the day and let me go. As she gave me the check, she said empathetically, "Make sure you keep your promise to yourself to go to college. Don't let this discourage you." I took the check and hopped a bus to Newark schools stadium to see a football game between Central and Ferris High, of Jersey City.

When I entered the stadium, I searched for and soon found some of my friends who were surprised to see me. Maurice said, "I thought you were working, man." "I was until I got fired." "Fired, what the fuck for?" "Just some bullshit, man. I really don't feel like talking about it." It was at that point that I noticed the score — 6 to 6 and we had the ball. I stopped talking to watch the action on the field, a run to the left that resulted in a touchdown; we even made the point after to make the score 13 to 6. My old friend from Clay Street, Larry, who played guard and from whom I had drifted, was voted the game's most valuable player. It was the only football game we won during my entire three years at Central and I had to get fired to witness it.

(15)

Because I had aspirations to attend college, I felt an affinity for Central's neighbor, NCE, and I would observe the overwhelmingly white male students walking back and forth to class. To a person, they all carried briefcases and slide rules. They didn't dress the way I expected college students would dress, but, I reasoned, it was because they were white and didn't know any better.

It wasn't long before many of Central's senior boys began carrying briefcases, causing Miss "The Redhead" Sullivan, the one Mr. Kruger went running to during the talent show, to remark cynically to one of her classes that, "Those boys don't have anything but comic books and candy bars in those cheap briefcases." When word got back to me, my reaction was to revive an old rumor about her and Mr. Franzblau. "Man, she's just still upset because Mr. Franzblau left her at the altar. And she's holding that against all men." I think I even called her a relic from the Victorian age.

I never took a course from Miss Sullivan, but I would often see her on hall duty as I passed to my history class with Mr. Cuozzo, who taught while sitting down behind his desk. He had very large eyes which he was constantly rubbing while he yawned. He never assigned any written homework and had not a single essay question on our exams. Instead, he opted for multiple choice and true/false tests. Once, three days in a row, instead of teaching, he instructed us to read a certain chapter while he studied for an exam for a course he was taking. He told us to read carefully because he would quiz us afterwards. He even justified his decision by informing us that he was "doing this for you." Smart-mouthed, I called to his attention that we would be graduating in a few months, so we wouldn't benefit from whatever he was learning. He didn't appreciate the remark and said as much. Sitting just to my right was Larry Hazzard, a well-known amateur boxer, who everyone thought would make it big as a pro. He was a Golden Gloves champion in his weight class and looked forward to turning pro. He ultimately became Boxing Commissioner for the state of New Jersey, replacing Jersey Joe Walcott after he died. I asked him how he felt about Cuozzo cutting us short. On our education, he merely hunched his shoulders.

Unlike my feelings about Mr. Couzzo, I longed to be in Mr. Thomas' class again. I had had him for history in my junior year and found him to be a dynamic teacher who dramatized his lessons. The one unit I recall most vividly was on Toussaint L'ouverture, the Haitian hero who led a guerrilla war against Napoleon to frustrate France's efforts to colonize Haiti. All I had read or heard about L'ouverture until then was negative. It had never occurred to me that he had been defending his own country against foreign invaders. Mr. Thomas made this fact abundantly clear as he exalted in his description of how Toussaint had "put a hurt so bad on the great Napoleon he could hardly wait to get back to France." It was the first time I had heard of a black man being victorious over a white man anywhere except in the boxing ring.

(16)

I was elected president of the senior class; Arlene Francis, a quiet, soft-voiced, brown-skinned girl with an engaging smile was elected vice president; Annette Tuosto and Delia Tucker, two of the most pleasant people I had ever known, were treasurer and secretary, respectively. We promptly went about forming committees — chief of which were the yearbook and the prom committees — to take care of the preparation and planning for graduation and all of the attendant activities. The committee chairs and I met with the class advisors from time to time to make sure we stayed on track. I was so busy with schoolwork, track, honor society meetings and my duties as class president, before I knew it, March was on me and at that late date, I still had no idea how I was going to pay for college. I had selected three schools to apply to, but I had difficulty writing the letter to request an application and catalog. I had learned how to write a business letter, but the business format seemed inappropriate. So, I called James to seek his assistance and he came by one day after school to help me. "What's the matter? Don't you know how to write a letter?" were the first words out of his mouth. "First of all, you don't send a letter. You send a postcard to the director of admissions and just say:

Dear sir or madam:

Would you please send me an application for admission and catalog for the 1961-1962 academic year?

Thank you.

Sincerely,

I sent this postcard to Rutgers and Pennsylvania State universities and Delaware State College, a school I had never heard of and do not, to this day, know how I came to apply there. Perhaps I would be fortunate enough to get a track scholarship -- a hope that turned out to be empty.

One of the carrots our track coach held out for us as an incentive to join and remain on the track team was the promise of track scholarships. It was this promise that lulled me into thinking that money for college would not be an issue, but during the indoor track season of my senior year, a raw reality set in for me. The only medals I had won were as a member of the mile relay team — a team on which I was either the slowest or next-slowest runner. My best outdoor time was only 50.8 seconds in a world where the top runners were consistently breaking 50. Earl Rogers, state champion every year I ran and our anchor runner, could coast the last 100 yards and still post a 49.5, and often did in his heats, so he could preserve himself for the finals.

Inspired by Villanova's Frank Budd, I wanted to go to Villanova or Penn State. I had mistakenly believed that Penn State was the University of Pennsylvania, home of the Penn Relays. I had been to the Penn Relays twice and seen the times the national competition was running and I began to doubt my chances of any school offering me a scholarship. *Wouldn't I have to compete with the same boys in college?* I thought. When I approached Coach Thomas with my concerns just the month before the Penn Relays, that neither Villanova nor any other college had contacted me, he advised me to write to Jumbo Elliott, 'Nova's track coach, and tell him of my desire to run for him. I followed his advice, but after hearing nothing for three weeks, I went to Coach Thomas again (yes, the history teacher). By this time, I was really stressed out. His advice to me was to just pack my bags and show up in September. "There is no way they would send you home." This advice left me feeling flushed and hurt. After three years of filling my head with false hope of a track scholarship, he was abandoning me! I could have accepted his telling me that he had assumed I would have significantly improved my time by my senior year and that was what he was basing his promise on. But this treatment? It was grossly unfair and harsh. My participation on the track team had helped his career, but not my chances for a free education.

Five months later I would witness three would-be freshmen basketball players from the Jersey state champion Trenton High being sent home by Delaware State College after only two weeks on campus.

I inquired but never found out why they left. I wondered what counsel their high school coach had given them.

I knew now that I was completely on my own. By mid-May, I had heard from all three colleges to which I had applied. Rutgers waitlisted me and Penn State and Delaware State (for Negroes) accepted me. Close to home, Rutgers was my first choice, but I did not want to run the risk of declining the others and have Rutgers come up short; so after discussing the situation with my mother, I decided to go Delaware State and if my grades were good enough, transfer to Rutgers to begin my sophomore year.

But first I had to be sure Rutgers would honor the courses I planned to take at DSC. I went down to the admissions office on Washington Street, DSC catalog in hand, and asked to see someone from admissions. After a short wait, I was greeted by a pleasant, olive-colored Italian woman with a captivating smile, who introduced herself and invited me into a small conference room. I showed her the first-year curriculum for math majors and asked which of the courses I could get credit for. She said if the school is accredited (new word for me), then all of them as long as I get a grade of C or better. I thought to myself, *I have no intentions of getting a C in anything.* Then she noticed a one-credit course called freshman orientation and said I would not get credit for that one. "You can't expect us to give you credit for their orientation." I agreed, thanked her and split.

On the way home, I stopped at the small record shop just north of S. Klein's and bought Miles' *Sketches of Spain* and *Saturday Night at the Black Hawk* as a reward for what I had accomplished. I was taking control of my own life. I went home quite pleased with myself. For the moment I did not think about how we would raise the money. Uncle Hugo was to intervene at another critical time in my life to help fix that.

My mother called him, and he advised her to "get him there and he will do the rest." I don't know all the maneuvering my mother had to do raise the money; I do know she either borrowed against or cashed in at least one insurance policy because I overheard her discussing the options with Uncle Hugo during a telephone conversation. (We had finally gotten a telephone by then.) I could tell from her end of the conversation; he had told her to raise what money she could, and he would make up the difference.

I notified DSC of my plans to attend in the fall and they sent me some documents that I had to complete and return by the stated deadline or they would assume I had changed my mind. Included among the documents was an application for a student loan. Unfortunately, the application required the signature of a working parent and at the time my mother, while employed, was a domestic and through some arrangement with her West Orange employer, she was off the books, so to speak. And my father refused to sign; I do not recall the reason. Crestfallen, I felt my chances of going to college begin to fade, despite Uncle Hugo's commitment. Not discouraged, I returned the other documents to DSC anyway.

I worried for the next month and then I got the surprise of my life when at senior awards day, I was honored with several awards and the Anna Mae Allen scholarship for $150. My mother was in the audience and hugged me afterwards, telling me I had no cause to worry now because this prize "means you are going to be able to go to college," but she would have to talk to Uncle Hugo to be absolutely certain. The tuition and room and board came to $850 for the full year, so the $150, almost 18%, was a significant amount of money. Then I got another surprise, an offer of a summer job at a Boy Scout camp in upstate New York.

Before I left for camp, someone called my mother and told her to pick up a copy of the Afro-American newspaper. My mother sent me to the corner store to get it, not telling me why. When I returned with it, she told me to turn to a certain page. Once I found the page, she looked over my shoulder and saying, "there it is," pointed to an article with the headline, "Central Grad to Attend Del. State." I eagerly read the article, which detailed my academic success at Central, noting that I had "compiled an enviable record," graduated in the top ten of my class and was the recipient of the Bamberger Medal for Excellence and the Anna Mae Allen scholarship, as well as being a member of the track team and various honor societies. I must have read the article "fifty-leven" times. It was the first time an article about me had appeared in the newspaper for anything other than sports. I never thought about how the Afro found out. I just figured it was the job of newspapers to know things.

Meanwhile, I learned that Larry, from my Clay Street days, had turned down a football scholarship. He told me he was not going to accept it because he had not taken his schoolwork seriously enough to handle college work. Two of Central's top ten, Patton, from my homeroom, and Leslie, who was the pianist for the group that played Benny Golson's "Blues March" at the student council talent show, had both declined full academic scholarships to a college in North Carolina because they did "not want to attend a Negro college." I was puzzled. *Was no education better than one obtained from a Negro school? Where had they gotten this notion?*

I ran into Patton ten years later on one of my campaign stops. He told me he was a bus driver and that Leslie, after working in the fall, enrolled at Long Island University in the spring semester, but split when his money ran out.

I was in touch with Leslie briefly by telephone during our 30-year class reunion. One of the organizers of the reunion had previously arranged to place a telephone call to him. He was in Los Angeles and in business for himself. Several of us took turns talking to him but no one thought to ask him if he had ever returned to college or what business he was in.

As I write this sentence, I have not heard from or anything about him since that phone call.

Chapter 9

From camp to college

(1)

Through a distant cousin, Bill Berkette, who lived in Jamaica, Queens, I was able to get a job - the one that I mentioned earlier -washing dishes at a Boy Scout camp in Brant Lake, New York. The need for kitchen help was so dire that he called me back and asked if I had any friends who might be interested. I was able to recruit Melvin and two Centralite friends: Phillip Parker, a rising senior, fellow track man, and one of my best friends; and Wiley Boulding, a brilliant 880 man (now 800 meters) who like me, was in the class of '61, but was on his way to Western Michigan University on a track scholarship.

Before I left for camp, I made an appointment at the Rutgers admissions office on Washington Street to explain I would be out of state for the summer and to mail all communications to me at the camp.

I decided I was going to major in mathematics only because I liked it and had done well in math. Moreover, James had been a math major who was then teaching at Newark's West Kinney Junior High School. I had no idea what I wanted to do for a living, but I knew I wanted it to involve math.

My former classmates and soon-to-be co-workers and I had previously arranged to meet my brother Melvin and me at the Greyhound bus station on Market Street in downtown Newark on the first Sunday after school was out. It would be an eight-hour ride to the camp. Except for

Melvin, we were all serious students and had brought along books to read on the long trip and over the summer. When we broke from our reading, we quietly sang R&B songs, trying not to disturb the other passengers. After the second song, one of the passengers asked us if we would mind singing a little louder. "You boys have real talent," he said. By the time we got to Newburgh, NY, we were the only ones remaining on the bus.

During the trip, I remember us stopping at a rest stop in Chestertown, NY. The driver had a deep Southern accent and when he announced the name of the town, it came out a drawling "chase-tah-towun." When we entered the well-kept men's room, the first thing we looked for was the urinals. There weren't any. Instead, there was a basin-like, granite structure that stood about three feet high, maybe five feet in diameter and about 18 inches deep. To flush it, you had to step on a rubber ring at the base of the structure that encircled it like a ring of Saturn. You were supposed to stand at this thing and relieve yourself with your penis in plain view of everyone trying to do the same thing. I wondered who in hell had designed such a device. What was the objective, to save money or water at the expense of travelers' modesty? We boys took our positions and did our business. But there was a white man who had also taken his place so that he was directly across from us; however, he was taking forever to get anything to come out. We watched him with great curiosity and amusement until, in frustration, he finally gave up. We figured he was embarrassed at the prospect of urinating in front of us and just could not relax. Given the myth about the size of the black male's penis, he was probably feeling self-conscious over the sight of four of them pissing opposite him.

After, we returned to the bus, we exchanged views about why he was unable to pee. Somebody's concluding remark was, "the dumb sucker should have gone into a stall if he was that nervous. And did you see how small his johnson was? That's what the problem was. He was ashamed that all of us had dicks twice the size of his." Even though that statement about relative penis size was exaggerated, no one contested it.

(2)

One of the camp administrators planned to meet us at the bus stop for the five-mile ride to the camp. We waited for a station attendant to unload our luggage. When I saw my suitcase, it had a rope tied around it and some of my clothes were exposed. *Oh, damn, these cats busted my suitcase. I need that suitcase for college. I don't have any money for another suitcase. I need it for school,* I thought. "You need to sue them, Dave," Wiley said. "Yeah and how do you do that, especially up here in these boondocks? If I don't even have money for a new suitcase, how am I going to get it for lawyer?"

After about fifteen minutes, a representative from the camp showed up in a van. He was a man in his early fifties wearing a Boy Scout uniform and sporting a crew cut, I believe. He welcomed us and immediately began to help with loading the luggage into the van. He asked us about our trip and where we were from. We answered his questions and I took that opportunity to tell him about my suitcase. "Those clumsy bastards; don't worry, we'll take care of it after we get to camp." He sounded so confident. *Was he just blowing smoke?* I wondered.

We approached a sign that read "Brant Lake Boy Scout Camp (I researched this and learned that it is now called Curtis I. Reed Scout Reservation) - one mile". We drove the mile and turned the van off the main road and made our way up the two-mile road to the camp. The driver stopped at our cabin and told me he would take me to the director's office once I got myself settled. "Okay, but won't I need the suitcase?" I asked. "I don't think so, but if we do, we can always come back and get it," he replied.

We drove the short distance to the director's office where I was introduced and given the opportunity to explain what had happened. "We'll just have to get busy and get them to replace your suitcase. Come over to my desk, we'll type the letter now." He called the Greyhound station and asked to whom and where he should send the letter. He hung up the phone and, on camp letterhead, began to embellish what I had told him. He explained that I would be up there for the summer and would be leaving right afterwards to go to college. Further, that it was imperative that the Greyhound corporation send a check at once to replace the suitcase. He said I had paid $50 for the Samsonite (it was not a Samsonite product and I had picked it up at the Goodwill for $5) suitcase just before I came to camp and that I did not have the receipt since I bought it at home. Unfortunately, he wrote, I could not get the receipt from home because I had not saved it. Then he asked rhetorically what had he done with his receipts when he was 16 (I was 17; but I guess he did not mind a little embellishment.). And finally, he wrote that I would be at the camp only until August 15 and therefore I would need a suitcase to get home and would need a check in enough time to buy another. He asked them to send the check to the camp's address and to his attention, made payable to Mr. David H. Barrett. He let me read the letter before he signed it.

I was impressed with the director's savvy, confidence, tendency to stretch the truth, and the sheer force of the letter's tone. He seemed to know they would pay. It was just a matter of when and how much. I thought, *so this is how these white people do things.*

Three weeks later, a check for $60, payable to me, arrived. That weekend, I cashed the check at the camp store, caught a ride into town and bought a new suitcase for $30. I got new suitcase and a tidy profit of $25. Anybody could understand that math!

(3)

Our Central crew was to be joined at Brant Lake Camp by three boys from New York City. It turned out that two of them had run, respectfully, for DeWitt Clinton and Bishop Cardinal Hayes, high schools against which we had competed at the Penn and Randall's Island relays. Two days after we arrived, my cousin informed me that one of the boys from New York had gotten another job and would not be coming. He asked if I knew of someone else who might want to work at the camp. I thought immediately of Gerald Parker, another rising senior (not related to Phillip) and best friend of mine. Gerald had the best work ethic of any of my friends and the only reason I did not recruit him in the first round was that he had not been on the track team as Wiley and Phil had. There was just a certain loyalty and camaraderie we track cats had developed for each other that made our friendships a little tighter. During my early teen years, my mother had told me when I was beginning to attach myself to some characters of whom she did not approve, "people will judge you by the company you keep." I would have been happy to be judged at any time by this current company.

Gerald arrived on the bus two days later. I went with the driver to meet him and we talked all the way back to camp. He was relegated to the bed in the least desirable location, right by the door so he was right in the line of traffic to and from the cabin. Gerald was a tall, dark-complexioned, handsome boy, but in those days of color consciousness among Negroes and when we had begun to refer to ourselves as colored, he was very sensitive about his dark skin. He was very much the romantic though. He told me of the time he lost his virginity, concluding the story with, "we took a shower and afterwards, shared a cigarette." I asked why he had done that. He responded, "that's how they do it in the movies."

Even though I had been at the camp only a few days, I had gotten a good assessment of the various personalities of the men on the work crew. A pot washer named Joe had retired from the Albany School System, where he had been a kitchen worker. He was 72 years old, somewhat cynical and always direct with criticism and compliments. It didn't seem to matter whether he had known you for a year or a minute. This tendency became evident when Gerald and I entered the cabin. Joe was sitting on what was to become Gerald's bed. The other men who had been upstairs came down to meet Gerald, and the other boys who had been napping woke up when we came in. Joe stood up to meet us and looked quizzically at Gerald as I introduced them. As Joe reached for Gerald's outstretched hand, he exclaimed, "Finally, I get to meet a nigger blacker than I am." A veil of uneasy silence engulfed the room following this remark and then everyone except Gerald, who was speechless, broke out laughing. Gerald appeared uneasy; he continued to hold Joe's hand though he was no longer shaking it. He looked at me as if to say "Aren't you going to say something to this man?" Bill, my cousin and the who made these job opportunities possible and who as chef, ran the kitchen and would be our boss, had not yet made it all the way downstairs; but apparently had heard the remark. He entered the room and, in an effort, to balance the scales said, "You might live a thousand years, Joe, but you will never meet anybody as dumb as you." More uncontrollable, boisterous laughter followed. This brought a tentative smile to Gerald's face. Joe had no retort; Bill's remark seemed to settle the matter.

Brant Lake was a camp that drew its campers and counselors from places such as Scarsdale, New York, and the Hamptons. The counselors were college students and former Scouts themselves, attending schools such as Bates College and Dartmouth. I was astonished at how confident and secure they appeared to be. It was as if the world was at their beck and call. For example, all of the counselors had cars and had had them since they were in high school. A few got new cars as high school graduation presents. For these boys, owning cars bought by their parents was just no big deal. When I expressed amazement after one of the counselors told me, matter-of-factly, that his parents had gotten him a new Corvette because he had gotten accepted to Harvard, he seemed a little embarrassed and tried to minimize it by saying lots of other kids had gotten cars when they got accepted to the their first-choice schools. I knew of no one whose parents had given him a car for any reason. Like me, most of my friends' parents didn't even have cars themselves! I didn't even have a driver's license and did not obtain one until my senior year in college. I did not get a car until I graduated and started working.

Some of the counselors had already mapped out their career plans. They were going to law school, medical school, business school (I had not known there was any such thing), going to work in the family business after college. "My dad wants me to join him at his firm." They would talk so confidently, as if there could be no obstacles to their goals. I never heard any conditions imposed, such as, "if I get a scholarship or loan." Or "if I get into law school." They just knew things would go their way, or more accurately, they came from families that would see to it that things did go their way.

The experience was to give me an up-close look at how kids and young men alike from wealthy families behaved and at the attitudes they held on a variety of subjects. They came from worlds that I had seen only in the movies and on television, unlike any of the worlds of white people I knew personally. I learned very quickly that we were strangers. In fact, I had more in common with the tormenting Italians of my old neighborhood and Webster Junior High than I had with these people, notwithstanding my embracing, among other middle-class values, the value of a college education.

(4)

One of the counselors, Mike Goldberg, a Dartmouth sophomore, befriended me and we spent a lot of time talking about civil rights issues. He had known only three Negroes in his life -- not counting his parents' housekeeper. His views about Negroes had been formed as a result of his interaction with them and what he had read in the newspapers. He had not read a single book by a Negro author — fiction or nonfiction — on any topic. So, it was pointless for me to frame my contribution to the discussion by referring to some points Du Bois had made in *Souls of Black Folk*. It was the only work of his I had read at that point, so I was not able to reference him beyond that. But then I didn't need to, since Mike was unfamiliar with Du Bois. He had heard the statement about the problem of the twentieth century being the color line, but did not know to whom it was attributed. I tried to embarrass him by pointing out that Du Bois was a graduate of an Ivy League school (Harvard) and that he is considered the first American sociologist. "What have they been teaching you at Dartmouth, anyway?"

Mike seemed to expect me to be an expert on Negroes in America. "Why do the majority of Negroes live in ghettos?" "Before I respond to that question, what is your source of information?" "What information?" "That the majority of Negroes live in ghettos?" "Oh, I don't know. I just assumed they do." "So, you want me to provide an answer to an assumption of yours? If I didn't believe you were serious, I'd laugh. Let me ask you a question. Why are the majority of Jewish men so short?" The expression on his face revealed that he was offended by the question. Before he could respond, I said, "Now you see why I would not respond to your question. I just made that up to demonstrate how ignorant your question sounded to me. I have never given a thought to the height of Jewish men."

In other discussions I made it clear that I didn't see why Negroes had to have special legislated rights already guaranteed under the Constitution to every American citizen. I laid out the argument that I supported boycotting businesses that discriminate based on race and more important, that I support Negroes forming an economic base so we wouldn't have to patronize white supremacists at all. He was taken aback by the term, white supremacists. I explained that racism and racial discrimination were but manifestations, the implementation, of the white supremacist ideology. "It's only if you truly believe you are superior to another human being that you can convince yourself that another human being is not even human at all, or at best sub-human. This was one of the justifications for slavery that the Christian church supported. Indeed, that is why they sent missionaries to Africa. They claimed they wanted to save the heathens so they would have a better life in heaven.

"When the white man came to Africa, he had the Bible and the Africans had the land. Now the Africans have the Bible and he has the land. And if that wasn't bad enough, he snatched some of Africa's sons and daughters and brought them here and made them property with the same status as a chair." Mike said, "but don't you think Africans are better off for the Western way of life white people introduced to them?" "You mean imposed on them, don't you? And you are talking about the same civilization that is responsible for WWI, II, and dropping the atom bomb on Japan. And is right now at the center of the conflict in the Congo. Give me one instance where an African country is better off because of Western civilization." "I don't know that much about Africa, so I don't feel comfortable answering that question." "Yet you would suggest that African countries are better off because of the West. You are guilty of expressing what my senior year English teacher called 'an uninformed opinion.' you would be right at home in some of the Negro barber shops I've been in." We both laughed at the idea of him sitting in such a barbershop.

We talked about girls, what Dartmouth was like, and how much I was looking forward to going to college. He spoke almost wistfully of a philosophy course he had taken, so much so that I made up my mind right then that I would take such a course too. I thought that these philosophers must have been people of leisure who had all of their needs met because how else would they have had time or disposition to contemplate their own existence, ponder determinism and free will and address other such abstract considerations?

(5)

During the first parents' weekend, Mike's parents came to visit. He had told me earlier that they were coming and he wanted me to meet them. At the time I thought, *why would he want them to meet me? I would never see them or him, for that matter, ever again.* I concluded that he wanted to show them he had added one more to the list of Negroes he now knew — and they could too.

Mike and I were sitting on the porch of the administration building when he pointed them out. They were driving a gray, 1960 Cadillac Deville sedan. I thought of Robey and the Bell Chords. Mike waved them to the parking area, and we strolled over to greet them. I was beginning to feel a bit uncomfortable but hid it under a Dunbar smile ("We wear the mask") as Mike made the introductions. His mother was an attractive slender woman, probably in her early forties. She had on what I thought was too much makeup and too much jewelry for a camp visit. His dad was stoic and stiff as he stood just behind his wife. "Mom, Dad, this is my friend, David. He's one of the Hobart engineers."

A company called Hobart manufactured the dishwashing equipment that we used. Thus, Phil and I were labeled Hobart engineers. Phil's job was to rinse, and otherwise, prepare the dishes for washing before I placed them in the rack that carried them on a conveyor belt through the washer. Gerald's job was to dry them. He did this by taking out the dishes once they had completed the rinse cycle. The law required the wash and the rinse temperatures to be 140 and 180 degrees Fahrenheit, respectfully; so the water quickly evaporated. And then he placed the dishes and utensils to rest in the cabinets and drawers until the next meal.

Mike's mother extended her limp hand to meet mine and as our hands met, she exclaimed, "Oh, you go to

Hobart?" Before I could get a chance to respond, Mike chimed in, "No, mom, he's the camp dishwasher. A manufacturer named Hobart makes the dishwashing equipment." Eager to let her know that dishwashing was not my chosen field, I quickly added, "I'm going to be a freshman at Delaware State in the fall." I had not expected she would have heard of the tiny school and would confuse it with the University of Delaware. She did and Mike corrected her as I had done for him during our first meeting. "Oh, I'm sorry. I misunderstood. Where's Delaware State?" I was growing anxious and wanted desperately to get away from her.

"Well, it was nice meeting you. I want to do some reading before lunch. Enjoy your visit." And I split.

(6)

All of the camp counselors and administrators were white, as were the campers. Like the Scouts, they all slept in tents. In stark contrast, the kitchen crew was entirely Negro except for one Puerto Rican, Deli. Four grown men, aged from 24 to 72, were the veterans of kitchen work. We slept in a large cabin that had a tin roof and on which a confused woodpecker pecked every morning at 6 a.m. All but one of the older men slept on the second level. The one exception was Richie, who was a cook at Pratt Institute (he pronounced it "Platt". He had a form of lisp that I had never heard before). I was comfortable with this arrangement because he was closer to our ages in maturity, even though he was 24. He was a muscular man who did 100 sit-ups and 100 push-ups every morning and kept us entertained with stories of his girlfriends and just general silliness.

His current girlfriend was named Virginia — he pronounced it "fah-jin-ya" — who had "big yellah legs" that he could not keep his eyes off. He would do anything she wanted as long as she would wrap her legs around him every once in a while. "If you care anything at all about her, you wouldn't put what happens between you and her in the street," I suggested. "Listen to chipmunk number one (he had named my brother and me the chipmunks because of our overbites)," Richie said. "He thinks he can give me advice about women." He was speaking to no one in particular. "Virginia is 500 miles away from here and nobody here knows her. So, there is no way anything I say can get back to her." "Richie, you never know who anybody knows. You know I have relatives in Brooklyn and Harlem. I could tell one of them and he might know Virginia. I've seen that kind of thing happen. I was at Jamesburg reformatory watching a baseball game between their team and the team of a friend of mine. It was a doubleheader and we had broken for lunch after the first game. One of the visitors, who had been sitting at my table, was boasting about a girl he had been with and it turned out she was the cousin of one of the inmates! The inmate called his cousin and told her. Can you dig that?" "I guess all I am saying is if you must tell us about your exploits, use a fictitious name or, better still, don't use a name at all. How would we know?" Richie closed the discussion by reminding me that I did not have to listen when he talked about his girls. I started to tell him he was missing the point, but I changed my mind and turned over for a nap.

Richie used to get on Joe's case because Joe walked as if he could hardly move his feet. I never saw him rush for anything. He said if he had somewhere to go, he always made sure he left "in plenty time" so he wouldn't have to rush. One night, Joe was sitting on my bed telling me a story about his childhood in Albany, New York. During the story, he stood up to demonstrate some point he was trying to make. As I recall, he was telling me about a fight he had had and was attempting to demonstrate what he had done to his opponent. Richie interrupted Joe's demonstration, shouting, "You can't beat nobody standing like that, Joe. You gotta stand strong like a man!" (He pronounced it, "main." I shouted back to Richie, "Will you let him finish the story? He's talking about what he did when he was fourteen, not what he would do now." It was no use. Richie jumped up, taking a boxer's stance and shouting at Joe to watch him demonstrate "how a main (man) fights." Joe, who had ignored Richie to this point, content to let me try to contain him, finally spoke up. "With your fast-living, skirt-chasing self, you be lucky to even be able to stand up at all when you get to be my age — if you get to be my age. Now sit your black ass back down and don't interrupt me again., you impudent mothah fuckah." Richie laughed and said, sarcastically, "please don't beat me up, Joe." And laughing, he turned and went outside.

Joe had two habits that annoyed everyone: he was a chain smoker, literally lighting the next cigarette with the one he was currently smoking. He would talk with the omnipresent cigarette dangling precariously from his bottom lip and slightly to the left side of his face, while the eye just above squinted continuously to keep the smoke out. I don't think he got rid of the cigarette until he felt the heat. Watching him, I sometimes wondered how long the ash would get before it dropped to the floor.

The second annoyance was his ritual of shouting every morning upon rising, "piss on the rock, boys." Now, Joe got up an hour before anyone else because he always allowed himself time enough so he would not have to rush. It was about 100 yards to the dining hall and it would take him every bit of twenty minutes to get there, whereas we young track stars would run the distance in 65 seconds or so.

I too was irritated over the premature wake-up calls; but I was also curious to know the origin of the expression. I asked Joe, when we had a private moment together, what it meant. He said when he was a kid in camp, he went on an overnight camping trip. Before they retired for the evening, the counselor would always remind them not to piss on the ground (because someone might step in the dampened area) when they woke up the next morning; but to walk over to the rocks and piss on them. When the counselor woke up, the first thing out of his mouth was the second reminder to the boys to piss on the rock.

One afternoon, I had been assigned to help Joe mop the kitchen floor. The floor was about 70 by 70 feet and made of smooth, gray slate. He was to mop one half while I did the other half. After mopping about ten minutes or so, he came to me and said, "you keep mopping like that, young blood, and your back will be no good in five years." I had been bending over and moving the mop in a forward and backward motion. Joe demonstrated what he called the back-saver method. He stood up straight, holding the mop at the top of the handle. Then with his arms stretched and parallel to the floor, he began to move the mop, left-to-right, in small arcs. Then he asked me to try it. I did and immediately felt the difference. I smiled broadly and thanked him for the advice. "Now you see how, at my age, I can still swing a mop and keep up with you youngsters."

Fortunately, we all had good work ethics so we had very few conflicts around work. The conflicts we did have usually grew out of our lifestyles and social interaction with each other. Night owls vs. early-to-bed, early-to-risers; neatniks vs. the slobs. These lifestyle differences were the causes of many intense, but short-lived, disputes. The one conflict that was ongoing was not among the kitchen crew but between Phil and the dining room steward, Dave.

(7)

Dave was a junior in high school and played a little Mozart on the dining hall piano every now and then. His job was to see to it that the place settings were correct, with forks, knives, napkins, all in their places. I remember referring to the dessert plates as saucers. He had corrected me before, but I had been accustomed to eating my dessert from saucers — in fact, I had never even heard of a dessert plate — so I just could not get used to the idea. On this occasion, he said, "I wish you would stop calling these saucers! They're dessert plates." I told him to lighten up, that it was no big deal. Phil had overheard the exchange and shouted out to Dave, "Who do you think you are, talking that shit?" Dave seemed stunned.

Furrowing his brow, he looked at Phil and asked what he meant. Before Phil could answer, I said, "It's no big deal, man. They are what they are. What does it matter what I call them?" Phil said, "he's acting like we're ignorant or something — like we don't know etiquette or something." "What do you mean by 'we', Phil?" I asked. "Dave was talking to me and I did not take it that way. How did you get into it?"

"I just don't like that cat, man, he thinks he knows so damn much," was Phil's response, as he crossed the floor, finishing his sentence while standing only a few feet from Dave. It was as if he was hoping Dave would say something so he could have a reason to hit him. But Dave simply backed away and continued to set the tables.

After that incident, Phil seemed to look for any reason to go up side Dave's head. It got to the point where we had to rein Phil in, advising him to back off Dave. I was convinced that given who he was, a Negro, and who Dave was, a privileged white boy, Phil would be sent home and possibly worse, if he hit Dave and word got to the administration. Thank goodness, Dave was smart enough to stay out of Phil's way and there never was a physical confrontation.

The most pleasant memory of the camp was my performing in the singing group we had formed. After Gerald arrived, it dawned on me that with him, Phil, Melvin and me, we had the makings of a credible quartet. Gerald was the only one who had not been in the Choristers, though he was a drummer in the school band and a member of the band that played Benny Golson's "Blues March" at the student council talent show. We knew he could sing because we used to hear him harmonizing in the school hallways. One Saturday afternoon, we got together to see how we would sound. Melvin had the best voice for lead so he was an easy choice. Gerald, Phil and I took the baritone, second tenor and falsetto first tenor, respectively.

We were pleased with the first session during which we selected two ballads for our repertoire: *"Crazy for You"* by The Heartbeats (the same group that had set the mood for Ernie and me at that Clinton Avenue party three years earlier) and *"Lovers Never Say Goodbye"* by The Flamingos. We later added *"Charlie Brown"* by The Coasters and *"See You in September."* The latter was a very popular song to whose lyrics many of the young Scouts, as well as we college students, could relate. It told of a (apparently college) couple who were leaving each other to go to their respective homes. They are at the train station and lamenting the fact that summer vacation was taking them away from each other. The singer wishes the girl a good time and is uneasy over the possibility that the summer could spell danger for their romance. He says he'll be counting the days to the start of school, counting the days till he'll be with her. He ponders how long the summer will (seem to) be and this reflection places doubt in his mind about the strength of the relationship. This is reflected in the lines:

> Will I see you in September?
> Or lose you to a summer love?

"See You" was recorded by The Tempos, who were from Pittsburg. By the summer it had hit the pop charts at number 23. Another group, The Happenings recorded it in 1966. My favorite version was by the Tempos, even though the Happenings were from Jersey. Both groups sang it in three-part harmony — no background singing — with everyone singing the melody. This style was the complete opposite of the R&B songs on which I had been nurtured and which made up our repertoire. The Happenings' style was more consistent with The Mills Brothers' style of singing than that of The Heartbeats. I believe one of the reasons I liked the Tempos was that they were not some sub-par imitation of an R&B group; rather, they had found their own voice and were singing from their own experience. The campers and counselors liked our version of the song so much that they often asked us to sing it again before we finished our set. For subsequent groups of campers, we made it the last song of the set and just extended it if our young audience called for an encore.

Most campers were there for just two weeks, while some stayed as long as the whole summer. We sang for them at the campfire, following the farewell banquet that occurred on the Friday night at the end of each two-week session. Those who stayed the summer got to hear us four times. One of the counselors recorded one of our performances — the recording caught the sound of an airplane passing overhead — and later mailed me a 33 1/3 rpm record of it as a keepsake. His father either owned or had access to a recording studio and had made the record from the tape his son had sent him. We were very appreciative and quite surprised at the gesture.

(8)

    Our chef, Bill, especially liked our singing and wanted to show his appreciation. A graduate of the Chicago Baking Institute, he was a person easy to work for -- he required only that we do our jobs and do them well. He did not micromanage us, but if we messed up, he would make us pay. He was not someone we wanted to have angry with us. I saw two sides of him that summer, both of them left me with my mouth agape.

    One late afternoon, during the second session, the maintenance crew had failed to empty the garbage from that day's lunch. As a result, the cans were teeming with the lunch-time garbage and emitting a horrible odor, made worse by the stifling heat. We had begun to prepare that evening's meal and Bill had arrived a little early to bake a strawberry shortcake for the two hundred or so campers and the staff. He had promised to put some extra aside for the kitchen crew and even more for the vocal group.

    Since Phil and I washed the dishes, we were the ones who scraped the scraps from them into the garbage cans before we placed the dishes in the dishwasher. When I went to get the cans, I discovered there were no empty ones. I reported the problem to Bill and he immediately went to the main office and summoned to the kitchen the supervisor of the staff whose responsibility it was to empty the garbage. The supervisor responded in about ten minutes and Bill confronted him about the garbage, demanding to know what was going on. The supervisor, a junior at the University of Connecticut, who took offense at Bill's tone, decided to ignore him and simply walked away. Bill followed behind him warning him that if he did not "empty the motherfuckin' cans now," he was going to pay. But the super kept up his pace. Then Bill sent me to get the camp director. I was anxious about the whole affair because I did not believe Bill would get away with talking to a white man, even a college student, like that, and he would surely be fired. Even though the super was clearly in the wrong, I thought when the rubber hit the road, his whiteness would trump his wrongness.

When I reached the main office, I delivered the message as I had been instructed and the director, sensing that things were about to get nasty, immediately raced with me to the kitchen. Along the way, he asked me what was up and I told him. As we approached the kitchen, I saw Bill pacing the rear loading dock. He was dressed in his baker's hat and long white apron, the uniform he always wore when he baked. He made a striking figure. The director and I climbed the stairs to the dock, but I continued into the kitchen, because I did not want to be anywhere near when the sparks began to fly. Showing no deference at all, Bill dramatically told the director what the problem was and how the super had responded. He concluded by saying if the garbage was not removed now, he would instruct his crew not to cook a goddamned morsel. The director told Bill to calm down and he would take care of it. Bill added, unnecessarily, "You better hurry up because the Scouts will be here in ninety minutes and we ain't cooking anything until we have some empty cans." Then out of lingering frustration and addressing no one in particular, he added, "I ought to put my foot up his narrow ass."

The director called the office from the kitchen phone and asked that the super be summoned to the kitchen. In a few minutes, the super appeared, coming down the road towards the kitchen. The director, apparently in an effort to spare the super any additional embarrassment, walked to meet him. I could see them both gesturing as they spoke. Finally, the super turned to leave, then showed up shortly afterwards with his crew in the pickup truck they used to haul away the garbage. When Bill heard the truck, he went to the dock and stood there, hands on hips, so he could see his will executed. That night the kitchen crew told Bill how much we admired him for what he did, standing up to the white people. We are agreed he was one bad mothafuckah. The other incident involving Bill was less flattering.

The older guys were so pleased with Bill that Lovejoy, Deli, and Bill decided to hit the racetrack at Saratoga the next Saturday night right after dinner. They had taken Bill's car, a 1955 Chevrolet, for the 100-mile drive, and assured us they would be back by 2 a.m. and would be ready for work after sleeping four hours and taking a nap after breakfast. The other older men remained at camp while we youngsters caught a ride into town to see a movie. We returned home about midnight and after talking for a while, went to bed.

Not long after we were in bed, we were awakened by loud voices approaching the cabin. I could distinguish one of them as Lovejoy's, he spoke in a unique staccato that would make him stand out in any crowd. "Take his clothes off. We can't take him in the cabin like this. After we get him cleaned up, you go get a bucket of water and start cleaning up the car. I'll help you once I get him into bed." I got up to see what was going on. I was not prepared for what I saw. Deli and Lovejoy were on either side of Bill carrying him down the pathway. Bill, our boss, for crying out loud, was wasted, stone drunk and babbling something about how he could take care of himself and imploring the men to release him so he could walk by himself. He was not wearing any pants. "What the hell is going on?" I demanded. I heard some of my cabin mates begin to stir. Someone turned on the lights. "Bill had too much to drink and shit all over himself, messed up the car and everything. We took off his pants and left them outside. We're gonna wash him and put him to bed but he's gonna have to wash his own drawers and pants." I was incredulous. I had so looked up to him that I could not even fathom his behavior.

After they got Bill settled and washed out the car, Deli and Lovejoy walked in complaining about how cantankerous Bill had been and anticipating what a time they were going to have getting him up in the morning. Bill slept until noon. Afterwards, though, we laughed among ourselves about the incident and no one dared mention anything about that night in Bill's presence. Moreover, it appeared as far as Bill was concerned, it had never happened.

(9)

On balance, Brant Lake was a positive experience for me. I learned some things about myself — mainly that I was in awe of the wealthy white people I met there; they really did exist and were not just on the silver screen. They were so confident and self-assured. Unlike the Italians of my earlier youth, they had showed no interest in talking like Negroes or imitating us in any way. Would I ever have their kind of self-esteem? Second, the experience prepared me for my years at Rutgers where my virtually monolithic view of white people, who were not Italian, was turned on its head.

And finally, it let me see greater possibilities for myself than I had ever imagined, notwithstanding my knowledge of racism at all levels of American society. I naively thought the education I was on a mission to get would remove, or at least neutralize, any reason for me to be discriminated against. I did not know how wrong the next few years would prove me to be.

The camp job enabled me to earn enough money for clothes, books, and incidental expenses for my first year of college. It was only the second time I had been away from home for a whole summer, but it was the first time I was not among relatives.

When camp was over, the Newark bunch took the eight-hour Greyhound bus ride back to Newark, said our goodbyes and good lucks and took public transportation to our respective homes.

About two hours after I arrived home, I received a telephone call from Wiley. He told me when he got home and put the key in the door; the security chain was engaged and had prevented him from entering the apartment. He had called out to his mother; thinking something was wrong, but it was his stepfather who came to the door and, without opening it, said, "you're your own man now, son." He told Wiley to take the clothes he had and when he found a place to live, to send his address and they would send him the rest of his things. I could not believe my ears. True, he was eighteen just like me and would be leaving for Western Michigan University in ten days or so, but he had not planned for anything like this. I didn't even wait for him to ask if he could stay with us. I figured he was already under tremendous stress and the call to me must have been difficult enough as it was. "Hold on a minute, Wiley." I covered the mouthpiece and told my mother, who had been standing only feet from me cooking dinner, what Wiley had just told me and I asked her if he could stay with us until it was time for him to leave for school. Without even hesitating, she said yes. I uncovered the mouthpiece and told him that if he wanted, he could stay with us until time to leave for school. "Oh, Dave, thank you man, thank you." I could hear the relief in his voice. I felt good and bad at the same time — good that we were able to help and bad because he must have felt sad and unloved that his mother must have been complicit with his stepfather in turning him away. The doorbell rang about thirty minutes later and I went down to answer it. Wiley had tears in his eyes as he thanked and hugged me. "It's no big deal, man." I said trying to conceal my own embarrassment at his physical expression of gratitude. "Need any help with your bags?" He had all of his stuff from camp: two duffle bags and one old suitcase. Another thing about being poor, you surely don't have a lot of stuff to cart around. I reached for the suitcase while he took the duffle bags. My mother greeted him as we entered the apartment. Wiley immediately launched into thanking her too. "Oh, shush boy; come here and give me a hug. What are friends for if they can't help you when you're in a tough spot?" "Yes, ma'am." Come on, I'll show you your room." She took him to my grandmother's old room. Before her death, she had lived with us for two years after my grandfather died. My father accelerated her journey to the grave by quenching their mutual insatiable thirsts for alcohol purchased with some of his father's life insurance money.

Wiley and I did not talk about his circumstances; instead we focused on how much we were looking forward to going to our respective colleges. I told him how brave I thought he was for going so far away from home. The words came out of my mouth before I realized that Michigan would likely be his home from now through college. I was embarrassed at my own insensitivity. "I'll probably just stay out there." "Yeah, that's probably a good idea."

Wiley left for Kalamazoo a week before I left for Dover. He said the track team had to get to school early so the coaches could get a good look at them. There were also three days of freshman orientation to go through. After he said goodbye to my mother, even offering to pay her for his stay (she refused the gesture), I helped him carry his bags to the cab. "Since you're going to be the first to get to school, drop me a note so I can have your address. And I'll write you when I get to Delaware."

Though we corresponded while we were in college, I did not see Wiley again until our high school 30-year class reunion. He had remained in Michigan and become an official in a labor union.

A week after Wiley left for college, I was listening to my mother as she was giving me advice I would need now that I was going to be almost on my own; she advised me of some of the temptations I was sure to be faced with and how I should deal with them. We were waiting for James to take me to the bus station and I think she did not want to give me this advice in front of him, so she was seizing this opportunity to do so. James had just called to say he was on his way and asked if I could be downstairs when he arrived. After I assured my mother that I had everything under control, we headed downstairs. I had my new suitcase and a trunk I used for my summer camp trips.

When James arrived, we unceremoniously loaded my luggage into the back of his '61 Peugeot and headed for Penn Station to wait for the Greyhound bus. It was only a three-mile drive, but it seemed longer. The car was quiet except for the music and loud commercials on WNJR ("Three rooms of furniture -- $299. No money down. Credit to everyone."). James switched to WVNJ, a station out of Patterson that played Hugo Montenegro, Henry Mancini, Percy Faith, Mantovani and Hugo Winterhalter, and sometimes, Basie and Duke. He had begun to listen to this station after he started college. I used to wonder why we never heard such commercials on that station. He pulled in front of the Greyhound bus station on Market Street; we unloaded the car and he went to park it as my mother stood guard over my luggage while I went inside to buy my ticket.

Shortly after the five o'clock bus arrived, James returned. I hugged my mother as an attendant began to place the luggage in the luggage compartment of the bus. She had tears in her eyes, but still smiled broadly. I guess I could understand why she was crying. I was the first to go away to college. I shook James' hand and my mother gave me my shoebox of food for the three-hour-ride. She did not want me to buy food at the rest stop, because she knew I would not be able to sit in the restaurant and eat it. I made my way onto the bus and looked for a seat. I wasn't sure if Jim Crow seating was still in effect in Delaware, but just in case, I made my way to a seat in the back so I would not have to experience the humiliation of being ordered to sit in the back of the bus at the state road stop in Wilmington. I sat on the side nearest the sidewalk so I could get one more glimpse of my mother. I checked the contents of the shoebox — fried chicken, potato salad, rolls, and a big slice of chocolate cake my mother had baked. I closed the box as

I settled in my seat, looked out the window at my mother, and released a deep, blue sigh.

End

Acknowledgements

This book grew out of a poem that I started around 1998 that was to be a tribute to my mother for her courage and dignity that belied her social and economic status. The poem was to recall an incident that happened in a butcher shop on Mulberry Street. I covered that incident in a reflection in chapter 1.

I wrote the book over a period of 21 years and finished it 21 days shy of my 76th birthday. During that time while on business trips, I wrote on airplanes to and from Germany, Hungry Croatia, Bosnia and domestically, St. Louis and Kansas.

I wrote through health speed bumps of prostate cancer, coronary heart disease, lymphedema and Parkinson's disease. My reacquaintance in the nineteen nineties with John Houston, III and the late Jerry Parker, a gifted pianist whom I knew from my high school days in Newark helped me to recall events that we had taken part or shared an interest in, such as interscholastic athletic contests and dances in the Central Ward at Georgie Hudson's Youth Canteen on High Street near West Kinney Street. Hudson was a popular disc jockey on radio station WNJR AM. The three class reunions, the last two organized by Delores McCrae Reed drew me into association with people I had not seen in 3 or 4 decades, some of whom I had known since elementary school. Conversations we had late in to the night that I had with my former classmates helped to fill in some holes and tie down some details in my developing story, a story that was then largely in my head as an idea. Afterwards email traffic between me and several of them provided even more detail.

Once I gained the confidence to sit at my computer and write; I got encouragement and support from Komozi Woodard, professor of history at Sarah Lawrence College, who invited me to speak to his seminar class; Professor Julia Rabig of Dartmouth College who was introduced to me by Professor Woodard when she was a student of his. I became a resource to her when she was researching her dissertation and she became a source of inspiration for me when she explicitly recognized the value of my story and encouraged me to finish it so she could assign it to her classes. And then the popular prolific and personable poet, E. Ethelbert Miller, who after reading an early draft of the manuscript advised me to "Make the city a character." I asked him how I do that. He said to study and reflect on the title I chose.

I thank my wife of 43 years, who demonstrated unwavering faith in me; especially when other forces were pulling my attention away from my writing. She was and remains my most severe and loving critic. She often concluded a criticism with the calming, "I know you can do better."

I am thankful to Angela Harris of Kokopelli Marketing Communications, to whom I've entrusted the critical tasks of marketing and public relations communications. In addition, she has worked tirelessly alongside me; guiding me through the self-publishing process including hours spent formatting the manuscript and getting this book into print. In fact, she was the first to encourage me to self-publish.

I am thankful, Angela, for your expertise and patience.

My fellow Gemini (for those who care) and frat brother, Ken Ojise Jennings, demanded I stay true to the story and to re-visit the important places I discuss in order to help rekindle my memory of them. He told me that not all research is done in the library or on the Internet. I struggled for a while with the meaning of" true" in story-telling. I decided, that it meant steeling myself to my own vulnerabilities and, that I had to maintain a state of reflection and self-criticism throughout all my writing. I have not told everything; but everything I have told is true.

Collectively and individually (In particular, Pat Kennedy, Laura Woo and Susan Thornton-Hobby) the board members of the Howard County Poetry and Literature Society (HoCoPoLitSo) with whom I have been meeting every second Saturday at 10:00 a.m. since 1988 and who "released "me from my ten-year chairmanship following my three life-threatening illnesses that had begun to distract me from my duties as chair as I sought the medical care I needed.

I am grateful to my first cousins, children of my late uncle Hugo: Hugo Junior and Patrice Parker. They got on board very early on and always made time to talk to me about the book and comment on certain passages. Patrice told me in 1999 that I could benefit from the services of a professional editor. I found such a person in Susan Thornton-Hobby.

I thank Susan Thornton-Hobby (again) for her tireless and patient editing of the manuscript. She used Google docs as our collaboration tool. I had had limited experience with it and that was when I collaborated with another teacher, Lisa Saula, on algebra 2 lesson plans and with my youngest son, Brandon, on a presentation I had developed the summer of 2018. I discovered Susan and I would be using Google Docs when I got an "Invitation to edit" email from her. She had not even asked me if I knew Google Docs, so I figured it was something I was expected and needed to know for us to have a minimum of pain through the process. In the email, she said she had completed only chapter one and wanted to know if the work she had done was what I expected. She took the silver I gave her and turned it into platinum. I hope my readers agree.

Thank you, Susan.

Finally, I am thankful to everyone who donated to my Go-Fund-Me campaign- especially in the first three weeks - the funds from which made this project reach the light at the end of the proverbial tunnel.

I wish only that my Uncle Hugo had lived to see this project to its conclusion.